MW01095035

3 1229

NOT RENEWABLE

946.081   Landis, Arthur H          1917-1986.
Landis      Death in the olive groves : American
          volunteers in the Spanish Civil War,
          1936-1939 / by Arthur H. Landis. -- 1st
          ed. -- New York : Paragon House, 1988.


            ISBN 1-557-78051-X (pbk.)


            1.Spain--History--Civil War, 1936-1939-
          -Participation, American. 2.Spain
          Ejercito Popular de la Republica.
          Brigada Internacional, XV. 3.Americans-
          -Spain--History--20th century. I.Title.
DP269.47.U6L33 1988          946.081
                             dc19
                                        88-3777
                             AACR2    CIP MARC

# DEATH
# IN THE
# OLIVE GROVES

# ꝺEATH
# iN THE
# OLiVE GROVES

American Volunteers
in the Spanish Civil War
1936–1939

ARTHUR H. LANDIS

PARAGON HOUSE
NEW YORK

First edition, 1989

Published in the United States by
Paragon House Publishers
90 Fifth Avenue
New York, NY 10011

A previous version of *Death in the Olive Groves* was published by The Citadel Press under the title *The Abraham Lincoln Brigade.*

Library of Congress Cataloging-in-Publication Data

Landis, Arthur H., 1917–1986.
  Death in the olive groves : American volunteers in the Spanish Civil War, 1936–1939 / by Arthur H. Landis. — 1st ed.
    p.    cm.
  Bibliography: p.
  Includes index.
  ISBN 1-55778-051-X
  1. Spain—History—Civil War, 1936–1939—Participation, American.
  2. Spain Ejército Popular de la República.  Brigada Internacional, XV.
  3. Americans—Spain—History—20th century.  I. Title.
DP269.47.U6L33    1988
946.081—dc19                                                    88-3777
                                                                    CIP

Manufactured in the United States of America

THIS BOOK IS DEDICATED to the 1,600 Americans of the Abraham Lincoln Brigade who gave their lives in defense of the Spanish Republic. It is also dedicated to those remaining veterans whose ranks have been thinned by the casualties of World War II and the normal ravages of time.

The volunteers of the Lincoln Brigade were a product of the very lifeblood of America, and they well deserve the recognition that their deeds and ideals have inspired. In essence, perhaps, they have added a single page to the meaningful history of their country—but that page has brought immortality and marked them forever as a part of America's heritage.

# Contents

# Acknowledgments

FOR PERMISSION TO QUOTE, the author is grateful to the following publishers and individuals:

Alvah Bessie for *The Heart of Spain* and *Men in Battle.*

George Braziller, Inc., New York, for *The Yoke and the Arrows* by Herbert Matthews. Copyright © 1957 by Herbert Matthews.

Chilton Books, Philadelphia and New York, for *American Commissar* by Sandor Voros. Copyright © 1961 by Sandor Voros.

Columbia University Press, New York, for *Spain and the Great Powers* by Dante A. Puzzo.

Doubleday & Company, Inc., New York, for *Not Peace but a Sword* by Vincent Sheean. Copyright © 1939 by Vincent Sheean.

Harcourt, Brace and World, Inc., New York, for *In Place of Splendour* by Constancia de la Mora.

Harper & Row, Publishers, Inc., New York, for *The Spanish Civil War* by Hugh Thomas. Copyright © 1961 by Hugh Thomas.

Alfred A. Knopf, Inc., New York, for *Freedom's Battle* by J. Alvárez del Vayo.

David McKay Company, Inc., New York, for *The Great Crusade* by Gustav Regler.

The Macmillan Company, New York, for *The Wound in the Heart* by Allen Guttmann.

Herbert Matthews for his *Two Wars and More to Come,* published by Carrick & Evans, New York.

Elizabeth Tinker Morrison for *Some Still Live* by Frank G. Tinker, Jr.

Thomas Nelson & Sons, Camden, N.J., for *The Story of an American Communist* by John Gates.

Paine-Whitman, Publishers, New York, for *The Struggle for Madrid* by Robert G. Colodny.

Princeton University Press, Princeton, N.J., for *The Spanish Republic and the Civil War* by Gabriel Jackson.

Putnam's & Coward-McCann, New York, for *The Civil War in Spain* by Robert Payne.

Mary Rolfe (Mrs. Edwin Rolfe) for *The Lincoln Battalion* and *City of Anguish* by Edwin Rolfe.

Sheridan Square Press, New York, for *The Story of the Abraham Lincoln Brigade* by John Tisa.

Simon and Schuster, Inc., New York, for *My Mission to Spain* by Claude G. Bowers. Copyright © 1954 by Claude G. Bowers.

The Viking Press, Inc., New York, for *The Last Optimist* by J. Alvárez del Vayo. Copyright © 1949, 1950 by J. Alvárez del Vayo.

---

I now wish to extend my thanks to all those who have helped me in the creation of this book. It is simply said, but terribly true, that without that help the book might have "died aborning." To the dozens of Veterans of the Brigade who gave generously of their time for personal interviews, my thanks. To Alvah Bessie, Robert Colodny, and to Mary Rolfe (for Edwin Rolfe), I wish to say that your knowledge of Spain, of the men of the Lincoln Brigade, and of the nature of the Spanish War as exemplified by the books you have written, has contributed greatly to this work, and I thank you. There were some, like Steve Nelson, Herman (Gabby) Rosenstein, and Larry Cane, who from the very beginning gave of their time and energies with no doubts or qualms as to the end result. To them it was well worth the try. And to them my thanks. There were others like Charles Nussar, Evelyn Hutchins, Harold Smith, Irving Goff, and Donald Thayer who arranged tape interviews and "bull sessions" over the years it has taken to complete this work. To them also my thanks. A very special accolade must be extended to Moe Fishman, National Secretary of the Veterans of the Abraham Lincoln

Brigade for his aid and personal participation, perhaps beyond the "call of duty." In my lexicon, for the years of his life given the organization of the VALB, he is listed as the authentic "long distance runner." And to him my thanks.

I wish to express my appreciation to Professor Jack Levine and to Jean W. Cirrito for their patient "ears" and "tireless eyes" in the assembling of this edition.

And lastly, my thanks and deep personal regards to one of the few men I have ever known who "put his money where his mouth was"—Manny Harriman (aka Sam Nahman), veteran of the Abraham Lincoln Brigade.

ARTHUR H. LANDIS

Redondo Beach, California

# Eulogy to the American Dead in Spain

## By Ernest Hemingway

*(Delivered in 1939 before the first convention of the Veterans of the Abraham Lincoln Brigade upon their return from the Spanish Civil War.)*

THE dead sleep cold in Spain tonight. Snow blows through the olive groves, sifting against the tree roots. Snow drifts over the mounds with the small headboards (when there was time for headboards). The olive trees are thin in the cold wind because their lower branches were once cut to cover tanks, and the dead sleep cold in the small hills above the Jarama River. It was cold that February when they died there, and since then the dead have not noticed the change of seasons.

It is two years now since the Lincoln Battalion held for four and one-half months along the heights of the Jarama, and the first American dead have been a part of the earth of Spain for a long time now.

The dead sleep cold in Spain tonight and they will sleep cold all this winter as the earth sleeps cold with them. But in the spring the rain will come to make the earth kind again. The wind will blow soft over the hills from the south. The black trees will come to life with small green leaves, and there will be blossoms on the apple trees along the Jarama River. This spring the dead will feel the earth beginning to live again.

For our dead are a part of the earth of Spain now and the earth of Spain can never die. Each winter it will seem to die, but in spring it will come alive again. Our dead will live with it forever.

Just as the earth can never die, neither will those who have ever been free return to slavery. The peasants who worked the earth where our dead lie know what those dead died for. There was time during the war for them to learn those things, and there is forever for them to remember them in.

Our dead live in the hearts and minds of the Spanish peasants, of the Spanish workers, of all the good simple honest people who believed in and fought for the Spanish Republic. And as long as all our dead live in the Spanish earth, and they will live as long as the earth lives, no system of tyranny will ever prevail in Spain.

The Fascists may spread over the land, blasting their way with the weight of metal brought from other countries. They may advance aided by traitors and cowards. They may destroy cities and villages and try to hold the people in slavery.

The Spanish people will rise again as they have always risen before against tyranny.

The dead do not need to rise. They are a part of the earth now and the earth can never be conquered. For the earth endureth forever. It will outlive all systems of tyranny.

Those who have entered it honorably, and no men ever entered earth more honorably than those who died in Spain, have already achieved immortality.

# Foreword

Before the war, in Berkeley, California, I was listening to the speeches in Nuremberg, in the middle of the night. Hitler was speaking on the radio. I was a student of Oppenheimer. My friends were in Spain: the Spanish Civil War seemed even more real to me than World War II. I know more people who were killed in Spain than were killed in World War II. We felt it was a prelude to the war in Europe. Had the Spanish Civil War been stopped, had the German and Italian aid to Franco been beaten back, the world war might have been aborted. Or so we thought.

PHILIP MORRISON, PHYSICIST, M.I.T.

"THE war in Spain is over in the field of action; but not in the field of thought." These prophetic words were written by the Spanish Republic's most illustrious soldier, General Vicente Rojo, not long after the Axis triumph in Spain in 1939.

Since then, over 25,000 books in all the languages of the earth have been written about this conflict. If one attempts to distill the essence of this immense literature, particularly now, as the world pauses to commemorate the fiftieth anniversary of the Spanish tragedy, one uncovers the following elements:

The resistance of the Spanish people and their allies to international fascism represented the last opportunity to avert the global calamity of World War II with its fifty-three million casualties. The Spanish Republicans, although aided materially by the geographically remote USSR, had been abandoned by the governments of Great Britain, France, and the United States, and were doomed to thirty months of valiant dying. During this bloody interlude, Germany, having already seized the Rhineland (March 1936), now occupied Austria and, with the connivance of Great Britain and France, dismembered Czechoslovakia. Italy, having conquered the only independent African state, Ethiopa, in 1935, dispatched a full field army to Spain and established bases in the Spanish Balearic Islands. Japan, bloated with the seizure of Manchuria in 1931 and correctly assaying the complicity of the West in the invasion of Spain, felt secure in launching a general war against China (July–August 1937).

In this dark and lethal global atmosphere, one bright light burned. It was kindled and held aloft by the 40,000 volunteers who formed the International Brigades. Organized by the Comintern and supported by a broad spectrum of left and liberal opinion, they gathered on the Spanish battlefields from fifty-three countries. In the early days of the war—late July 1936—they participated in small groups (*centuria*) with the civilian militia columns, battling the regular army units led by the insurgent generals Franco, Mola, Goded, and Queipo de Llano.

The rebellion had been triggered by the electoral triumph of the Popular Front parties in 1936. It pitted most of the Spanish armed forces and police units against an unarmed people. It arrayed the land-owning aristocracy, the bourgeoisie, and the Catholic church against a government which drew its main support from a coalition of socialist, communist, and anarchist masses and their trade unions. Spain's most prestigious intellectuals rallied to the side of its people.

Had the legal government been given minimal access to the foreign arms market; and had the Fascist powers kept their bloody hands off Spain, the Republic controlling the great cities of Madrid, Barcelona, Valencia, Oviedo, and Bilbao would have suffocated the rebellion in a few weeks.

If we stop the clock of history at Summer 1936, we can see that not just Spain but humankind stood at the crossroads of destiny: it was four years before the Allied disaster at Dunkirk; five years before Pearl Harbor; and six years before Hitler and his followers began to implement the so-called Final Solution.

The most potent military units pledged to the rebellion were the army of Africa—the Moroccan and Riffian troops, the battle-tested Spanish regulars, and the Spanish foreign legion. These forces were under the command of General Francisco Franco. They were isolated in their African encampments across the Mediterranean. It was this army, transported by German and Italian aircraft to rebel-held enclaves around Seville, that saved the Fascist cause.

Compounding the Republic's agony was the response of the Western powers. Pressured by Tory Great Britain not to aid the legal Spanish regime, the French, under Socialist Premier Leon Blum, called into existence what was to become known as the London Committee of Non-intervention—a diplomatic fraud that in fact organized an arms embargo against the Spanish Republic, knowing full well that the arsenals of Portugal, Italy, and Germany were being placed at the disposal of the rebellion. When, shortly thereafter, the United States Congress passed the Neutrality Act, Spain stood naked before her enemies.

Spearheaded by German and Italian airplanes and tanks, fueled with American gasoline supplied on credit by the Texas Company, the mechanized armies of Africa slashed through the southern provinces of Spain and thrust armored fingers toward Madrid. It was not so much a war as an organized massacre. Then, in late September, the nature of the conflict changed again. The USSR denounced the Non-intervention Committee (which it had joined at France's request) and declared its support for the legal Republic. Pilots, tankists, artillery experts, naval advisors, and experienced staff officers arrived in Madrid and brought some order out of the chaos plaguing the amateur Republican army. Also, in formal agreement with the Republican government, the decision was made to raise a corps of volunteers to fight under the command of the Republican general staff. In the first week of November 1936, as the Fascist army started to close a steel ring around Madrid, the first column of the International Brigades marched through the beleaguered city and took up positions. Thirty-five hundred strong, made up of battalions called Edgar André (German), Commune de Paris (French), and Dombrowski (Slavic), they halted the rebel drive. Soon they were joined by the Twelfth Brigade (Italian, French, and German), the Thirteenth (Slavic), and the Fourteenth (French and Belgian). In the first five months of continuous and desperate action, the International Brigades saved Madrid. They paid for it with thirty percent dead and thirty-five percent wounded.

It was to join this embattled brotherhood in arms that the Americans, Canadians, British, and Irish, who formed the Fifteenth International Brigade, departed their homelands in late 1936. It is their story that Arthur Landis recounts in the pages that follow. Already well known and respected for his previous books, *The Abraham Lincoln Brigade* and *Spain: The Unfinished Revolution*, Landis wrote this book because he felt that a great deal that has been written about the Spanish conflict in general, and the American volunteers in particular, is often too technical, lacking in archival support, and somehow fails to convey the intimate, human detail that might make the lives and deaths of these men in Spain meaningful to the current generation. Arthur Landis died on January 27, 1986, and we who knew him and worked with him fulfill one of his last wishes by dedicating this book to all his comrades of varied origins who at one time or another were brigaded with the Americans. Thus, when the name Abraham Lincoln Brigade appears in this text, it should be understood to refer to this international brotherhood.

ROBERT G. COLODNY
XV International Brigade
Professor Emeritus,
History
University of Pittsburgh

# Introduction

ON July 18, 1936, Spain's military, backed by a triumvirate of Rightists, great landowners, and Fascist Falange, led the armed forces into revolt against the popularly-elected government of the Spanish Republic. The fighting spread quickly from the Protectorate of Morocco to every province and city of the Spanish mainland.

Loyal units fought back, but it was the direct action of the people alone that proved decisive. Workers of the powerful unions, students, peasants, fighting units of the Basque, Catalan, and Left political parties, all stormed the arsenals of the major cities with little else than their bare hands and antiquated hunting rifles. They then attacked the rapidly deploying battalions of the Army and the paramilitary Guardia Civil. In what seemed but a matter of days they were transformed into a militia, the first fighting columns of the Spanish Republic!

Sailors of the fleet seized a majority of the ships from their officers. High passes of the French-Spanish border in the Pyrénées were recaptured. The greater part of the Mediterranean and Biscayan coasts as well as the major cities (Madrid, Valencia, Bilbao, Barcelona) all fell into the hands of the people. By the end of the eighth day, the Republic had won solid control of an ever-expanding area of some 350,000 square kilometers of the country, as opposed to the 175,000 controlled by the Fascists.

A poll by England of its thirty-two consulates in Spain found thirty suggesting a triumph for the Republic. On the eighth day, the German Ambassador sent a message to Hitler: "Unless there now occurs something out of the ordinary, it is difficult to understand how the rebellion can succeed."

Some generals already thought of capitulation, others of suicide. General Mola, defeated in the Sierras, prepared to retire from those heights and to accept the disaster that seemed inevitable. "Their hopes," wrote the Franco historian Arraras, "were dissolving in complete defeat."

In essence, the war in Spain was civil only for the first eight days, *and it was won by the Popular Front of the Spanish Republic!*

The *de facto* leader of it all, however, General Francisco Franco y Bahamonde, seemed strangely unperturbed. His reply to Mola was that he should resist just a little longer. For El Caudillo knew something that Mola didn't; he knew the total plan, the total commitment to be made by Nazi Germany and Fascist Italy. He also had direct links, plus aid, from British Intelligence, and therefore knew of the negative role that England had assigned to itself. Hiding cautiously in the Protectorate of Morocco, sheltered by both the Straits of Gibraltar and a newly-arrived squadron of the German fleet, led by the pocket battleship *Deutchland*, Franco had prepared his second phase and greatest treason—the invasion of his homeland by the armed might of the Axis powers.

There then began one of the bloodiest conflicts of modern times. A holocaust, plotted in the chancellories of Rome and Berlin, was unleashed against the Spanish people, against those who had dared depose the centuries-old monarchy, institute land reforms, and bring to the Cortes a program to bridge the chasm between the remnants of feudalism and the benefits of an enlightened democracy. The war would cost one million dead. It would last almost three years. And it would end in a Fascist victory.

The Nazi Condor Legion, with upward of 25,000 pilots, tankists, artillerymen, and technicians from the German army, some 150,000 Moroccan troops from the Army of Africa, including the Spanish Foreign Legion, two full divisions of the Portuguese army, 100,000 troops from the Italian army and air force, plus the greater part of the original Spanish army and the Guardia Civil; all of these forces, together with massive armaments and materiel supplied by the Fascist powers, were now hurled against what rapidly became an unarmed, unaided, blockaded, and starving people.

But the true tragedy was that Spain's legal government, from the first moments, was denied its right under international law to purchase arms for its defense—from *any* source. And this by the democracies of the Western world!

The excuse? To confine the war to the Iberian peninsula and to thus prevent the conflagration from spreading. The result of this planned appeasement of the Axis powers, however, was precisely the opposite. As any thinking human being now realizes, the opening guns of the Spanish Civil War were actually the opening guns of World War II.

Within just ten days of the outbreak of the revolt, and with flight after flight of Junker-52 bombers already landing at Seville's airport, the infamous "Pact of Non-intervention," initiated by England, agreed to by a reluctant France, and given the nod by a confused and perplexed President Roosevelt, was in effect. For the democratically-elected government of the Republic, there would be nothing from that point on. For the insurgents of Spain's Fascist military, there would be everything!

Only Mexico sent aid to the Republic—a single shipment of 20,000 rifles.

The Soviet Union, contrary to all prevailing propaganda, was not even granted recognition by the Republic until the second month of the war. Moreover, the Spanish Republic, reeling before the invading Axis armor in the first critical months, still sought by every means to purchase arms from any country *but* the Soviet Union—to no avail.

Not until the third month of the war was a letter requesting aid sent to the Russians by Spain's Socialist premier, Largo Caballero. And this only when Franco's Army of Africa, spearheaded by Italian armor and canopied by bombers of the Condor legion, was smashing toward the gates of Madrid.

The Russians agreed. It is generally recognized by historians today that the foreign policy of the Soviet Union, as it applied to the Axis threat of that time and its manifestation in

Spain, was a correct one; England's policy, to the contrary, was crudely designed to maintain a Europe free of any liberal or socialist threat to its ruling classes. That such a Europe, cleansed likewise of socialism and democratic capitalism, would then be fascist, bothered British conservatives not one bit. That their burgeoning Axis monster might get out of hand was, they said, a risk that they would have to take.

Not so for the majority of the British people, who demanded aid for Spain and denounced the infringements of Italy and Germany upon the borders of their neighbors. Winston Churchill, then out of office, initially supported the appeasers. A long-time friend of Alfonso XIII, the one-time and future First Lord of the Admiralty did not change his opinion until Italian subs began to sink British merchant shipping. By then, 1938, it was too late.

Still the madness grew. How else can one explain the assertions of Lord Plymouth before the Non-intervention Committee—and the world—that "No proof exists of Italo-German violation of the accords of Non-intervention"? This, when every news source in the West, including England's own media, was reporting from the battle fronts on the waves of Fiat-Ansaldo tanks, the horrendous barrages from newly arrived 88mm guns manned by German gunners, and the fleets of trimotored Junker and Caproni bombers over Madrid, Valencia, Barcelona, and Bilbao.

How, indeed, can one explain the invincible British navy allowing its merchant ships to be attacked on the high seas by "pirate" submarines with no counteraction? In the month of August 1937 alone, ten ships, half of them flying the Union Jack, were sunk by these submarines. In that same month, the British destroyer *Hancock* was itself attacked by the Italian pirate submarine *Iride*—and did nothing.

Not until three critical months of war had passed did Russian aid begin to arrive in Republican ports. In the two-and-one-half ensuing years, fifty-eight ships carrying Russian arms were sent to the bottom of the Mediterranean. Italian and German freighters, on the other hand, were simply convoyed to rebel ports by the naval units of their respective countries. British and French patrols would monitor their arrival and report the facts to their governments, who would then promptly deny that the event had occurred.

The resulting disparity in arms was critical. It is estimated that, except for a few months in 1937, the rebels "possessed at all times a superiority of at least twelve to one in numbers of medium and heavy cannon; seven to one in numbers of light cannon; and an advantage of fifteen to one in bombers and ten to one in attack planes."

The outright intervention of Germany and Italy, however, did generate a form of support for the Republic. Though the governments of the Western world refused to help a country whose constitution was more conservative than that of the United States, their people reacted otherwise. Mass meetings were held in every country. Food and medical equipment was sent to the embattled Republic. Volunteers stepped forward to join the ranks of the Spanish militia. Their declared intent? To stop European fascism just there—in Spain—and thus to disperse the burgeoning war clouds of a second world war.

They came from factories, fields, and universities, from prisons and concentration camps, crossing borders bristling with bayonets. Some 42,000 men volunteered to serve in what became known as the International Brigades. Of this total it is estimated that there were never more than 17,000 in Spain at any one time, and no more than 6,000 involved in any single campaign; this, in comparison to whole divisions of the Italian, German, and Portuguese armies.

A significant percentage of these men were Socialists and Communists. And, though an evaluation of this phenomenon is beyond the scope of this work—this writer would rather allow the Internationals, and especially the Americans, to be judged against the living background of their times—this participation of progressives remains central to an understanding of history on the perilous eve of World War II.

Herbert Matthews, writing of the Internationals for the *New York Times*, said of them: "To those of us who were there, who knew these men, who saw them fight and die, they brought a glory and enrichment to the life of our times."

History suggests this as a true evaluation, for the survivors were among the outstanding personalities of World War II.

Their names are legend: Colonel Rol Tanguy, a commissar of the Franco-Belge Brigade, commanded the Free French Forces that liberated Paris. André Malraux, author of such works as *Man's Fate* and *Man's Hope*, was the organizer of the International Air Squadron in Spain. Malraux, a captain in the French Underground during World War II, became a Minister of cabinet rank in the government of Charles de Gaulle. Randolfo Pacciardi commanded the anti-Fascist Italian Garibaldi Brigade. A middle class republican, he became a member of the first postwar Italian government under Premier Alcidi di Gasperi. Competing with him for votes were two other members of the Garibaldis, Pietro Nenni, leader of the Italian Socialist Party, and Luigi Longo, Communist, who led the Italian partisan movement in the north of Italy against the Germans. The list seems endless: Josip Broz (Tito) of Yugoslavia, Sabi Dimitrov, partisan hero of Bulgaria, and Norman Bethune, the Canadian doctor who originated the blood-bank system. Together with the American volunteers of the Abraham Lincoln Brigade, they fought in what is often called "the last pure cause."

There were five brigades in all. Ernest Hemingway wrote of the Eleventh, the Thaelmann Brigade, that: "They were all anti-Nazis . . . and they marched like the *Reichswehr.* They also sang songs that would break your heart and the last of them died on the *muela* of Teruel, which was a position they sold as dearly as any position was sold in any war."

The Twelfth Brigade was Italian; its members used the name Garibaldi for obvious reasons. And because of them the myth of Fascist invincibility was smashed forever on the plains of Guadalajara, where they met the enemy head-on and contributed to the ignominious rout of Mussolini's prized Littorio and Black Arrow Divisions.

The Thirteenth was an all-Slav Brigade made up of Poles, Czechs, and Eastern Europeans. They called themselves the Dombrowski Brigade, honoring a hero of Poland's struggle against the tyranny of the Czars. Included in the Dombrowski Brigade was a company of Jews. The majority came from Palestine, others came from European countries. It was called the Botwin Company of the Polish battalion. Research has shown that there was a substantial participation of Jews in almost all of the five International Brigades. They were the premature anti-Fascists who wanted to defeat Fascism before it engulfed the world.

The Fourteenth was French and Belgian. Its banners, like its songs, blazed with the names of the French Revolution and the Paris Commune. It was said seriously that when one walked in the I.B. cemetery in Madrid that "it looked like a street in Paris."

The last, the Fifteenth Brigade, was English-speaking. Except for the early defense of Madrid, there was no major battlefield in all of Spain on which its flags and banners did not appear. Its composition varied at the beginning, having had attached to it, when first organized for the battle of the Jarama River Valley, a Slavic battalion, Dimitrov, and a French Battalion, the Sixth of February. Its final make-up was four battalions, three of them English-speaking, one Spanish. These were the Saklatvela Battalion, the Canadian Mackenzie-Papineau Battalion, the 59th Spanish Battalion, composed of Cubans, Mexicans, Latin and Pan-American volunteers, and the Abraham Lincoln Battalion from the United States of America.

In the first days the name, Abraham Lincoln Brigade, referred to the total grouping of Americans in Spain: the hospital and medical units, transport units, the John Brown Field Artillery Battery, plus the thirty or so American flyers in the air force. In areas of combat, however, the press and radio usually referred to the volunteers as the ABRAHAM LINCOLN BATTALION!

PART I

# the hills
# of Jarama

*Add horror to horror,*
*Add fighting to waiting;*
*Add manhood to childhood,*
*Add singing to weeping!*
*Oh, hills of Jarama,*
*White House over Morata!*
*We have said the hour*
*Will not find us sleeping.*

ANONYMOUS
JARAMA FRONT, FEBRUARY 1937

AT 3:00 P.M. on Saturday afternoon, December 26, 1936, some ninety-six Americans sailed for Europe on the *Normandie.* Their destination was Spain; their objective, to offer their services to the cause of the Spanish Republic.

The gathering together of these first volunteers was a simple operation. The climate for it was marked by an overwhelming American sympathy for the embattled Spanish people—seventy-six percent, according to a Gallup poll of the day. Moreover, spiritually and emotionally there had been no cause since slavery to evoke such a need for urgent, personal participation.

In the first months of the war, Spain's Washington embassy reported a flood of American applications to fight for the Republic. In effect, there was no lack of volunteers. The problem was how to get them to Spain. Where was the apparatus and the funds to do the job?

The American Socialist Party, in full sympathy with the Republic, openly advertized in its press and in the pages of the *New Republic* for recruits to a Eugene Debs Brigade, honoring an outstanding leader of the socialist and trade union movements. It came into instant conflict with hastily devised State Department restrictions and was forced to desist.

The American Communist Party, in its "popular front" form of that day, which then enjoyed a degree of respectability, moved rapidly to fill the vacuum. Without fanfare, its members offered themselves as the apparatus. The Spanish Republic would provide the funds. The way to Spain was open!

The word went out through unions, campus groups, left-liberal organizations, and the like, that one could now volunteer for the Republic through the Committee for Technical Aid to Spain, a sub-rosa and partially Communist–controlled division of the quite broadly-based North American Committee for Spanish Democracy. The volunteer had only to go to that organization in any major city to sign up.

Obviously, not all volunteers were acceptable. A close check was run on each volunteer. Considering what they would eventually have to face—war at its most brutal and barbaric—no adventurers, mercenaries, or derelicts could be accepted. The basic requirement of any man was that he be pro-union and strongly liberal. One hardly need add that, in the dynamic America of the thirties, this simple condition was easily met by three-quarters of the population. As for non-Party volunteers agreeing to Party administration, as one man put it, "Our purpose was to get to Spain to defend the Republic. We didn't give a good Goddamn who bought the bus tickets."

The first ninety-six recruits were highly representative, coming from all areas of the country—San Francisco, Los Angeles, Chicago, and so forth. There was no cloak-and-dagger nonsense. Each man from each minigroup was given a limited amount of money for expenses; his elected group leader an address to report to in New York, a union hall or one of the various organizations of that day. The final American address of a majority of volunteers was the YMCA. The rates were reasonable, the accommodations clean, the location convenient.

The volunteers docked in Le Havre, France, on New Year's Eve, and went immediately to customs for baggage inspection. One man, William Wheeler, recalls that it was a comical sight to watch the expressions of the customs officials as they opened identical suitcases holding khaki clothing and odds and ends of military gear. The poker faces of the young Americans (average age, twenty-two) proved too much. Customs officers simply threw up their hands and muttered, *"Vive la République! Vive l'Espagne!"*

At 5:00 P.M. they boarded the boat-train for Paris. By noon of the next day they had passed through the small towns of southern France and had arrived at the border town of Perpignan. Fortunately for this first group, the border had not yet been closed. They crossed into Spain by bus. The majority of those who would follow were quite often forced to run a gauntlet of the French *Garde Mobile,* searchlights, machine guns on every bridge, patrol dogs, and the like; and all this before crossing the Pyrénées Mountains on foot!

The first stop for these first recruits was the ancient Catalan town of Figueras, with its spectacular, eighth-century fortress, moat, and drawbridge. Its gray walls would soon be marked with the names and messages of hundreds of Americans in transit.

At two points, New York and Paris, the recruits had been given the chance to return. Now, at Figueras, there could be no turning back.

Under lowering snow clouds and a chill wind, they continued by train through Barcelona and on to the highlands of central Spain and the International Brigade base at Albacete. The date of their arrival, January 6, 1937, was marked by local headlines reporting additional Italian troop landings at the rebel-held port of Cádiz.

Albacete, a provincial capital with a population of 40,000, was located in the southeast section of the Republic. A hundred miles from the nearest battle front, it was well situated for the purposes of the International Brigades. All around it, like the terminals of uneven spokes on a wheel, were villages housing the training bases of the various units. It is to be noted that this was the province of La Mancha, Don Quixote country!

The Albacete base itself was under the command of the French Communist André Marty, famed for his leadership in the 1919 mutiny of the French Black Sea Fleet against orders to aid the White Russian army in the Civil War against Lenin's Bolsheviks. Any controversy notwithstanding, there is no doubt that such control of the base existed. To deny it would be a perversion of history, especially since the brigades were, at the time of their greatest strength, organized and maintained by the Comintern.

5

This was not true in the beginning, however. Indeed, the International Brigade base, as a Comintern project, was not established until the fourth month of the war, and only after many thousands of Europeans had already volunteered to serve the Republic and many hundreds had already shed their blood at Irún, Madrid, Aragón, and Estremadura. Robert G. Colodny, in his book *The Struggle for Madrid*, explains it this way:

> The concept of the war in Spain as a crusade against fascism was born in the West, *not in Moscow.* . . . The first *"Centuria"* [in Spain] were spontaneously formed by the men on the spot and these were continuously reinforced from France. The news that foreign volunteers were fighting with the Militia, that Germany and Italy were supporting the Rebels, was spread across the continent by the socialist, anarchist, and communist press, and served to stimulate the volunteers. That this took place before the Soviet Government denounced the Non-intervention agreement is an indication of the wide response the first armed resistance to fascism evoked in the European working class in general, and among the German, Italian, Austrian, and Polish emigrés in particular.

The problem of an apparatus working outside Spain to maintain the flow of volunteers existed in Europe, too. The French-Spanish border was already in the process of being closed, and problems of every kind were being created by the governments of England and France to impede the free flow of volunteers. The Comintern offered itself to the Spanish government as the apparatus. The Republic, in the absence of any similar offer from any other source, was forced either to accept it, along with the Red-baiting propaganda that would ensue, or in the long run, lose even those who would volunteer their lives in its defense. An agreement negotiated by the Left Republican Martínez Barrio, for the Spanish Republic, and Luigi Longo for the Comintern, was then concluded.

The first recruits arrived in Albacete in mid-October 1936. A singular percentage, if not a majority of them, were Socialists, Communists, left militants and anti-Fascist Germans and Italians. Though they no longer had a choice in the matter, they accepted the new leadership from Moscow for a very important reason. It was now the only guarantee that anti-Fascist volunteers of all persuasions could continue to aid the Spanish people in their confrontation with the ultimate enemy—the armed might of European fascism.

Herbert Matthews, who covered the Spanish war from its tragic beginning to its tragic end, knew many of the leaders and men of the International Brigades personally. In an effort to keep the historical record straight, he wrote of them:

> No one will ever persuade me that the men who came from all over the world to fight in Spain were clever or cynical or hypocritical, or that they were mere robots obeying orders (except for the few Russian leaders involved). I still say they fought against fascism and—at the time—for the democracy we know. I still say that a vast majority of them fought and died for the highest sort of moral principles.

Writing of the American volunteers, who would also be victimized by the Red baiting of the pro-Fascists of that day, Matthews had this to say:

> "You cannot dismiss these youngsters with the contemptuous label of "reds." They are not fighting for Moscow, but for their ideals and because they would rather die than see a Fascist regime under any shape or auspices installed in the United States. The American Battalions are unique in one respect; among all the Internationals *they remain American to the core.* None of the Internationals are so conscious of their nationality."

The General Commissariat at Albacete, a multilingual command apparatus, was now joined by Philip Bard, the elected leader of the American contingent. He would work with his counterpart, Peter Kerrigan, of the British Battalion, as the American liason with the brigade base.

On the second day, after exploring the town and drinking in the small cafes, they returned to the barracks, the Guardia

Nacional, to be duly identified and registered. Bard and Kerrigan were then driven in newly arrived French Matfords (Fords), to the tiny, picture-postcard village of Villanueva de la Jara. Of all the training villages, it was the smallest. It was also, at thirty-two kilometers, the most distant from the base.

There was a light snow on the ground and an invigorating bite to the air. The pervasive, resinous smell of wood fires was everywhere. Greeted by the *alcalde* (mayor), they were quartered in a long-deserted monastery with walls weathered by the winds and rains of many centuries. The steps of its bell tower were deeply worn by the abrasion of countless sandals. The whole village, as one man put it, seemed lost between the feudalism of the Cid and the relative modernism of Napoleon. It boasted of but four telephones and an equal number of radios.

Left to themselves and unaware of the exact format of a "people's army," they settled on an embryonic battalion organization along the lines of an American union, with elected officers and meetings conducted according to *Robert's Rules of Order*. The concept, though admirable, was patently unsuited for the creation of the iron discipline they would need to face the trained troops and superior weaponry of the enemy.

At the first meeting, they sought a name for their battalion. The vote was overwhelmingly for Abraham Lincoln, the American president most representative, they agreed, of their own ideals and principles. The machine gun company, being somewhat special, was also given a name—Tom Mooney, a famed American labor leader then serving a life sentence in Alcatraz.

Within a few days, Robert Hale Merriman arrived from Albacete to become battalion adjutant under the elected commander, James Harris, a seaman with a military background. Merriman, six-foot-two and twenty-eight years old, was the son of Scottish-American parents. A graduate of the University of Nevada, where he had majored in economics, he had won both a Newton-Booth Traveling Fellowship and a post as economics instructor at the University of California at

8

Berkeley. Completing his studies in Europe in the winter of 1937, however, he disassociated himself from academic life to offer his services to the Spanish Republic.

Within a few days of Merriman's arrival, Colonel Vidal of the brigade base accompanied the newly-appointed American Commissar, Samuel Stember, to Villanueva. Vidal seized the occasion to inform the volunteers that the new Loyalist (People's) Army did *not* function like a union local. It was an army, he told them, like any other army, but more so. Its structure embodied not just an imposed discipline, but more so. Its structure embodied not just an imposed discipline, as with national armies, but a self-discipline as well. He then explained the role of the "commissar," a rank which had first appeared in England during the reign of Cromwell. Today, the office varied: for example, in the Soviet Union commissars represented a single political party, but in England, France, and especially Spain, the opposite was true.

John Gates, the last American commissar to the Fifteenth International Brigade (a position equivalent to that of a lieutenant colonel) defined the commissar thus:

> The office of commissar was by now an institution in the Spanish Army. It had been established because of the nature of the war and the problems faced by the army. Since the old army had gone over to the enemy, this was a completely new army, created from scratch. When the fascist revolt broke out, the people spontaneously formed a militia, which took political form as the various political parties and union federations organized their own units.
>
> This worked for the early days of the war but it soon became apparent that a regular army with a unified command was needed, that political subdivisions were impossible. This was a delicate matter since the new set up brought opposing political trends into direct contact and often conflict with one another. The government therefore created the office of commissar—officers entrusted with unifying all political factions with the aim of saving the Republic. Fighting against great military odds, the army would have to make up for this with its unity and

with the average soldier's understanding of the profound issues of the war.

The commissar was entrusted with this job of education. In rank he equalled the officer in command of a particular unit and they signed all orders jointly as a symbol of the unity of the army and government. While a military officer in combat, the commissar was a combination morale officer, chaplain, information and education officer in the rear. His province included relations between soldiers and civilians, and with illiteracy wide-spread in Spain, he organized classes in reading and writing.

It is not true that the commissars were representatives of the Communist Party. They were subordinate to the government and charged with the duty of *subordinating the political differences among the soldiers to the common goal of victory.*

The Americans accepted the commissar system at its face value. For most, good-naturedly or otherwise, the word was rendered as "comic-star." The Americans themselves were highly political; that is, they would have had discussions on the war and the issues behind it whether or not there had been a commissar to chair the meetings. A good commissar could make life easier: finding cigarettes where there were none, keeping the *Intendencia* (quartermaster service) reasonably well-stocked, seeing that reading material and mail arrived promptly, and so on. An inept commissar or CP hack, however, was openly disliked.

From the first day, the Americans sought good relations with Villanueva's villagers. Fiestas were held. Six thousand pesetas were donated to the *Socorro Rojo*, the Spanish Red Cross. A projector was brought from Albacete and films were shown: in the morning for children, in the afternoon for adults, and a late show before taps for the men. The only clinic ever to be seen in Villanueva was set up and administered by William Pike, the Lincoln Battalion's first *médico*. The crowning event of one affair was the raffling of a homemade American apple pie. It brought 200 pesetas and was eaten, reputedly, by two Finns from Minnesota. All in all, the volunteers did such an excellent public relations job that, for the villagers, nothing was too good for them. The *Intendencia* suddenly had a choice of the best winter vegetables; charcoal and wood became instantly available; and the *ayuntamiento* (city hall) was offered as additional space for the battalion headquarters.

More men filtered in to Villanueva, many with military skills, such as Paul Burns, John Scott, Martin Hourihan, Fred Lutz, Dave Jones, Oliver Law, Walter Garland, William Wheeler, Eugene Morse, Douglas Seacord, and Eli Biegelman. Robert Merriman had unofficially replaced James Harris as commander, and, at an early date, a solid military unit had begun to take shape. There were classes in mapping, scouting, fortifications, and so on, all the subjects that Merriman, Seacord, Morse, Scott, and the dog-eared manuals could competently teach. Each day the companies would maneuver through the olive trees and vineyards surrounding Villanueva; each day they would scout the frozen pine groves, all touched with a winter rime, and storm the crossings of the little Río Valdemembro. What had been an amorphous group of civilians was fast shaping up as a hardened, disciplined, military unit.

Douglas Seacord became commander of the machine gun company. Company 1 went to John Scott (aka Inver Marlow), a slender, bespectacled British expatriate journalist whose wanderings had brought him to Spain via India and the United States. Company 2 went to Stephen Daduk, an American pilot who had flown for the Republic in the defense of Madrid, in the dark days of November and December 1936.

Daduk had reputedly brought down a Heinkel-111 while flying an antiquated Briguet bomber. He was later shot down over the capital's Tetuán district while flying a patched-up British Air-Speed. His thigh was broken. The leg mended; he heard the Americans were organizing and hastened to join them.

The training became still more rigorous, spurred by the news that a fresh division of the Italian *Corpo Truppi Volantari* (CTV), was strongly attacking the southern coastal city of Málaga. The defending militia possessed but a few thousand rifles, six antiquated field pieces and a handful of machine guns. Despite the peril, no aid had been sent to Málaga, nor was a similar massing of insurgent troops to the south of Madrid given serious attention by the War Ministry, now located in Valencia. Pleas from the worried Madrid Army Group were ignored.

On the eighth of February, word circulated that the newly formed British Battalion had entrained for the Madrid front. The day was also marked by the fall of Málaga. It was learned, too, that just three days previously, February 5, a second great rebel offensive had been launched to seize Madrid. The rebel High Command, Generals Orgaz and Varela, under the guidance of the Reichswehr officers Von Thoma, Von Faupel, and Sperrle, had unleashed some 40,000 troops on a twenty kilometer front to the south of the capital. Their immediate objective was the town of Arganda, in the Jarama-Tajuña river triangle. They would then seize Alcalá de Henares to the northeast, thereby severing the Madrid road to Guadalajara and Valencia to effectively isolate the capital.

The coup de grace for Madrid and perhaps the Republic itself would then be launched. To the north of Guadalajara was the newly-arrived Italian Army Corps under General Mancini Roatta. When and how it would attack depended in part upon the success of the rebel commitment along the Jarama.

As of the eighth, the town of Ciempozuelos had been taken, and the defending Republican Eighteenth Brigade destroyed. The strategic height of La Marañosa overlooking the Valencia road had been overrun, and its defenders slaughtered to a man. Moroccan *tabors* of Ifni and Mehil La, advancing behind a wave of Ansaldo tanks, had then smashed through to the Jarama. The weakly-held Republican line was crumbling everywhere.

With the British had gone the other battalions of the Fifteenth, the Czech Dimitrov, and the French Sixth of February. Also, the Twelfth, Eleventh, and Fourteenth International Brigades, decimated from the battles of attrition at Madrid, were again being ordered into the breach.

On February 12, the Americans were alerted. The battle

now raging on both sides of the Jarama was fast assuming the proportions of a new Cambrai. Jack Shirai, the Lincoln Battalion's lone Japanese-American volunteer, was ordered to Albacete for new, camouflaged kitchen equipment. Doctor Pike received the complete medical supplies given to all units going into battle.

On the fourteenth, a joint battalion-civilian farewell party was held in a building adjacent to the barracks. It was a kaleidescope of decorations, with posters of popular heroes and crepe paper everywhere. There were refreshments, dancing, and movies. Villanueva de la Jara had never witnessed a happier event—or a sadder one.

By 3:00 P.M. of the following day, the battalion had been convoyed to Albacete, first to the *Guardia Nacional*, then to the bull ring where they were addressed by André Marty, Peter Kerrigan, and Vidal. They were told that the Fascists had crossed the Jarama but were being held, stubbornly, heroically. Kerrigan and Marty spoke of what would now be expected of the Abraham Lincoln Battalion.

More trucks rumbled into the ring while they spoke. Case after case of rifles were unloaded, distributed, still bearing their protective cosmolene. They were Remington rifles, made in the United States for the Imperial Russian Army of 1916. Cartridge belts came with the guns—the leather-box, three-to-a-belt kind—plus a trianglar, stiletto-type bayonet. French steel helmets were passed out. A final item was 150 rounds of ammunition per man, the standard European battle ration.

It was then that the volunteers were met by members of the American Medical Bureau, who had come to see them off. Under the leadership of Doctor Edward Barsky and Frederika Martin, head nurse of the contingent, they had been in Spain just a few weeks, had visited the Jarama front, and were already setting up a first American hospital at Romeral. Standing in a line with Kerrigan, Vidal, and Marty, they silently shook each man's hand as he reboarded the trucks to move out. Darkness had fallen. The *camiones*, passing one-by-one beneath the arc of the huge gates, were fleetingly outlined by a single dangling lightbulb, tossing in the slow wind.

*13*

In the bitterly cold hours before dawn, some ten kilometers from the front, the convoy halted while Merriman and John Scott continued on to report to division headquarters at Morata de Tajuña. Colonel Vladimir Copic, the Yugoslav brigade commander, agreed that the men be given time to clean their guns and to fire them, for as yet *the majority had never actually fired a weapon.*

Outside the village of Chinchón and shivering in the cold, the men, most of whom had been in Spain but two short weeks, tore strips from their shirts to clean the Remingtons. In groups of fifty they then fired five rounds each into the hills on the opposite side of the road.

Underway again, they experienced their first air attack, a flight of Heinkels coming in low in a strafing run. The trucks stopped. The men hit the dirt. There was no panic; no casualties. A flight of spanking-new *Moscas* (Spanish for flies), the Soviet monoplane Polykarpov L-16 disrupted the run.

In the air over the Jarama on that same day were the American pilots James Allison, Ben Leider, Whitey Evans, and Frank Tinker, in a flight of eleven L-15 biplanes or *Chatos*, a Spanish endearment for small, snub-nosed children. Their logs show an engagement with a squadron of twelve trimotored Ju-52s, protected by thirty-five Heinkel fighters in the area of Morata de Tajuña in the late afternoon. Two Heinkels were credited to their group—one downed by Leider, the other by Allison.

Dawn found the Lincolns under a sporadic shelling in reserve positions. The first to die was Charles Edwards, killed by a sniper's bullet. Shortly after, Michael Chelabian, a New Yorker, was decapitated by an incoming shell. Light casualties continued for the next few days.

An account of the ensuing Lincoln Brigade disaster can be best understood, if at all, against the background of preceding events. By February 10, the rebel Army of Africa had smashed through to the Jarama. Madrid units, the Spanish Brigades of Enrique Lister and the peasant commander El Campesino, plus the Twelfth International Brigade, were just then racing over the hills to spread themselves in a thin line along the destroyed front. The French Battalion of the Twelfth Brigade reached the Pindoque Bridge just as dusk fell. A company was posted to guard it. Moroccan units, taking advantage of the moonless skies, surprised and knifed the bridge sentries, then butchered the remainder of the company asleep in slit trenches. By dawn the Moroccans had crossed the bridge in strength. Squadron after squadron of cavalry deployed upon the plain.

The remaining companies of the French Battalion fought desperately to the south of the bridge, retreating finally to the first range of hills, where they held the cavalry at bay. The Twelfth Garibaldis then arrived to drive instantly for the bridge. The Moroccans, however, had already seized a dominating height and brought up a score of mountain guns. Nevertheless, the anti-Fascist Italians stormed through a hail of shells and bullets to roll the Moroccans back, and to bring the crossing under fire.

Insurgent infantry and tanks continued to cross in great numbers. At that point, newly arrived Russian tanks, under their commander, Pavlov, destroyed the mountain guns and drove the enemy tanks and infantry back across the river. Pavlov's tanks in turn were given a drum-fire barrage from the massed 88mm guns on the captured heights of La Marañosa, and were forced to retreat.

Again the insurgents advanced in great numbers.

The full strength of the Moroccan cavalry then turned on the depleted ranks of the French, who had just four machine guns left. Shells from La Marañosa now ranged their line and rear. They were effectively cut off from all aid.

The first charge of some 1,600 cavalry sabers was driven off. The French then fell back to the next range of hills, carrying their wounded. They placed their guns as expertly as they could, knowing there could be no further retreat; they now had but two belts per gun.

The cavalry in the valley below was reinforced. When they charged again they numbered well over 2,000. The guns of the French cut the horsemen down in swaths until their ammunition was exhausted. They were then overrun by one last attempt of the cavalry, and by a swarm of Moroccan infantry infiltrating the Chinchón Road from the south.

The Poles of the Thirteenth Brigade, racing desperately over the hills to aid the French, arrived to see the last of them being butchered before the Moroccans continued their advance. The Poles, too, then fought for each line of hills. Casualties among the Moroccan infantry and cavalry were terrible. The rebel historian Manuel Aznar observed that in some instances only one sergeant and perhaps two men would be left from whole sections.

The Poles fought desperately to stem the avalanche of numbers. By mid-afternoon they had lost half of their original thousand. Then Spanish units arrived, and they, with a handful of tanks and the remaining Poles, secured the last line of hills before the vital Arganda Road.

To the south, behind waves of Ansaldos, the rebels stormed the village of San Martín de la Vega, crossed the Jarama in force, and captured the strangely undefended heights of Pingarrón. The southern rebel flank was now obviously driving for Morata de Tajuña.

On the morning of the twelfth, the battalions of the Eleventh and Fifteenth International Brigades were thrown into the maelstrom. The British dug in on a knoll to the south of the San Martín Road to bar the way to the advancing Moroccans and Foreign Legionnaires of the *Tercio*. It was their valiant defense of this position for the first seven hours of the day that masked the weakness of the Republican front, preventing the rebel command from discovering that for a space of three miles to the south there was a gap in the Republican lines.

The British stood firm against repeated charges by the Moroccans, as did the Sixth of February Brigade to the north. Further north, the Czechs were also under heavy assault. By noon, the French, their companies decimated, their antiquated Colts jammed and out of action, were forced to retreat, thus exposing the British on their knoll. A few tanks were rushed up. The exhausted French advanced again. But the tanks quickly retired, leaving the British, French, and Czech battalions to defend themselves against Fascist tanks, massed artillery, and complete batteries of machine guns with nothing but bolt-action rifles. Not a single hand grenade remained in the entire brigade.

The Czechs then received the full force of the Moroccan

*tabors* deflected by the British and French. Five times they were driven from their positions in the olive groves—and five times, with bayonets alone, they took them back. To the north the anti-Nazi Germans of the Eleventh Thaelmann Brigade repeated the heroism of the Czechs. And so it went, all along the line of the assault.

There are few battles of World War II that can even begin to equal the ferocity of the clash of opposing forces on those few square kilometers of the valley of the Jarama. Battalion after battalion, brigade after brigade, were hurled into the inferno by both sides. The unceasing action of attack and counter-attack exacted a toll upon rebel and Republican alike that can only be described as horrible. The rebel General Varela lost two-thirds of his effectives; the Republican General Pozas, likewise. Varela, however, knew that given another day, Republican reinforcements might stabilize the positions. So he launched one final attack with all the forces at his command.

It began at dawn of the fourteenth, with the usual massive barrage. On the right the Moroccans and Legionnaires were stopped cold by newly-deployed Spanish troops. But the rebel Colonel Asencio, after heavy losses, joined with the rebel Colonel Buruaga to shatter the entire Republican southern flank. The depleted forces of Enrique Lister and the Internationals of General Gal were driven back. One hundred eighty survivors of the British Battalion—which had originally numbered 600—drifted stunned and dazed toward Morata. On a sunken road they were met by the area commander, who begged them to return. There were *no* reserves, he told them. Unless they themselves could stop the oncoming Moroccans, the vital road to Arganda and Alcalá would be lost—and Madrid as well.

The story of their return is legend. The remnants of the Fifteenth rallied, picked up all stragglers, even its walking wounded, and drove gallantly back in one last great effort toward the heart of Asencio. Aided by a fast-falling darkness, they, together with Colonel Lister's remaining men, formed an advancing line of bayonets and bursting grenades. The Moroccans would not wait for their steel—they broke and ran. By 12:00 midnight, under a bright moon, the Fifteenth and Eleventh Brigades held the exact positions they had held on February 12.

That same night the Fourteenth Franco-Belge Brigade arrived to launch a dawn attack that would clear the road between Morata and Arganda. Four decimated International Brigades were now in line, holding the center of the Jarama front.

A series of Republican counter-attacks was then initiated. The entire area northeast of the Manzanares juncture with the Jarama was cleared of the enemy; the heights of La Marañosa that had been captured and lost again. On February 21, the action was extended to positions opposite the ford of San Martín. On the twenty-third, Republican units stormed the heights of Pingarrón and retook it. Before they could fortify the crest, however, or bring up sufficient machine guns to protect their gains, the *Regulares of Tetuán*, with the aid of a storm of artillery, took it back; this, in the late afternoon.

Just one hour before, at 3:00 P.M., the Abraham Lincoln Battalion had been given its baptism of fire, in an effort to draw strength from the counter-attacking Moroccans.

Taking over positions from the Seventieth Spanish Brigade to the north of the San Martín Road, they had simply moved out as ordered. Their support? Four vintage World War I Maxim machine guns, two of which were out of action before they had fired a single belt. Perhaps the sheer audacity or madness of it, combined with the winter sun rapidly setting behind the Jarama hills and casting long shadows over the vineyards and olive groves, was all that saved them from heavy casualties. In some places, they made it to the enemy wire and lobbed grenades over rebel parapets to silence the guns that were peaking in intensity. A few groups dug in within ten to fifteen meters of the enemy and exchanged individual rifle shots with Moroccan machine gunners.

It has been said, with some reason, that with any kind of support, the Lincolns could have seized the trench line. If so, ensuing events might have been different. As it was, with the coming of darkness they withdrew, as per orders, to their original positions.

Rough data shows casualties of forty wounded and twenty

dead. Among the latter were John Scott, Company 1 commander, Rudolfo de Armas, leader of Company 1's Cuban *Centuria*, and Eugene Morse, commander of Company 2.

On the following night the Lincolns crossed to the south of the road, with the British, French, and Dimitrovs to their left, in that order. The Seventieth Brigade reoccupied its old position. Losses had necessitated new appointments: Douglas Seacord replaced Daduk as adjutant and William Henry of Company 1's Irish James Conolly *Centuria*, now commanded the company. Company 2 passed to Lieutenant Martin Hourihan.

Hourihan, from Towanda, Pennsylvania, had left parochial school at sixteen to go to sea and then spent six years in the United States Army, from which he was finally discharged for radical leanings. After graduating from the Alabama Polytechnical Institute as an engineer, he began to teach and to help organize poor southern sharecroppers. It was thus a quite "natural thing" for Hourihan to volunteer for Spain in 1937.

Another teacher, Paul Neibold of Katonah, New York, was advanced to section leader, as was Lieutenant Robert Thompson. Oliver Law, in his early thirties, was given command of the machine gun company. An ex-Army man, Law was the first Black to ever command an almost all-white American military unit—a truly historic event. Two of his gun crew leaders, Walter Garland and Douglas Roach, both of New York, were also Black.

A bright sun shone on the morning of the twenty-sixth, a respite from the rain of the previous two days. Captain Merriman, with Seacord and the commanding officers of the other battalions plus the Spanish Seventieth, were again called to Morata. A last coordinated attack was to be launched the next morning; its objective, to breach the rebel line of fortified hills, roll up their flanks, and destroy their bridge head.

The plan was General Janos Galiez's. Known as General Gal, he was an ex-officer of the People's Army of Hungary during the short tenure of Bela Kun's socialist government. The attack would begin at 7:00 A.M. The artillery would lay down a barrage. Planes would bomb the rebel positions. A company of scarce tanks would clear a way through the wire and knock out the enemy guns. The Seventieth would move out first, then the Lincolns, British, and Dimitrovs. This was all very pat—indeed, classical. However, in Spain there was no assurance that the expected infantry support would materialize.

Considering the Republic's always limited means, plus the ominous presence of the Italian Army, poised to strike at any hour, northeast of Madrid, it is doubtful that such support still remained in the proximity of the Jarama river front.

On that same day, an additional seventy-three men joined the Lincoln Battalion from Albacete, the majority of them having been in Spain just three days. More Remingtons were issued, and they, like their comrades before them, fired five shots into the nearest hillside, then marched to the trenches to be divided between the three companies and to get what rest they could.

Dawn broke on the twenty-seventh with a heavy dew on the ground and a cloudy overcast. The men were wide awake. Red coals of cigarettes glowed dully all along the length of trench. The command post had been moved to the center of the Lincoln positions, and the officers were clustered around a single phone. Merriman was alert, outwardly relaxed, and confident.

Jars of coffee, brought up from the kitchen a kilometer distant, were passed down the line. The men drank, ate their bread and jam, and stared at the gray sky. Some peered through the firing points at the vague line of enemy trenches. They then checked their gear: boots, clothes, and cartridge belts, anything that might impede their freedom of movement. Each man had attached three or more grenades to the shoulder loops of his cartridge belt.

The new recruits were in full pack, musette bag, and blanket roll. With their French helmets and slender bayonets, they seemed like vague still shots from the Battle of Verdun, or like the young poilus in *All Quiet on the Western Front*.

At exactly 7:00 A.M., a light firing began from the Loyalist positions, sharp and clear in the still air. The order to join in came down the line. Oliver Law's six operating machine guns opened up, joining the flat rhythm of the British and Czech guns to the south.

A single battery of 75s unlimbered and began firing. The shells dropped beyond the trenches facing the Republican Spaniards. It was full daylight. No tanks appeared. The firing from the Republican Spaniards died. The rebel gunners, alerted to the impending attack, began an organized and effective reply. Their bullets ripped the sandbags all down the Lincoln line. Merriman, noting that the Seventieth had not moved out, sent runners to all companies to advise them to cease firing. The British and Dimitrovs did likewise. The men waited, puzzled. Merriman called Copic. What the hell was happening? Where were the planes? Where were the tanks? Where was the artillery—sufficient to make a difference? Copic's reply, in English, was vague, dissembling. The tanks, he said, would be coming. The Lincolns must be ready. And did they have an aviation signal out? If not, why not?

Two volunteers, Joseph Streisand and Robert Pick, both from New York, raced out upon the macadam road signaling with a white cloth. The point of the "V" would indicate the enemy. Attempting to return to the trenches, they were literally cut to pieces by machine gun fire.

The Seventieth started up again. The process was repeated. In the midst of this new firefight, Merriman received a repeat of the previous order—but now there was no mention of *any* support.

Enemy fire, in the meantime, had increased to such an intensity that it seemed nothing could live above the parapets. Firing from the loyalist Spaniards had fallen off again, a possible indication that they had left their trenches. They had! But a runner from Company 2 arrived to state that the Seventieth was pinned down, as close as thirty meters from Spanish trenches.

Minutes later two armored cars advanced from between the cleft of hills toward Morata. They fired a number of rounds toward the rebel lines, and retired. Still, no tanks or planes. At this juncture, a runner from the brigade brought a written order for the Lincoln Battalion *to go over alone*—"to set an example for the others."

Now the planes arrived, three of them, not bombers but fighter planes, in a simple strafing run. And that was that. Spanish cadres who could, returned to their trenches. Only desultory firing could be heard from the British and Czechs. It was then agreed by the Lincoln staff that to go over now would be insane, even criminal!

Merriman called brigade headquarters, demanding to speak to Copic or Gal. Gal was not available, but his orders were explicit. The Lincolns had made it to the enemy wire on the twenty-third without support, they could do it again now! The argument veered back and forth. Copic would not oppose Gal. Merriman was overruled. The order remained: Attack! It was then almost noon.

Copic, fearful of Gal and angry at Merriman's defiance, sent the British Captain D. F. Springhall, together with Lieutenant George Wattis, another Britisher, to the American positions, ostensibly to see that the order was carried out. Springhall and Wattis, making the trip by motorcycle, entered the communication trenches, rounded the hill, and clambered along the Lincoln positions where, according to English historian William Rust, "In most places the parapets had already been blown to pieces."

Wattis remained with Company 2. Springhall arrived at the Lincoln headquarters just in time to accompany Merriman and his entire staff over the top.

No one knows how Springhall felt about Gal's orders after he had seen with his own eyes the impossible attack conditions. In any case, it was too late. Merriman had challenged the authority of the general of his division and the commander of his brigade, thereby risking the charge of insubordination and cowardice. He had done all that he could short of mutiny. When he could do no more, he personally led the Lincolns over the parapets beneath the scanty covering fire of Law's machine guns. Captain Springhall followed, perhaps to expiate his own questioning of this young commander's courage.

All down the line, above the fury of the rebel guns, came the

Lincoln cheers as they went over singly and in groups to meet a hellish fire. Within seconds Springhall was shot dead. Merriman and two others of his staff were caught in the same burst; Merriman went down with a bullet through the shoulder which broke the bone in five places. Fortunately, he was hit within just a few yards of the trenches and was quickly pulled to safety. In great pain, Merriman agreed to leave the command post only when the British and Slavs had been informed of his condition, and when the command had been transferred to Seacord in the field and to Lieutenant Cooperman at headquarters.

Merriman had no way of knowing that Seacord and both his runners had been cut down just thirty meters from the trenches. Everywhere it was the same. William Henry of Company 1 had also fallen, his body riddled with bullets. Adjutant Eamon McGrotty, lying beside Henry, arose to order the advance to continue; he was instantly killed. Whole groups of men would barely reach the top of the parapets before being smashed back into the trenches by the withering fire of the opposing guns. Of those who had reached the olive groves, half were already dead. Each time the line arose to continue the advance, the direct and cross-fire of whole batteries of guns cut into the men, thinning their ranks so that squads and sections simply melted away in death and agony.

The British Battalion, some 120 men commanded by Captain Jock Cunningham and Commissar Aitken, gallantly followed the Lincolns over. The fire in their sector was severe, but nothing to that confronting the Americans. The British, however, recognizing the insanity in time to do something about it, ordered an immediate withdrawal. With no support in sight, the Czechs, too, withdrew. *Only the Americans continued!*

According to one Lincoln machine gunner, Court Bevansee, half the guns were useless after the first few belts. The crews then grabbed rifles and followed the infantry over. There was, at this point, no command at all. With the exception of Lieutenants Hourihan and Robert Thompson, the Lincolns had lost all their officers. Still the advance continued. There were some on that afternoon who got to within ten meters of the Fascist wire before they fell. One of these, a young boy from New York, Milton Rappaport, fell face forward, still holding his rifle, and with an unexploded grenade in his right hand. Others dug in within thirty meters of the rebel strong points. Again they fought with individual rifle shots against nests of machine guns.

Finally, from somewhere, the order came to return to the lines. Perhaps it wasn't an order at all, but simply a reaction, a return to sanity. Or perhaps it was the rain that was the deciding factor. Some made it back before darkness fell, each with his tale of men wounded and dead. Most were wounded themselves.

Robert Klonsky, who had been in Spain just seven days, has stated that when he and others returned, they found rage and anger rather than demoralization in reaction to these events. Some wept bitter tears of frustration. Others wandered aimlessly, cursing the "bastards" who had forced the attack.

There are a myriad of stories told by survivors. The consensus is that the attack was a tragic, criminal error which, at a later date, figured strongly in Gal's dismissal from his command. Robert Colodny, historian, teacher, and a veteran of the Spanish war, wrote this analysis:

> The final attack against Pingarrón, an act of monumental stupidity, was organized by General Gal on February 27. Parts of two Divisions, the 15th and the 11th, took part in the operation, which was clumsily planned but executed with great gallantry. Planes, tanks, and artillery promised for the support of the infantry failed to materialize; but General Gal gave his commanders the senseless orders to "take Pingarrón at all costs." The battalion assigned to lead the attack was the fresh though mostly untried Abraham Lincoln Battalion, commanded by Captain Robert Merriman. . . .
>
> The Rebels had covered the approaches to Pingarrón with a triple line of interlacing machine gun positions. . . . And through this curtain of fire the Americans tried to advance.

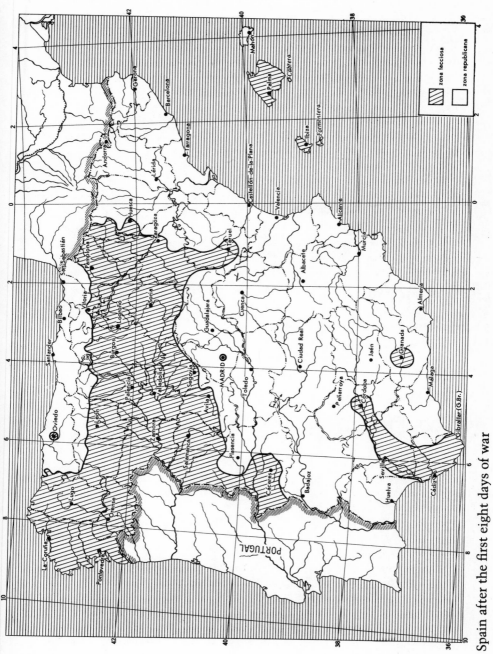

Spain after the first eight days of war

*Mosca*—Soviet fighter plane

Group of U.S. volunteers

Arthur H. Landis, volunteer

Ernest Hemingway, frequent visitor to the front lines

(from left) Gates, Brigade Commissar; Thompson, Mackenzie-Papineau
Commander; Doran, early Brigade Commissar

After the storming of the Fascist barracks

Dolores Ibarruri, "La Pasionaria"

Evelyn Hitchins, the only
woman truck driver

Preparing detonators

Dismantling and cleaning machine gun

Professor J.B.S. Haldane considers a gas mask

University of Madrid, destroyed, holds out from 1936 to 1939

In the darkness and rain of the Lincoln trenches, the survivors were alerted to the possibility of counter-action. No
one slept. All stayed at their posts or volunteered to search for
the wounded and the dead. The rain turned to sleet as the cold
of the night settled in. There was no food, no dry clothes.
There was nothing to blunt the edge of the horror that had
happened. In the trenches there were perhaps sixty men. The
search squads numbered another forty. They were all that was
left of the Abraham Lincoln Battalion.

More than 200 wounded were being evacuated. In the mud
of the olive groves and vineyards, and out upon the slopes of
the slight hill beneath the Fascist fortifications, were the
bodies of 127 students, teachers, union activists, and young
blue-collar workers, a small part of the best of America. They
had not thought to die so soon, nor for so little reason.

United Press, Madrid, March 2, 1937. A violent assault
was launched late last night against Government positions southeast of Madrid, but was repulsed with heavy
losses.

The assault began at 8:30 P.M. on positions near Morata
de Tajuña, at Perales del Río, and at a point south of
Vallecas.

Enemy tanks approached the government lines pouring
heavy machine-gun fire into the defending trenches. The
battle was especially bitter between Pingarrón Hill, and
Morata de Tajuña.

The remnants of the Lincolns were involved in this battle.
One man describes the attempt as a gigantic firefight with
every rifle and machine gun on both sides sending out a hail of
bullets. Bodies of attacking Moroccans, seeking to repeat the
night victories of the Pindoque and San Martín bridges, dotted the fields before the Republican lines.

The attack, according to the rebel historian Aznar, was
designed to pin down the Internationals and the Madrid units
of Lister and Rojo in preparation for the unleashing of the
Italian offensive. But rebel General Orgaz failed—with 6,000
or more casualties. Moreover, the Eleventh and Twelfth Inter-

25

nationals were already at rest at Alcalá, while the Fourteenth Franco-Belge was on its way south to join the Thirteenth in Andalucía.

Only the decimated Lincoln Brigade, together with new battalions of raw, young Spanish troops, still held the Jarama line. It had been *they* who had disrupted Orgaz's venture.

The Italians could wait no longer. In just eight short days after the Lincoln disaster of February 27, General Roatta Mancini's offensive began. Five Italian divisions, the Spanish Soria division, a mixed brigade of Spanish-Italian infantry, a brigade of German infantry, 4 companies of motorized heavy machine guns, 100 planes of the Italian air command, upward of 250 tanks, and 180 pieces of artillery, *all* were hurled against the weak Republican line below Sigüenza.

The Italian's pathetic attempt to seize Guadalajara has been likened historically to Caporetto, Italy's greatest disaster in World War I. Suffice it to say that Mancini's divisions, after shattering the Republican line on March 8 and 9, then advanced thirty kilometers to capture Brihuega, Torija, and Masegozo—and were stopped cold!

On March 14, while Republican tanks began the counteroffensive by smashing the Italian spearhead at Trijueque, General Orgaz again attacked on the Jarama. The Lincolns were hit hard. Artillery ranged their lines. A full company of Ansaldo tanks led the assault. The new Spanish battalion on their left, mostly young recruits, broke in the face of the tank attack. British and American bombing squads then drove into the occupied trenches to blast the enemy out with grenade and bayonet. The Americans were led by Captain Hourihan, Commissar David Jones, and the new Company 1 commander, Robert Wolk. The trenches were cleared. The Ansaldos were forced back by armor-piercing bullets from Law's new Maxims, as were the attacking Moroccans and Legionnaires.

Robert Wolk, a twenty-year navy man and a former chauffeur to Admiral Stirling of the Brooklyn Naval Yard, was the only American killed. There were many wounded, including Max Krauthamer, a young lawyer from New York, and Robert Raven, from the University of Pittsburgh, who lost both eyes.

By the end of March 1937, the Republican counter-offensive then literally hurled the Italian Black, Blue, and Green Arrow divisions, plus the Littorio division, back to their starting point; this utilizing mostly the same units that had smashed the Jarama offensive.

Captured Fascist war materiel lined the highways. Ernest Hemingway, on the scene, wrote of "mountains of ammunition, shells, grenades and provisions." Thirty-six pieces of artillery and over 200 heavy machine guns were listed in the booty of the first days. Italian losses were approximately 3,000 dead, 6,000 wounded, and upward of 2,000 taken prisoner.

Republican Spain had proven that even the limited arms received from the Soviet Union had sufficed to defeat a vastly better-equipped enemy. A heightened confidence was evident among the soldiers of the new People's Army. After all, German and Italian intervention could now no longer be denied by the appeasers of the London Committee; or so reasoned the leaders of the Republic. They were still not aware of the depths of iniquity to which their betrayers would sink. Even after the exhibition of the first hundreds of Italian prisoners in Madrid, the parading of the many captured tanks, the presentation of mountains of captured documents, after all *that*, the English Foreign Office could still announce matter-of-factly that there was no official confirmation of the *rumor* that Italian troops were on the Madrid front.

The inability of the Spanish Republic to exploit the victory at Guadalajara was a part of that bitter frustration and defeat with which it was constantly met. A student of those times will clearly see how the path to Munich followed an almost hypnotic and preordained pattern. All the world knew that whole divisions of the Italian and German armies fought in Spain. All the world knew that the preponderance of arms from those same countries was the only thing that kept the forces of Franco in the field. Only the chancellories of state, of the Quai d'Orsay, and of Whitehall claimed they did not know what all the world knew.

The cold March rains had set in along the Jarama. The lowering clouds extended over the breadth of the Castilian plateau. Along the arc of the Sierra de Guadarrama to the west, north, and east, rain turned to snow flurries. Only on rare occasions did the sun peep out to confuse those who planned the deployment of continued battle.

To the Lincolns in their muddy, waterlogged trenches, it seemed incessant. Aside from an occasional artillery salvo, or lengthy machine gun burst, the monotony of the chilling downpour was broken only by the biting wind from the mountains.

Paul Wendorf, who would survive until the last battle, wrote in his diary of this period:

> We awoke in the mornings to find mud in our dugouts, blankets soaked, tunics damp. The coffee was carried in urns—we had no hot containers in those days—up more than a mile of mountain path. We often crawled back to our dugouts without drinking it. Most meals were cold. The wind whirled in eddies, and mud joined the food on the way to our mouths.

The rains continued. So did the legitimate anger of the men at the handling of the disaster of February 27. Meetings were held. Demands were made that General Gal be called to account. Their words fell on deaf ears; the Brigade Commissariat would do nothing. To all the Commissariat's efforts to defend Gal, the curt rejoinder was, "The bastard did it, didn't he? Get rid of him!" Finally, the appointed Lincoln commissar, Stember, was dismissed—the volunteers would have no more of him. His place was taken by David Jones, one of the oldest and best-liked men in the battalion.

Captain Allan Johnson, who was the highest-ranking regular U.S. Army officer to volunteer in Spain, arrived at the Fifteenth's headquarters the following day. He states now that if he had not been held up in Paris, and then in Figueras, he could perhaps have averted the debacle. A graduate of the U.S. War College, General Staff School, he was a regular Army captain of the headquarters of the Twenty-sixth Division of the Massachusetts National Guard, and a small arms instructor at M.I.T. Requesting a year's leave from his duties, he had offered his considerable services to the cause of the Spanish Republic.

Gal did nothing to help the situation. In April, for example, when the Lincolns were granted a long-overdue rest, they were allowed out of the trenches for only *two days*. During this time, they were taken along with the British to the town of Alcalá de Henares to parade for the townspeople, to be reviewed by the general after a few glasses of cognac, and then to be returned to the very same trenches!

Steve Nelson, probably the best-liked American commissar to survive the Spanish war, became embroiled in the Gal controversy immediately upon his arrival at Lincoln head-quarters in April. According to Nelson, the meaningless slaughter of the twenty-seventh continued to hang over the heads of the officers of the Fifteenth like a Damoclean sword. He resolved to do something about it once and for all. A meeting was held, and it was decided that he would go directly to Gal with the request that the Lincolns be given relief or allowed to transfer to another brigade or division. Nelson relates:

When I came into his [Gal's] headquarters, lo and behold, I see a big room without anything in it except a couple of maps and a large-size picture of General Gal. It was a freshly painted picture, approximately life-size, and it hung right in the back of him with the epaulettes on his uniform staring out at me. The whole thing floored me. I had walked in in a pair of old I/B. britches [ski-pants tied at the bottom], and an old shirt and an old brown beret. I took the beret off, figuring that I was in an office and that I shouldn't sit down with my cap on. The painting plus my immediate awareness of the man's vanity didn't help mat-ters any. I was afraid I wouldn't get very far with him, but I presented our arguments anyway. A very sharp conversa-tion developed.

It became instantly apparent that instead of being a man, instead of being willing to see the guys, face up to them and tell them: "Look! A mistake was made—I made it, or the division made it, or the army made it—it was a mistaken decision," he preferred to ignore their mood

entirely, insisting that they stay in the same trenches. He
insisted, too, that they were showing all kinds of weak-
nesses, particularly American superiority, *imperialist
superiority*, if you will, and that he wasn't going to let
them get away with it.

Nelson was a newcomer. Gal had his way; the Lincolns
remained on the Jarama. That the situation was resolved at all
can be credited not to the commissariat, but rather to the
men's own American spirit of anti-Fascism and their desire to
get on with the job they had come to do.

With the coming of spring many United States notables
visited the American positions, including many reporters.
Herbert Matthews writes, "The Battalion section of the Brigade H.Q. was in a little house not far from the main square of
the village of Morata, and it was like a corner of home to us
newspapermen."

Martha Gellhorn visited the Lincolns on a number of occasions. She arrived the first time on April 5, in the midst of an
attack, and was forced to spend the day at the brigade's first-
aid post, watching the bodies of the dead and wounded being
brought in. Afterward, she memorialized the day in an article
for *Colliers*, a few copies of which reached Spain and were
avidly read by the volunteers.

The attack of April 5 was the last the Lincolns would make
on Jarama. The objective was to straighten a small section of
the line still held by the insurgents as a result of the March 14
attack. The job was accomplished, but that was the extent of
it; no further advance could be made. Hy Rosner, with
wounds still unhealed from the earlier battle, tells of commandeering an ambulance and aiding in the evacuation of
wounded, under heavy enemy fire. Among the wounded
were Captain Johnson, Hourihan, David Jones, and a number
of leading cadres. Oliver Law was advanced to command
the Abraham Lincoln Battalion, filling the gap left by the
wounded officers.

Other journalists, notably Herbert Matthews of the *Times*
and George Seldes of the *New York Post*, were frequent visi-

tors to the American lines, as was J. B. Haldane, the eminent British scientist, whose two sons were fighting with the British. Haldane had been an infantry bombadier with the British Army in France during the First World War. He gave valuable tips to the British volunteers about the techniques involved in tossing hand grenades into enemy trenches.

Haldane's semi-official mission was to study the effects of the Fascist air raids on Madrid. He also advised the Spanish authorities on how to set up defenses against chemical gas attacks. The Republican forces had captured cylinders of mustard gas during the rout of the Italian divisions at Guadalajara. Thereafter, Soviet experts on chemical warfare had flown hurriedly from the USSR, and a secret school was established to train Republican officers. The Fascists never actually used these weapons; but Haldane's reports from Spain on the effects of air raids became quite useful to the British War Office three years later, when the German Luftwaffe appeared in the skies over London!

Matthews writes of one of his visits:

> I found them all healthy and reasonably happy, with plenty of zest left for fighting. . . . As usual they all jumped on me for news from the States, of what Americans thought about Spain, of how the strikes were getting along—and what about the baseball season. The old complaint about not receiving American cigarettes was made a dozen times. That always was an unsolved mystery. Cigarettes were sent from New York often enough, but somehow they never got past Barcelona and Valencia.
>
> The trenches were very well built—even deep enough for my height. As I walked along, one young chap impulsively offered me his rifle and asked me if I would like to take a shot. When I refused he said, "of course, that would jeopardize your non-combatant standing." It never occurred to him that anyone would not really care to take a shot at Fascists.

Edwin Rolfe, editor of the *Volunteer*, organ of the Fifteenth Brigade, writes of Hemingway:

Among the best loved by the Lincoln boys, was Ernest Hemingway. The presence of this huge, bull-shouldered man with the questioning eyes and the full-hearted interest in everything that Spain was fighting for instilled in the Americans some of his own strength and unostentatious courage. They knew he was himself a veteran of one war, that he still carried the fragments of an old wound in his body; and the fact that such a man with so prominent a position in the world was devoting all of his time and effort to the Loyalist cause did much to inspire those other Americans who were holding the trenches.

The Lincolns, entering into action in February, had no idea that their tour of duty would be longer than that of any other battalion serving in Spain. They made the best of it. John Tisa, of New Jersey, writes:

A library was created with books by Jack London, Sinclair Lewis, Fannie Hurst, John Dos Passos, and many other well-known writers. Magazines were passed around. Still, there was so little reading material that the print was almost worn off the pages by constant thumbing. God! how we longed for more books from home. A hole in the ground deep enough to offer protection from stray bullets, and a barber [Steve Troxil] with a sharp razor did a lot to keep the men in good spirits. A radio was purchased. Loudspeakers arranged at proper distances made it possible for the whole battalion to listen in. A "wall-paper" was made up of two iron posts with a canvas shelter stretched between them. It was called *The Daily Mañana*. The paper included news of the day, humor and cartoons sketched by local talent, special notices, letters of interest, etc.

Best of all in terms of morale was the arrival of sports equipment. It was a common sight, in back of the low hill, to see ping-pong being played, or a softball catch, or a soccer game with the Lincolns pitted against the British. William Rust of the British writes:

Overhead the bullets whistled so that a player jumping to "head" a ball might easily have stopped a bullet. A dozen or so chaps, pretty well naked except for boots, would be playing with perfect indifference while a sharp artillery-tank duel was taking place just a few hundred yards away.

Among the many songs, ribald and otherwise, that epitomized the thinking of the men during the weary months along the Jarama, was one written to the tune of the "Red River Valley." It remains as one of the more popular songs of the Abraham Lincoln Brigade:

> There's a valley in Spain called Jarama;
> It's a place that we all know too well,
> For 'tis there that we wasted our manhood
> And most of our old age as well.
>
> From this valley they say we are leaving,
> But don't hasten to bid us adieu!
> For e'en though we make our departure,
> We'll be back in an hour or two.
>
> O, we're proud of the Lincoln Battalion
> And the marathon record it's made.
> But if you would do us a favor
> You will take our last word to Brigade:
>
> You will never be happy with strangers,
> They would not understand you like we;
> So remember the Jarama valley
> And the "old men" who wait patiently.

On June 17, 1937, after four months, or 120 days, of frontline duty, the Abraham Lincoln Battalion was relieved. Within two short weeks after the luxury of baths, haircuts, and passes to Madrid, the troops received new orders: to stand ready to participate in the first major government strategic offensive of the war.

The standards of a host of valiant men have colored the pages of American history. Since the first shots at Concord bridge which "rattled the thrones of privilege and kings," Americans have always been counted in the ranks of fighters against tyranny. That the U.S. media would be quick to avail itself of the scanty International Brigade releases as to this new American phenomenon was certain. The headlines, as if disclosing some heretofore well-kept state secret, were startling: *American Volunteers Spearhead Jarama Attack! American Shock Troops in Violent Government Offensive!* The effect was traumatic. A palpably living entity had been created with which all Americans could now identify.

It was an about-face for a significant section of the media, since most had previously given a quasi-endorsement to the Franco "crusade." The terror bombings of Spanish cities, however, plus the now open invasion of the armed might of Italy and Germany, had begun to change all that. The threat to world peace was clearly evident. That some Americans had chosen to oppose the challenge of Nazi Germany and Fascist Italy on the battlefields of Spain was the catalyst that tipped the scales.

*Time, Life, Newsweek,* and *Fortune* magazines now expressed open sympathy for the Republic. *Newsweek* went so far as to print in its entirety G. L. Steer's dramatic description of the obliteration of the Basque holy city of Guernica by flights of Ju-52s. And, too, countering the blatantly right-wing, pro-Franco *Chicago Tribune, Washington Times, New York Journal,* and the Hearst press, were the stories of George Seldes for the *New York Post,* Richard Mowrer for the *Christian Science Monitor,* Matthews for the *Times,* Hemingway for *Esquire Magazine,* and Martha Gellhorn for *Colliers.* All extolled the courage of the Spanish people, denounced the Axis attacks, and openly warned of the peril to the Western world if Fascism was allowed to win in Spain.

No better example of the sympathy for Republican Spain exists than that embodied in the heading of a release appearing in the *New York Times,* March 1, 1937, just three days after the Lincoln attack on the Jarama:

"Ninety-eight Writers Score Spanish Rebels! Despite U.S. Neutrality, Our Citizens Should Condemn Insurgents. . . ."

The accompanying article is lengthy but to the point. A glance at just some of the signatures reveals a collection of the greatest names in American letters: Franklin P. Adams, Brooks Atkinson, Robert Benchley, Erskine Caldwell, John Dewey, Clifton Fadiman, Dorothy Canfield Fisher, Sinclair Lewis, Lewis Mumford, Christopher Morley, Genevieve Taggard, Thornton Wilder, and a host of others who could scarcely be shrugged off with the tag "Communist." Nor was it an accident that the American Medical Bureau, a unit independent of the volunteers and the International Brigades, was now operating three complete hospitals within twenty-five kilometers of the Madrid front—at Romeral, Tarancón, and Villa Paz—plus a beautifully equipped and staffed mobile unit on the southern, Córdoba front.

A list of those participating in the Medical Bureau's organization, plus its sponsors, indicates the support of prominent Americans from virtually every professional walk of life. Among them were Henry Pratt Fairchild, Paul Douglas, Albert Einstein, Walter B. Cannon of Harvard Medical School, James B. Peters of Yale Medical School, and a host of others representing virtually every university medical school in the United States.

American trade unions also supported the cause. Both the CIO and AFL had come out strongly for the Republic and for their beleaguered brothers in the great Spanish unions, the Unión General de Trabajadores (UGT) and the Confederación Nacional de Trabajadores (CNT). At the request of the International Federation of Trade Unions, the American Trade Union Committee for Relief to Spain (representing both the AFL and CIO) dispatched 100,000 much-needed dollars to Spain in mid-June of 1937. An additional $125,000 was sent in mid-July, at the height of the Government's Brunete offensive. This was but a part of the flow of funds to aid the Republic. In that same period over $800,000 was raised by Spanish Republican supporters in the United States, $170,000 by the American Medical Bureau, $152,000 by the Spanish Socialist Confederation, and an additional $275,000 by the North American Committee. An equivalent sum today would approximate 10 to 20 million dollars—no small feat in that depression year of 1937!

Nor were the Lincoln volunteers overlooked. By April of 1937, the Friends of the Abraham Lincoln Brigade was organized, with functioning chapters in every major city. Its list of national sponsors also read like an honor roll of the best in America. California, for example, had among its sponsors Ellis Patterson, state assemblyman, Los Angeles Supervisor John Anson Ford, the distinguished writer Upton Sinclair, Leo Gallagher, the only American attorney to observe the infamous Reischtag trials, and the eminent actors James Cagney, Frederic March, and Mary Astor, among others.

Needless to say the problem of cigarettes and "things from home" had been solved. Indeed, the men of the International Brigades as a whole shared in the American largesse, including all those from Fascist countries for whom there would otherwise be no packages, for whom there would be nothing, not even letters.

> The New York Times, June 12, 1937. The formation of a new battalion of Americans, the George Washington Battalion, fighting on the side of the Loyalist Government of Spain was announced by the Friends of the Abraham Lincoln Brigade at their headquarters at 125 West 45th Street, New York City.

A week prior to the Lincolns' withdrawal the "new" Washington Battalion had arrived at Morata to take over reserve positions and await orders. Its commander was a Yugoslav-American, Mirko Markowitcz, who, like the Lincoln's first commander, David Harris, seemed to play a minimal role in the affairs of the unit. David Mates, a Chicagoan, and steelworkers union organizer, was his commissar, and Captain Trail, an English officer, his adjutant. Lieutenant Hans Amlie, a Wisconsin mining engineer, member of the American Socialist Party executive, and a brother of the progressive congressman Thomas Amlie of Wisconsin, commanded Company 1. Lieutenant Cecil Smith, a Canadian with a Princess Pat regimental background, commanded Company

2. Lieutenant Yardas, another Yugoslav-American, commanded Company 3. The twice-wounded Black Lieutenant
Walter Garland of the Lincolns had been appointed commander of the machine gun company. The company commissars were, respectively, Bernard Ames from Washington, DC,
Morris Wickman, a Black from Philadelphia, Harry Hynes, a
west coast seaman who was very popular with the men, and
Carl Geiser, a university student from Ohio.

Organization of the Washingtons had begun immediately
upon the departure of the Lincolns for the front. Since that
date, February 16, well over a thousand additional Americans
had passed through Albacete. With the closing of the border,
most had been forced to climb the Pyrénées. A few came
by ship. On May 30, the small steamer *Ciudad de Barcelona*, from Marseilles, with 280 Internationals aboard (80 of
them American and 20 Canadian) was torpedoed off Mal-
grat, Spain.

"We were hit," relates Abe Osheroff,

> At about 2:00 P.M., and about three hours from Barcelona.
> There were two torpedoes. The first blew a tremendous
> hole in the side; the second missed and wound up on the
> beach. The ship went down within fifteen minutes, with
> few lifeboats being launched. Volunteers from the Ameri-
> can National Maritime Union kept their cool and threw
> everything floatable overboard for the dozens of men
> struggling in the water. A Republican seaplane, which had
> followed us most of the way while keeping an eye on the
> Italian cruiser paralleling us on the horizon, dropped its
> bombs in the general area of the submarine and then
> landed on the water to help in the rescue of the Interna-
> tionals. Fishermen too were coming out with all speed
> from Malgrat.

Osheroff, a strong swimmer, together with a Canadian, Ivor
Anderson, boosted as many as fourteen men to the seaplane's
lower wing. The plane then taxied the mile to shore, with
Osheroff and Anderson swimming in its wake. Over fifty men
were drowned, fifteen of the American and Canadian Internationals. [Anderson himself would be killed in the Battle of the

Ebro, and Osheroff retired from action at Fuentes del Ebro with a shattered knee.]

Of the many Americans who had passed through Albacete, some had joined with returning wounded to flesh out the Lincoln Battalion. Others became a part of the rapidly expanding International Brigade transport services, artillery unit, ambulance units, and the like. Some sixty Americans joined with forty English and an equal number of Cubans and Latin Americans to form Company 2 of the Twentieth Battalion, Eighty-sixth Mixed Brigade. They were sent south to help contain a limited rebel offensive in the Córdoba-Espiel-Peñarroya sector.

The Anglo-American Company, as it was called, was commanded by Lieutenant Rollin Dart, an American whose background was as an officer with four years service in the U.S. Army Air Corps. He had come to Spain to fly. Unable to do this for the moment, he accepted the command of the Anglo-American Company. The company's commissar was John Gates, from Youngstown, Ohio. Gates was to remain with the Eighty-sixth Brigade long after its foreign cadres returned to their respective countrymen. He moved rapidly from company to battalion to brigade commissar, "because," as he put it, "of my effectiveness with burros and public relations."

The story of the Twentieth Battalion's commandeering of a train and their chasing the Moroccans through Andalucía is legendary. In mid-May 1937, a new "Government of National Unity," headed by the Socialist Juan López Negrín, had replaced the altogether chaotic Largo Caballero government, responsible for so much of the debilitating confusion of the previous critical months. Negrín's first act was to dispatch a military staff to the aid of the Basque-Asturian enclave in the north, then under attack by Navarese divisions and the Italian CTV, recovered from its debacle at Guadalajara. There were few if any planes in the north, no tanks at all, and a bare minimum of artillery.

On June 11, 1937, the Fascist northern command renewed its offensive. Preliminary barrages from some 150 guns were devastating. The waves of Ju-52s and He-45s from the Nazi Condor Legion were the paradigm for future Rotterdams,

Coventrys, and Dunkirks. On June 20, the Basque capital, Bilbao, fell. The Basque remnants retreated toward the final redoubts of Santander and Gijón.

The second act of the Negrín government was to unleash a major offensive designed to save those last cities of the north while simultaneously breaking the seige of Madrid.

The "Brunete Offensive," as it was later called, lacked neither audacity nor wisdom. It was a classic pincer movement, south from the Madrid-Escorial road and west toward Boadilla del Monte from just north of the village of Villaverde. Had it succeeded, Madrid would have become the anvil upon which some of the best enemy troops could be crushed. Such a victory, however, would be wholly dependent upon the speed and *skill* of the attacking troops; for the conditions, the superior weaponry and cadres of the enemy demanded a closing of the pincers within forty-eight hours. After that would come the counter-attack—the deluge of foreign steel and explosives.

July 2, 1937: In the first hours of darkness, trucks appeared in all the villages of the Fifteenth Brigade. The ensuing convoys encircled blacked-out Madrid, heading north and west. From the first moment, the Americans were aware of a massive movement around them—artillery, tanks, field kitchens, battalions of marching men. "It seemed," as one man later put it, "that all the Republic's resources would be committed to the battle."

United Press dispatches from Hendaye, France, had previously reported that the Republic's Central Army Commander, General José Miaja, had "cancelled all furloughs and ordered his men back to the trenches. The American Lincoln and Washington Battalions," the dispatch said, "had returned to their posts on the Jarama."

Not so! By the following morning the Americans were encamped to the northwest of Madrid in the proximity of Torrelodones on the Escorial Highway. July 4th was celebrated accordingly. American troops were in high spirits, as were those of the other battalions, invited to share in the Yankee Independence Day. Jack Shirai, the Lincoln cook, together with Lou Zlotnick from the Washingtons, prepared an unusually good meal. Each man was also issued double rations of chocolate and cigarettes—an invariable indication that an offensive was in the offing.

The meal finished; at precisely the moment when all had settled back to enjoy its aftermath, motorcycles roared through the swift-falling twilight. The orders were: "Battalions! Prepare to move out!" The Brunete Offensive had begun!

July 5, 5:30 A.M.: With the first fingers of dawn greeting the rising ground mists, the men of the Fifteenth found themselves situated on a ridge peering down into the open expanse below them. The Lincolns, the last to come up, moved into position just as the roar of Republican guns signaled the formal beginning of the offensive.

Actually, the forward movement had begun many hours before. Beyond the ridge there was a collage of movement against the panorama of rolling plains and occasional hills or *barrancas*, all sloping down from the Republican high ground. To the west was the Perales River; on its far side the rebel-held village of Navalagamella. Southwest, at twelve kilometers, was the village of Quijorna. Due south, at perhaps four kilometers, was the village of Villanueva de la Cañada, and much further, at thirteen kilometers, the village of Brunete. To the east was the Guadarrama River and the village of Villanueva del Pardillo. To the south of Pardillo, the vague slopes of the Guadarrama rose gradually to a long crest and disappeared in the distance.

It was a Dantean montage, a sweeping vista of war. Government and rebel planes were overhead. An ammunition dump had been hit in Quijorna; columns of black smoke joined the dust and cordite of exploding shells. Lines of men advanced over the fields and along the roads toward the far villages, some in column, others in open formation, and already taking casualties. Squadrons of cavalry flushed the ravines of the enemy. From everywhere came the pervasive crackling of countless machine guns and rifles. Even as the Lincolns watched, the fingers of a killing heat began to touch them. They reached for their canteens. By 7:00 A.M. the canteens were almost empty.

A number of T-26 tanks which seemed to have been moving

toward La Cañada came under the fire of enemy antitank guns and shifted south. This movement, reported to brigade and division, apparently prompted General Gal to order the Fifteenth to advance and take Cañada! The original plan, the rapid penetration east and south for a quick seizure of Mosquito Crest on the far side of the Guadarrama River, was thus put aside. Gal's decision was to prove disastrous. As the Republican General Vicente Rojo suggests, the Fifteenth was then "lost to the attraction of fire." An assault on La Cañada instead of bypassing it simply meant that 3,000 crack troops were now missing from the exact spot where they would be needed the most—Mosquito Crest, which dominated the village of Boadilla del Monte, the last stronghold on the way to closing the pincers.

Villanueva de la Cañada was a front-line fortress: concrete bunkers, triple lines of barbed wire—the works. It had batteries of 10.5s, antitank guns, mortars, and machine guns everywhere. It was defended by a battalion of between 800 and 1,000 hand-picked Falangist volunteers.

By 10:00 A.M., the British, Lincolns, Washingtons, and Dimitrovs, having advanced down the long, ravine-slashed slopes, had encircled the village. By noon the Lincolns to the west and the Washingtons to the north had infiltrated to within a hundred yards or so of the first bunkers. The advance continued, slowly, all afternoon. Some units reached the first houses of the village, took the first machine gun nests. Others, pinned down in a partially harvested wheat field, could only listen to the cries for water from the wounded and the dying. Again, the assault was being carried forward with little or no artillery support, and no tanks or friendly aviation.

As dusk fell, the rebels tried to break out to the south—and ran head-on into units of the British Battalion. The Fascist officers, desperate, used civilians as shields, firing from behind them into the advancing British. The British, in turn, not wishing to risk the lives of civilian women and children, charged the Fascists with *arma-blanca*, the bayonet. The fighting was instantly brutal. The British, enraged by the Fascist tactics, granted no quarter. William Rust writes:

It was all over in minutes. The enemy lay dead everywhere on the road, and mingled with their drab uniforms were the brighter dresses of the women and children. Fortunately most of the civilians got away. Many of the women helped to dress the wounds of the British casualties.

Simultaneously with the hand-to-hand combat on the road, the Lincolns stormed into the streets with bayonet and grenade and began taking their first prisoners. As they advanced, they could hear shouts, hurrahs, and exploding grenades marking the advance of the Washington and Dimitrov battalions. The bitter fighting went on all night, house to house, street by street. It was not until 7:00 A.M. of the following morning that the last pocket of resistance was overcome and the village secured.

The enemy had paid a heavy price. Of the 800 or so Falangists, less than 300 were prisoners. Many machine guns were captured, as well as the battery of 10.5s and a half-dozen antitank guns, many mortars, and hundreds of rifles. But the battalions of the Fifteenth had also suffered, losing as many as twenty men each. The British had lost George Brown, a company commander and a beloved veteran of Jarama. The Washington adjutant, Captain Trail, had been killed, as had Max Krauthamer, the twice-wounded Jarama veteran. John Oscar Bloom of Canada, who had gone into the attack waving a straw sombrero and yelling, "Come on Mackenzie-Papineau!" was instantly killed. Also dead were Joseph Armitage, another Jarama veteran, and Bryce Coleman, a young recruit to the Lincolns. The list of wounded was long: Lieutenant Daniel Lepo, Lincoln machine-gun company commander. Captain Martin Hourihan was hit again; this time both an ankle and thigh were smashed by bullets. Lieutenant Walter Garland was hit for the *third* time. Other casualties were John Givney, Norman Duncan, Frank Martin of San Francisco, who survived a dangerous stomach wound, and Moe Fishman of the Washington's Company 1, who lay for twelve hours exposed to the blazing sun with a smashed leg bone and without water or medication.

The knowledge that twenty-four precious hours plus an important part of the brigade's strength had been spent in the assault was cause for some concern, especially since it was now known that the Republican Colonel, Enrique Lister, operating wholly in enemy territory, had seized Brunete in the early hours of the previous day and, not waiting for the arrival of the Thirteenth and Fifteenth International Brigades, was now within two kilometers of Sevilla la Nueva in the south. With a skirmish line of scouts thrown out behind a screen of a dozen tanks, he had struck to the very outskirts of Boadilla del Monte—a penetration of twenty kilometers. And beyond Boadilla was Madrid. Another dozen kilometers and the battle was won! "General Varela," the rebel archivist Manuel Aznar writes,

> could see the Republican tanks advancing from his command post. Some had penetrated to the first houses of the town, and to within six hundred meters of Varela's H.Q. Varela could be reached with a rifle shot. A little more and he would have been within grenade distance.

Of the rebel counter-measures in the face of the Republican loss of momentum, Aznar says:

> The 13th Division of Barrón is hurled into battle almost blind. The 150th follows, commanded by Colonel Sans de Buruaga. The two commanders take advantage of the hours of pause that the "reds" have given them—hours which would contain the secret of the battle of Brunete. The 12th Provisional Division of Guadarrama, consisting of nineteen units under General Asencio, is also thrown into battle. Hour after precious hour the necessary reserves are mobilized. Aviation from the North flies immediately to the Center. The 4th and 5th Brigades of Navarre, in line before Santander, are given orders to move south—to Madrid!

With but a few hours sleep, the Lincolns again set out for their original destination; this beneath a shelling from new enemy batteries in Quijorna. For whatever reasons, no guides were forthcoming, so that the day of July 6, too, was wasted in endless marches across fields and *barrancas* in search of orientation points for further advance.

On the morning of the seventh, they arrived before Mosquito Crest, a height dominating the village of Boadilla, where they should have been by noon of the first day. On that first day, the fifth, the height had been penetrated and flanked by limited elements of Lister's Ninth Brigade. It was now held by the enemy, since the hard-fighting Spaniards, with no support, had been forced to retreat.

The lost hours were truly gone forever. With the crack of dawn, the enemy air arm had appeared in massive strength. At each flank of the pocket—in the south below Brunete, and all along the length of the heights of Romanillas and Mosquito, Italian and German batteries were now in position.

Indeed, the Americans, moving now to the assault of Mosquito Crest, were actually confronted by a swarm of rebel infantry advancing down the slopes from the ridge. The two American battalions kept right on going, a thin line of advancing bayonets in the face of which the enemy broke and ran, back toward the dominating ridge some 2,000 meters to the east.

Manuel Aznar states that these troops were elements of the Eighth Bandera of the *Tercio*, spearheading Asencio's Guadarrama Division. The heavy machine guns of the Americans, firing over the heads of the advancing infantry companies, cut into the fleeing Legionnaires with deadly accuracy.

Established on a line with a small knoll, and fronted by a declivity or ravine, the Lincoln staff—Law, Nelson, Adjutant Vincent Usera, Lieutenant Paul Burns, and the new machine gun company commander, Lieutenant Sidney Levine—decided to push the advance from the captured knoll. Law, Burns, and Usera would take the men over. Nelson would go only as far as the opposite ridge until the forward movement had attained some degree of success.

At that precise moment, the Lincoln line came under a severe fire of antitank shells and mortars. The few Republican tanks in the area had disappeared.

Down into the ravine went the attacking companies, and

out onto the open slopes of the far side. The fire from the heights was heavy, the casualties in the first hundred yards severe. As at Jarama, to advance without support became impossible. The men dug in, protecting themselves and their wounded as best they could.

Harry Fisher of New York describes the death of Oliver Law:

> We were to attack and take the ridge, which was about 600 meters away. All I can remember is that I was a little shaky, knowing that we were going over the top again. I was to be a runner for Paul Burns. Johnny Powers would be his second runner. We lined up for the attack and we were very thirsty. At 10:00 sharp Burns waved his pistol and shouted, "O.K. Let's go, fellahs!" We crossed the ravine and as soon as we reached the top of the ridge all hell broke loose, machine guns, shells, everything. After going ahead for about a hundred yards, I hit the ground, breathless. Again, like at La Cañada, I heard the cries for first aid and the moans of the wounded and dying. To the right I saw Powers. He had a bad leg wound. Oliver Law got up then. He was about twenty yards ahead of us, standing there yelling and waving his pistol. "O.K., fellahs, let's go! Let's go! Let's keep it up. We can chase them off that hill. We can *take* that hill. Come on!" He got hit just about then. That was the last I saw of him. Some of the guys got to him and pulled him off the field, but he died before he could reach the hospital.

Stretcher bearers sent to take Law back say that he didn't want to go, that he kept saying not to waste time with him. He finally said, "No use lugging me any longer, boys. I'm finished. Put me down." They buried him there, made a makeshift plaque, and hung his helmet on it. The plaque stated his name, the fact that he was thirty-four years old, and that he was the first known Black to ever command an almost all-white American military unit.

The Lincoln dead numbered between fifteen and twenty. Another thirty or so were wounded. Among these was Paul Burns, the very able Company 1 commander. Steve Nelson assumed command of the battalion in the absence of the adjutant, Vincent Usera. Lines were established. A link was made with the Washingtons. The battalions dug in.

Harold Smith of the Washington's Company 1 describes their attack against the ridge:

> More action over to the left front. Detro [Philip] pointed out a ridge three hundred yards ahead and said that we were going to take up positions there, that I was to take a unit out and establish an outpost in the valley below it. [Detro now commanded Company 1. Hans Amlie, upon Trail's death, became battalion adjutant.] We move out. With me are Dick Ruciano, Felix Kusman, Johnny Mills. We had a light Dictoryev MG, and twelve men in the group. Heavy fire to the left [Mosquito Crest]. We see men and some tanks maneuvering to fire. Suddenly we are confronted by Markovicz. He waves a machine pistol and yells something in broken English, like: "On to Madrid!" He points toward the hill. I wave my rifle and yell, "*Adelante!*" The guys follow. We run up the ravine in the direction of the firing. In the open we come under fire. We take cover and Felix opens up against the enemy positions some six or seven hundred yards away. Johnny Mills, the ammo-carrier, runs up with the pans. He's hit instantly. I figure there isn't much sense in staying there. We continue the advance. The *barranca* up which we are going keeps narrowing. Then it takes a sharp turn to the right. I find Sam Stone, who is a section leader from another company. He says we are attacking the hill and I call to the guys and we take the right turn out of the *barranca* and into an open field on the hill's slope. It was a long open slope, cultivated, wide, and it led up in the direction of that big black hill. The slope had a line of men on it, all driving toward its crest. They were charging and a lot were already down. It seemed utterly chaotic—very heavy MG and mortar fire. All I could think of was to keep myself going forward. I forgot completely that I was a squad commander. I continued on for some distance with Dick Rusciano and a couple of others. We passed Harry Hynes, Company 3 commissar. He was mortally wounded, blood pumping arterially. We bandaged him hurriedly and continued on—could see others coming over the same terri-

tory. We stopped at an olive tree. No one was in front now except the enemy. The crest now was just a hundred or so meters distant and the fire was terrible. Ernie Arion was with me and Ray Tycer and Vaughan Love and a seaman whose name I can't remember; also a guy named Bauer, an artist. Someone called for help a short distance in front of us. We went to get him and found it was Herb Hutner. He had a smashed thigh-bone and while the other guys pulled and dragged, I held the two sections of his leg together. Joe Stone and Phil Detro joined us, and there was now about fifteen men around the olive tree. Ernest Arion, seeing Hutner's blood on me, thought I'd been hit. When he raised up to take a shot at the Fascist trenches he took a bullet through the heart and was killed instantly. Under Detro's command we concentrated our fire upon a part of the crest which dominated the terrain in a direct line with us. I, acting on Detro's orders, reported to Battalion H.Q. Irv Fajans was badly hit at the time. I was told that we were to hold our positions until the tanks came up, and to follow them in an assault on the hill. When I returned I found that of the fifteen men around the olive tree, eight were down, mostly dead. One, I remember, was Joe Stone. It was impossible to get men out of the place. Saw tanks coming up to the right rear. Saw one tank take a direct hit. The tank attack never developed, and it became evident that we were not going to move any further that day. Detro ordered the men to dig in and establish a line.

The greater part of the Washingtons suffered the fate of Detro's company. Harry Hynes, the west coast seaman-commissar, was dead. Hans Amlie, battalion adjutant, was wounded, dragged from the field by Roger Hargrave of the machine gun company. The battalion had taken more than a hundred casualties. Most were wounded, but an irreplaceable number were dead.

The British, attacking due east along the Boadilla Road, ran into a barrage from newly-arrived rebel guns. They were pinned down for a number of hours. Among those killed was Charles Goodfellow, battalion adjutant. His place was taken by Sam Wilde, who, within minutes, was a casualty himself.

Starting on the morning of July 9, the Fascist military had a superiority in arms, due to the reinforcements that they were constantly receiving. On each ensuing day the weary Internationals of the Fifteenth were bombed and strafed; still they maintained their pressure against the hill. Five times in as many days they probed the heights, and each time they were repulsed. The Americans, occupying extremely disadvantageous positions, were as close to the enemy as it was physically possible to be. The terrain to their rear was mostly exposed and open. One of the men wrote in his diary:

> Down from our positions into the valley, and up the hillside behind us, ran the lines of communications. They were raked night and day by snipers and machine gun fire, artillery and aviation. The ration parties ran the gauntlet, using mules when they could be used; and when these were killed, running, ducking, stumbling down the hillside, laden with sacks of grub. The boys in the trenches could see them coming—and laid bets on whether they would get through.

The wounded simply couldn't be taken out until nightfall. Yet many times in a single day, with desperately wounded men bleeding to death, the ambulance men loaded their mules—already covered with blood from previous wounded—and flogged the wretched animals along to give the men a chance.

On July 11, the rebels counter-attacked along the entire length of the Guadarrama, using elements of three divisions. The Lincoln Brigade received its share of attention. By day's end, however, it had not ceded a single foot of ground. And this time it was the enemy whose bodies littered the slopes below the trenches.

Jack Shirai, the lone Japanese-American from California, was killed on that day. He'd kept his promise, which was to join the battalion in the lines when the action began and "to hell with the kitchen." Like Oliver Law, they buried him with just a headstone, noting his ancestry and his courage.

A random sampling of media communiques from the United States reveals the strong interest in America's committment to the Lincoln volunteers:

*Milwaukee Journal*, Madrid, July 18, 1937. Hans Amlie, a native of Wisconsin and a brother of Congressman Thomas Amlie, was among the wounded when twenty Americans gave their lives in a charge against the Spanish rebels, July 9th. Eighty other Americans of the George Washington Battalion, of which Amlie was adjutant, were wounded in the fighting—but the Loyalist lines were carried forward.

*San Diego Sun*, Madrid, July 18, 1937. Sixteen miles west of Madrid the pick of the Nationalist and Loyalist Armies fought it out today with every arm of warfare from airplanes to trench knives and fists, the most savage and perhaps the most important battle of the Spanish Civil War.

[U.S.] Volunteers of the Abraham Lincoln and Washington Battalions, who a year ago were clerks, students, and workers back home, were thrown into the most dangerous areas of the fighting. Sources close to the General staff estimated that between five and six thousand men of both armies were killed and wounded yesterday. Ambulances fought for space on the roads back to Madrid.

The greater metropolitan newspapers—the *New York Times*, the *San Francisco Chronicle*, the *Chicago Sun*, the *Washington Post*—all gave wide coverage to each communique containing news of the American volunteers.

On the night of July 12, the Lincolns withdrew to the far side of the Guadarrama. On the fourteenth, following a couple of good meals plus a bath in the rapidly evaporating pools of the little river, the two battalions were merged. Their combined strength now numbered less than the original 525 men of the Washington Battalion. Markowicz took the place of the fallen Oliver Law. Nelson was commissar, Captain Rollin Dart, adjutant, Lieutenant Leonard Lamb, chief of the headquarters company. Lieutenant Sidney Levine retained his command of the machine gun company, with Carl Geiser of the Washingtons as his commissar. Alec Miller, Canadian, and Owen Smith became commanders of Companies 1 and 2, respectively. Lieutenant Yardas continued in command of

Company 3, with Henry Eaton as his commissar, replacing the fallen Morris Wickman. Eaton was the grandson of a former mayor of Los Angeles.

On the following night the Lincoln Battalion was ordered to the aid of Spanish units defending captured Villanueva del Pardillo. The march was a forced one, up the dry bed of the Guadarrama River.

"It was rough," Harold Smith relates. "Guys discovered they could walk in their sleep. One man would stop and the rest would domino against him. The officers would have to kick the men awake."

Reaching the La Cañada-Pardillo Road at dawn, they marched three kilometers to enter another wide *barranca* with steep sides. Louis Zlotnick's food trucks caught up with them. Just as the food was being apportioned, however, shells began to land in the *barranca*'s shallow bottom. The men, exhausted from both fatigue and hunger, tried to ignore the flying shrapnel while digging in and eating at the same time. Then came the menacing sound of planes.

During the ensuing hours the rebels, having pinpointed the Lincoln positions, sent flight after flight of bombers over the *barranca*. "The earth trembled and shook in continuous upheaval," Steve Nelson writes.

> Whole trees were uprooted and flew through the air. The blast of the concussions was like a wind-storm. It was impossible to believe that anyone but yourself was still alive; impossible that you could live so long in such an inferno. In the seconds-long pauses you listened for voices, screams, for any *human* sound, and there was nothing. And then a shell burst, and you heard the roar of motors and the scream of bombs, and again the earth was ripped to fragments around you.

Harry Fisher recalls,

> They came in low, hour after hour. The bombs fell everywhere, saturating the place. Nothing could be seen because of the smoke and dust. I remember we had a helluva time just staying on the ground. We had to hold on

to the grass to keep from rising in the air. I remember thinking that everyone else must certainly be dead; that no one could possibly live in this chaos.

Henry Eaton describes the scene in a letter to his family,

> We dug our faces into the earth, our bodies prone. No thunder could be so deafening; the stench of high, sulphurous explosives choked in our mouths. Then crash, and a weight is forcing me into the soil. A faint moan—I knew then that the comrade lying next to me had been thrown on my back. A slight convulsion and the moaning stops. Shoving, I am free of his weight. The air is thick, a gray sulphurous fog, almost impenetrable. I look at the body of my comrade. It was as if a giant biscuit-cutter had been plunged into his back, his skull, his buttocks, and left gaping holes, clean and bloodless. The seven letters from his sweetheart in Detroit, which I had delivered to him the day before, are all around him. My own possessions have been blown to shreds.

The bombs and shells all landed in an area less than three city blocks in length. The battalion command post, with Nelson, Bernard Addes, and Alec Miller present, was under an oak tree in the *barranca*. The tree's limbs and a part of its bole had been clipped off by white-hot shrapnel. Then a Spanish runner from the lines ahead appeared with the information that they were under heavy attack, *that the Lincoln commander was to come instantly with any of his men who had survived the bombing!*

Nelson, Miller, and Lamb ran along the top of the *barranca*, peering desperately into the cloud of smoke and dust, calling to the men to form up, that the lines were breaking ahead, that they must go to the aid of the Spaniards. And out of that pall of smoke came men, stumbling, faces black with the grit of cordite and ashes, eyes staring, shocked, stunned by the weight of bombs and shells—but still willing. Section after section came together, then company after company—on the double, moving straight to the lines ahead.

To quote Nelson again:

It was the miracle of the war. Just nine men were dead and sixteen wounded. All that day the Spanish comrades had watched the death-fires flickering over the hollow where the Americans lay. They too had believed that it was impossible that many, or *any*, could have survived. They watched with amazement and joy the *Americans* streaming into their lines. More. They cheered, wept openly, wringing the hands of their Lincoln comrades.

But there was no time for greetings. The third rebel attack of the day was just then beginning. Though the previous attacks had been driven back with considerable losses, the effect of the rebel artillery had been devastating. Trench walls, parapets, and defending machine guns had been destroyed in whole sections of the line. The depleted Republican battalion, a unit of Colonel Enciso's Second Brigade of the Tenth Division, had suffered maximum casualties. The Lincoln machine-gun company, with the heavy Maxims from both the Washington and Lincoln Battalions, quick-mounted these guns all down the twisting trench line to deliver a withering, killing fire into the advancing Legionnaires, driving them instantly back. Not stopping there, the Americans then hit the entire area of enemy strong points, enfilading the supply road to Las Rosas, and all visible points of rebel communications.

Daniel Groden of New York tells of one last attempt by a Moroccan *tabor* of some 150 men to mount a night assault. The Americans hurled grenades and fired into the advancing wraiths. Groden, taking out a patrol in the predawn hours, found many Moroccan bodies among those of the Legionnaires—plus American-made Mills grenades.

The Lincolns remained in the Pardillo sector for another two days, moving from threatened point to threatened point to give support by their presence and élan to the decimated battalions of the Second Brigade. On the night of the seventeenth, they returned to the general rest area of the Fifteenth Brigade.

On the eighteenth, the full rebel counter-offensive was set in motion. Six fresh divisions were literally hurled against the exhausted Madrid Army. Irving Pflaum, United Press correspondent, filed the following report:

> Madrid, July 19, 1937. There has been no such concentration of men and material in any previous battle of the war. . . . The attack broke Saturday evening with a terrible bombardment from Nationalist planes, masses of bombers and pursuit ships of the German and Italian air fleets.
>
> At dawn yesterday there was another air bombardment, the heaviest perhaps that any troops have ever experienced. . . . Artillery joined in the fire and Madrid, sixteen miles away, awakened to the thunderous echo of the explosions and knew that the big battle was on.

Rebel archives tell of mountains of dust and battle smoke to darken the sun. They tell of crushing the defending Republican Brigades before Navalagamella, of Asencio resuming the attack at Villafranco del Castillo, and of Brunete changing hands four times in a frightful carnage of shells, plunging tanks, and hand-to-hand battle. In the end, however, the Republic still held Brunete.

The counter-offensive continued.

During those days, from the seventeenth to the twenty-fourth of July, the men of the Fifteenth lost all track of time. One day merged with another in intensity and chaos. The battalions were sent individually into every area of danger, into each wavering line that had been shot up, decimated or, in many cases, destroyed. The courageous Spanish brigades of Modesto, Lister, Jurado, Enciso, and El Campesino, as well as the Internationals, were reduced to companies, sections, before the continuing onslaught of the hordes of Moroccans, the cannon fodder of unwilling conscripts, the pick of the Navarese, and the massive force and weaponry of the Axis powers.

Each volunteer's story of the last days of Brunete is of vague but bloody actions in undetermined time and space: fire fights, hand-to-hand conflicts, the bombing of ambulances, the destruction of the clearly-marked American evacuation hospital unit by nine Ju-52s. In this last attack, Robbins, the courageous young doctor from California, was killed, as was Doctor Sollenberger of New York and two of his aides. Twelve were wounded.

Harold Smith tells of nights listening to the weird chants of the Moroccans in the trenches opposite; the Americans would counter with compositions of their own, arranged and led by Harold Malofsky of Queens, New York.

In retrospect, it was at Brunete that the name of the Abraham Lincoln Battalion began to assume the proportions of legend. It fought any and everywhere. There was no Spanish line battalion that was not aware at one time or other of the Lincoln's fighting support either directly or on its flanks. Young Spanish troops, with their innate ability to romanticize the commonplace, soon equated the deeds of the Fifteenth Brigade with the Americans alone, so that the deeds of all, rightly or wrongly, became mostly those of El Batallón Lincoln.

On July 24, when Brunete fell again, this time to such a hail of bombs and shells that the town itself was obliterated, the Fifteenth received orders to retreat across the Guadarrama. The decimated Spanish brigades of Enrique Lister simultaneously counter-attacked in order to aid the Internationals in their withdrawal from the Vado-Mosquito line. Lister reentered Brunete and was again driven out. Rebel archives tell of heavy losses along the full length of the attack perimeter. In some cases the Moroccans, Navarese, and Foreign Legion suffered sixty to eighty percent casualties before the defending Republican guns.

For the Lincoln Battalion, the day of the twenty-fourth began with an intense fire fight which touched off an enemy ammunition dump. Rebel soldiers, attempting to save the munitions, were cut down by the Lincoln's guns.

The Dimitrovs, on the Lincoln's left, led off. Sidney Levine relates, "They retreated back over the ridges in perfect order, each company covering the rearward movement of the other with its fire-power."

To the south, on the other hand, the retreat had caught the British and French in untenable positions. Cut off, they were forced to fight a running battle through all the hours of the day before reaching the safety of new Republican positions.

The Lincolns began their withdrawal with the Moroccans pouring across the ridges and ravines on either flank. The race to the river began. Company after Lincoln company filtered back through the terrain. On Nelson's orders, Lieutenant Levine, with a few light machine guns, brought up the rear, discouraging close pursuit and doggedly holding the enemy at either flank.

At the last assembly point in a *barranca*, and with fire now coming in from all angles, Nelson's attention was drawn to a line of stretchers by the questioning eyes of the wounded. Time was of the essence if their lives were to be saved. Nelson quickly detailed a squad of men to each wounded man, all under the command of Dennis Jordan. They moved out immediately, the remainder of the battalion placing itself in a protective arc between the wounded and the enemy. There would be no repeat of the massacre of the French wounded by the Moroccans at Jarama's Pindoque Bridge. One injured man, a young volunteer from Chicago named Graham, grasped Nelson's hand in silent gratitude before the stretcher bearers moved off. They headed toward the river, where they again dug in—just in time to beat back the first of an hours-long series of enemy attacks.

> United Press, Madrid, July 24, 1937. The fighting today was on a scale unequaled even in the attacks that began the siege of Madrid. Losses were frightful on both sides. All through the late afternoon until early evening U.S. Volunteers threw back wave after wave of the pick of the Nationalist Army, holding fast to the lines assigned to them and caked in sweat, dust, and blood. . . .
>
> Many stories of heroism are told by the Volunteers. One American was lying wounded on a stretcher. A doctor said: "We don't have enough stretchers for everyone. Is anyone strong enough to walk?" "I think I can," the American said. Seconds later he died.

On the night of the twenty-fourth, the British Battalion ceased to exist, as did the French Sixth of February.

The Fifteenth, when it was finally ordered to retire from the front, left the trenches at night. It was daylight, however, before they reached the La Cañada-Valdemorillo Road. The Lincoln Battalion, numbering less than 300 men, walked on the macadam as though drunk. They were bearded, dirty, emaciated—and exhausted.

A Spanish major, seeing their condition, stopped a number of trucks loaded with fresh young Spanish troops at pistol point and directed the drivers to take as many of the Americans as they could to their destination.

Once more the Lincolns found themselves in the pine-forested Castilian Eden, the original kick-off position near Valdemorillo which they had labeled the "Pearly Gates." There they were bombed one last time—within a few hundred meters of Lou Zlotnick's kitchen and the invigorating smell of his stew.

There was just one casualty here, Major George Nathan, the courageous British chief of staff. Nathan had become a legend in his native Ireland during the so-called Irish Troubles of 1916–1923. There he had fought the notorious British "Black and Tans." He had fled Ireland with a price on his head. In Spain, Nathan was just as great a hero as he had been in his homeland. Mortally wounded, Nathan, in his last moments, asked softly of those around him that they "sing him out of life." They did. The song was the Socialist anthem, "The Internationale," and the eyes of the singers streamed with tears.

A last act was played on the following night. A motorcyclist came up the road from Quijorna with a dispatch for Lieutenant Colonel Klaus, who now commanded in place of the wounded Copic. Orders were that the Fifteenth and Thirteenth Brigades return immediately to Quijorna, where Spanish troops had suffered serious losses and were under heavy attack and in danger of being overrun.

The officers of the two brigades were stunned! A staff meeting was called, and a heated discussion developed. Colonel Klaus called for the opinion of all the battalion commanders. Chapaiev, for the Dimitrovs, shook his head. His men must first be spoken to. Captain Crespo of the Fifty-ninth Spanish said briefly, stiffly, that his men were exhausted, that he did not think they could make it. A young French lieutenant, speaking for the Sixth of February's Captain Forte, who had lost an eye on the last day of action, also refused to commit their men without discussion. Klaus turned to Nelson, and Nelson said, "Our men feel the same as the others. But if the lines are breaking, we can't just sit here and let it happen."

The battalion commanders then went to speak to their units—and the men agreed to return. But they were devastated. Where three weeks before the Fifteenth Lincoln Brigade had numbered close to 3,000 men, it now numbered fewer than 600. Where three weeks before there had been 900 Americans in two battalions, now there were 280. Where there had been 360 effectives in the Sixth of February, now there were 88. An assembly of 93 exhausted Czechs and Yugoslavs were all that was left of the 450 men of the Dimitrov Battalion. And only 125 Cubans and Mexicans could be counted from the 400 men who had gone into battle under the gallant Captain Crespo. Wally Tapsall, commissar of the British Battalion, led the last of the original 360 Britishers to join the Americans on the road. There were 37 of them, hardly enough for a rifle section.

Still they were going back, prepared to fight. Then a miracle occurred: a motorcyclist arrived with a second dispatch. The message: "The Spanish comrades have extricated themselves from encirclement and have the situation in hand."

For the American volunteers, the campaign of Brunete was over.

# PART II

# ARAGON

Rich in bankruptcy, to the World
I leave my heart, to the Republic my gun
To men's slow eyes my unvanishing footsteps.

JAMES NEUGASS
WITH THE LINCOLNS AT
BRUNETE, JULY 1937

THE MESSERSCHMIDT-109, the deadliest of all German fighter aircraft in World War II, was the first one introduced on the "proving ground" of the Spanish war. The first Me-109 ever to be shot down is credited to Lieutenant Frank G. Tinker, an American volunteer in the Republican air force, on July 17, 1937, at the Madrid front. He and two Russian wing men flying single-winged Mosca L-16s repeated the deed the following day, catching five of the new 109s flat-strafing the trenches, and downing them all!

In the final months of 1936 a handful of Americans, like André Malraux's famed International Squadron, were already in action. They flew the old French Dewoitine D-373 fighters, the Nieuport NiD-52s, and the antiquated Breguet bombers. They fought strictly for pay, and their service, in some cases of questionable value, ceased altogether in December. Those who remained and those who came after did so for reasons other than money. Frank Tinker, of Dewitt, Arkansas, was one of these. Annapolis and United States Army trained, Tinker had a real love for freedom. James Hawthorne, a correspondent in those days, wrote of him that, "Democracy to Tinker spells popular independence, and *Fascism* its destruction."

In like manner, Major Frank I. Lord, an American ace of World War I who had twenty-two German planes to his credit, became a bomber pilot for the Republic. He was too old for *Chatos. Life* magazine quotes Lord as saying, "The struggle of the Spanish people changed me from an adventurer to a zealous patriot."

Frank Tinker and more than thirty American pilots continued flying through the late Fall of 1937. The eighty-plane armada (a good number of them civilian planes held together with baling wire) that blasted the Italians on the road to Guadalajara; the great air battles over the Madrid front in the blistering heat of the Republic's first offensive; the battles of Málaga, Huesca, and Teruel; the Aragón—Quinto, Belchite, Zaragoza: in all these battles the Americans pitted their stubby-winged fighters against the mass of the constantly growing rebel air arm. At the time of the Republic's greatest strength—Jarama, Guadalajara, Brunete, they, together with the young Spanish flyers called *La Gloriosa* by the people, accepted odds of four and five to one and still swept the skies of the vaunted Fiat-32s and the Heinkel 51s of the Nazi Condor Legion.

American casualties were not many. The losses, however, were deeply felt. Ben Leider, his snub-nosed *Chato* riddled with bullets, crash-landed and died on almost the same day as the Lincoln disaster on the Jarama. Leider—he had two Heinkels to his credit—was an ex-flying reporter for the *New York Post* and a founder of the American Newspaper Guild. Once during a strike, he had flown his plane to Seattle, Washington, to picket Hearst's *Post Intelligencer*, with huge banners attached to his tail assembly.

Sidney Holland, of Chicago, was brought down over Segovia while flying an unarmed cabin plane refitted as a bomber. Chang Selles of the original, mostly American, Lacalle squadron, was lost at Brunete. Eugene Nolte and Glen Finnick were both shot down over Navalcarnero while flying single-motor Soviet Rasante bombers. Finnick survived, but Nolte's plane became his funeral pyre. Some, like James Allison, were shot down and lived to fly again. Whitey Dahl was downed twice. The last time, he was captured and sentenced to death by a Fascist military tribunal. He was later freed, reputedly because of poignant letters sent to Franco by his wife.

With the end of the fighting in Aragón, the Republican air force became purely Spanish. The Internationals, however, were not forgotten, especially the Americans. During their short service of six months or so, they had destroyed upward of forty-three assorted Heinkels, Junkers, Fiats, Capronis, and new Me-109Bs.

Three American aces were born of the Spanish war. Frank

Tinker had eight verified victories, Orin D. Bell seven. Bell, like Frank Lord, was already a World War I ace, having shot down six German aircraft while flying with the Royal Canadian Air Force. In Spain he had flown mostly on the Granada-Córdoba fronts. The third ace was James Peck of California, one of the few Black pilots even to be licensed in the United States at that time. Peck flew *Chatos* for a number of months on the Aragón front, along with another Black pilot, Paul Williams. At the end of his service in Spain (during his last flight he protected Republican bombers attacking the Italian air base on Majorca), Peck had five verified kills to his credit.

The following is the only known list of Axis aircraft shot down by Americans in Spanish skies. It does not include bombers or fighters downed by the efforts of two or more flyers in the same engagement.

| | | |
|---|---|---|
| Frank G. Tinker | Guadalajara | 2 Fiats |
| | Teruel | 1 Heinkel |
| | Segovia | 1 Fiat |
| | Huesca | 1 Heinkel |
| | Brunete | 1 Fiat |
| | | 2 ME-109bs |
| Orin D. Bell | Estremadura | 7 Heinkels |
| Albert Baumler | Guadalajara | 1 Heinkel |
| | Segovia | 1 Fiat |
| | Brunete | 2 Heinkels |
| Charles Koch | Málaga-Córdoba | 2 Heinkels |
| Harold (Whitey) Dahl | Guadalajara | 1 Heinkel |
| | Segovia | 1 Heinkel |
| | Brunete | 2 Heinkels |
| Ben Leider | Jarama | 2 Heinkels |
| James Allison | Jarama | 1 Heinkel |
| | Teruel | 1 Heinkel |
| Stephen Daduk | Madrid | 1 Heinkel |
| James Peck | Aragón | 2 Fiats |
| | | 2 Heinkels |

And so it went. American flyers operated out of all airfields in Republican Spain: San Xavier, Manises at Valencia, Al

Cantarilla at Murcia, Guadalajara, Barajas—and all the military fields surrounding beleagured Madrid.

On many nights Madrid's Hotel Florida saw the flyers reunited in drinking sessions and gabfests with Hemingway, Matthews, and the officers and men of the Lincoln Brigade on leave from the front. These last were ever present, going in and out of Hemingway's rooms, trading news, using "Papa's" flowing tub, tapping his reputedly bottomless flask, and trying, conscientiously, not to disturb him in the hours when he wrote.

After Brunete, there was no more of Gal. Indeed, he seems to have disappeared at that point from brigade archives. Americans arrived in Madrid by the truckload, and the capital took them to its heart. Their stalwart, colorful figures in brigade ski pants, boots, and berets were everywhere. They filled the hotels, the Florida and the Nacional, and thrilled the *Madrileños* with their cheery and sometimes garrulous presence at Chicotes and the Aquarium, the nightclub haunts of American and Western press representatives. They could also be found at the Capital *cine*, where the Marx Brothers played to capacity crowds in *A Night at the Opera*, or at another movie house off of the Gran Vía, where *Madrileños* stared wide-eyed at Jimmy Cagney's famous grapefruit scene in *The Roaring Twenties*.

A featured entertainment, unique to Madrid under siege, was a visit to the trenches by streetcar, costing ten *céntimos*. In some places, Republican and Fascist machine gun positions were within fifty meters of each other. The American movie star Errol Flynn, who claimed Republican sympathies, was actually grazed by a stray bullet on one of these guided tours. Some Lincoln men spent the greater part of their leaves examining Madrid's fortifications.

In a sense, the capital was but an extention of Brunete. It was constantly being shelled by the many German guns installed on Monte Garabitas, the highest point of the Casa de Campo on Madrid's western outskirts. Edwin Rolfe writes:

> The artillerymen on Garabitas knew when the theatres on the Gran Vía closed, late in the afternoon; and they

timed their bombardments and set their range accordingly. Across the years of the siege many hundreds were killed this way.

But though the roar of the guns continued, so did the life of the defiant capital. The cafes were open, the markets teemed with what little there was to buy. Peddlars hawked *matcheras*, raisins, and cigarette papers (but no tobacco), and the shells never really kept anyone from his or her proper business or the variety shows and movies. As Rolfe put it, "Madrid was still the liveliest, proudest city in the world, the best to wake up in."

England's reply to the courage and strength of Republican forces at Brunete was to increase its appeasement of the Axis powers. Foreign Secretary Eden boasted that if Francisco Franco could be given the victory he, Eden, was sure he could reach agreement on an "eventual German and Italian withdrawal"; this, while the new Prime Minister, Neville Chamberlain, made personal contact with Benito Mussolini and the Italian divisions renewed their drive against the desperate Basques and Asturians in the northern enclave.

In the south the German pocket battleship *Deutchland* shelled the defenseless Republican city of Almería, an act of deliberate murder promptly denounced by the United States and completely ignored by Britain and France.

In the meantime, the Lincolns, in their base villages along the Tajo River, continued their rest, leaves, and reorganization. Early in August, it was announced that the Fifteenth would now be an all-English-speaking brigade, pending the arrival of the Canadian Mackenzie-Papineau Battalion, then in training at the village of Tarazona de la Mancha, near Albacete.

Wounded Americans were scattered throughout the capital's hospitals. The overflow was sent to the new American hospitals at Tarancón, Castillejo, and Villa Paz, this last comprising two vast landed estates, formerly summer homes of the Bourbon royal family. A general departure of wounded Jarama veterans had also begun. Captain Paul Burns was one of these. An American journalist, he had become successively, during the war, a section leader, company commander, and battalion adjutant. Twice wounded, he was being invalided home to Boston along with the three Flaherty brothers, whose exploits had been dramatized in many American newspapers.

The twice-wounded Lieutenant Walter Garland was also returning home. Other repatriates were Joseph Gordon, who had lost an eye; John Sims, who had lost an arm; David Mates, commissar of the Washingtons; and David McKelvey White, son of George White, a former governor of Ohio and then acting national chairman of the Republican Party. David White, ex-Lincoln machine gunner and former professor of English literature, was to become the first executive secretary of the Friends of the Abraham Lincoln Brigade in the United States.

The Washington Battalion would not be reconstituted. Captain Hans Amlie, recovering from wounds, would now command the Lincoln Battalion. Lieutenant Leonard Lamb would be adjutant, and an American seaman, John Quigley Robinson (Robbie), would be commissar. Like the other battalions, the Lincoln was still not up to strength. With its returned wounded, its new Spanish company, and as many as a hundred new volunteers, most of them seamen from the National Maritime Union, its roster was fewer than five hundred men.

For the first time, however, American ascendency within the structure of the brigade was becoming an established fact. Steve Nelson was now brigade commissar. Major Robert Merriman, returning from the hospital and a stint in the officer's training school, was brigade chief of staff. Captains Rollin Dart, Carl Bradley, and Eli Biegelman were now staff officers. The Fifteenth's Auto Park (transport) was now commanded by an American, Lieutenant Louis Secundy, with a majority of his drivers and mechanics American as well. The brigade quartermaster service, too, was American led and staffed.

On August 12, 1937, Lieutenant Quentin Durward Clark, commanding the mostly American Second Esquadrón of the First Regimiento de Tren, Fifth Army (transport), his commissar, William Sennett, and two American sergeants, Lindfors of Minnesota and David Thompson of San Francisco, were given *salvo conductos* to Aragón, in the northeast sector of Spain. Their job: to lay out a convoy route across some 300 kilometers of terrain. At the Fuencarral transport base again, they made their report and joined in the job of readying the trucks for the journey. An interesting sidelight to this particular base was that there were fighting bulls in the hills surrounding it. Donald Macleod, one of the drivers, remembers the time that he, Clark, Hemingway, and others went on "safari" one day to bag bulls. They got two, and a most marvelous feast was had by all.

On August 18, the Fifteenth Brigade, composed now of but four battalions and attached to the Thirty-fifth Division of the Fifth Army, was alerted. By the nineteenth the men of the battalions, picked up from their base villages and rousted out of every hotel and club in Madrid, were on their way to Aragón!

The Aragón front stretched from the French-Spanish border through Huesca, Zaragoza and south to the Franco-held bastion of Teruel, just ninety kilometers above Valencia. Unlike the brutal, bloody fighting on the northern, southern, and central fronts, no major battle had ever been fought in Aragón. Largely Anarchist controlled, the area had generally lain quiescent since the first months of the war.

Analysts today agree that had the Anarchists launched an offensive in October and November of 1936, when the poorly-armed militia of the center front was being literally cut to pieces by the sheer power of Franco's oncoming Army of Africa with its mass of newly arrived Axis weaponry and men, the capital might never have come under siege. Indeed, the Tajo River valley itself might well have been saved and the very course of the war changed! The weapons existed in Catalonia to do the job, as did the manpower. The Anarchists themselves admit to close to 100,000 rifles plus 100 pieces of artillery from the park of San Andreas alone; and all this with a plentitude of shells and munitions.

To repeat: while the rest of Spain fought desperately, against insuperable odds, there had been no shortage of weapons in Catalonia; nor had there been the slightest effort by the Anarchist chieftains to aid their comrades of the center fronts.

The disparity between the thinking of Republicans, Basque and Catalan Separatists, and Socialists and Communists of the Republic's Popular Front Government, on the one hand, and the *Federación Anarchista Ibérica* (FAI), on the other, has often been described as an unbridgeable abyss. For Spanish anarchism in its childlike simplicity—or worse—thumbed its nose at both bourgeois republicanism and socialist-communist Marxism as being different equal manifestations of the State, which it professed to abhor. No matter that the simple worker and peasant may have preferred, the Republic with all its faults was the only alternative to Franco's firing squads and a return to the dark ages.

Diego Abad de Santillán, Anarchist ideologue and leader of the FAI executive, put it piously:

> For we of the Spanish social vanguard, whether Negrín [the Socialist Premier] triumphed, or Franco won, the results would be the same. . . . If the leaders of the Libertarian organizations [the FAI] had ever *seriously* resolved to send *all* their armaments, their war materiel and their best men to the front, the war would easily have been over in a few months.

De Santillán was writing, of course, of the first months of the war, before the full weight of Axis intervention was felt. That the Anarchists acted as they did proved disastrous; and when the course of events forced a reevaluation of strategy, it was too late—for them and for Spain.

Weakened by dissention within their own rank-and-file and within the great *Confederación Nacional de Trabajo* (CNT), which they had controlled at the war's beginning, but which, in the main, had broken with them because of what they had done, they continued in a negative role until the war's end.

In Aragón at this point in time, the excesses of the FAI and its ruling body, the Autonomous Council of Aragón (now dissolved by government degree), had contributed to a fast-waning influence. Still, the Americans found themselves in a countryside whose inhabitants continued to equate the Republic with the forced collectivization of the Anarchists.

They were billeted in villages where the people were silent, cynical, and not at all sure that the oppression of a Fascist dictatorship was worse than the prevailing chaos under the Anarchists.

On the sector of front assigned to the Fifteenth, a few kilometers to the south of the village of Quinto del Ebro, Commissar Nelson accompanied Captain Bradley to the Anarchist positions. "It is customary," Nelson relates,

> in all armies to go out to greet the officers of the relieving forces, to explain the positions to them, and to point out the danger spots, the water supply, pass on any information regarding enemy positions, habits, and so on. But these officers explained nothing. They were clearly hostile and made no effort to conceal it. The commander, who like the rest wore the red and black insignia of the FAI, spoke with cold and brittle politeness. He was anxious only to get away.

The Americans found the few miserable attempts at trenches, situated at least two kilometers from the rebel strong points, to have been used principally as latrines. In this same sector, according to Herbert Matthews, football games had been arranged between the opposing sides. To cap it all, the very excellent hospital to the rear at Pueblo de Híjar was staffed and equipped to handle the casualties of a major offensive. Yet in the six months of its existence, it had received exactly *two* wounded.

The offensive the Republic had planned in Aragón was both audacious and ambitious. Tactically, it sought the seizure of the city of Zaragoza and the subsequent, total investment of the cities of Huesca and Jaca in the northeast, preparatory to their capture. Strategically, it was the simultaneous objective of again forcing a halt to the Franco offensive against Asturias that would guarantee that section of Spain for the Republic while activizing the Aragón front under the central government, and thus laying the base for a military unity, without which the war could not be won.

August 24, 1937, broke with a bright sun and a cloudless,

azure sky. As at Brunete, the view from the Lincoln positions was impressive. The plain ahead was interminably flat, with here and there an outcropping of low, eroded hills. Enemy lines, at a distance of two kilometers, were being shelled by a single battery.

Only the church steeple of the village of Quinto del Ebro was visible, since it lay below the plain and along the Ebro River. On the plain, to the west of the church, was a walled cemetery. Circling the cemetery and the invisible village were the enemy trenches. Southeast of Quinto, at a little less than a kilometer, was a large hill called Purburell. It was approximately 600 feet in length, with steep sides sloping to the plain on the west and to the river and the Azaila Road on the east. Its top was ringed with cement and steel fortifications, all bristling with machine gun nests and even a few pieces of artillery. It was garrisoned by no fewer than 800 men. The Lincolns watched as the Dimitrov Battalion advanced toward Purburell's southern approaches.

The time was 6:00 A.M. The Dimitrovs came under heavy fire and quickly withdrew. The maneuver had been a feint to draw reserves from the village to the hill.

By 9:00 A.M. the Dimitrovs had circled the face of the insurgent front to position themselves to the north of the village; this, while the Lincoln Company 1 advanced to positions facing the cemetery from the west.

A first probe against the cemetery drew heavy fire, though casualties were light. Alec Miller, the veteran Canadian commander, shot through the head, walked a full kilometer to a first-aid post and survived to go home to Canada. Charles Nussar, appearing somewhat unmilitary in a sleeveless white shirt, took command.

A realignment of Company 1 placed the bulk of the battalion squarely in front of the enemy line fronting the cemetery and church, at a distance of some 400 meters. Rebel positions were now being hit by shells from as many as twelve 7.5s and 10.5s, marking the first time the Lincolns had ever had such direct support. A flight of a dozen bombers, too, made an appearance, plus a line of eight T-26 tanks.

What happened, according to the consensus, was right out

of the manual. Despite the fact that they, too, were receiving heavy mortar and machine gun fire, plus bursts of overhead shrapnel from the enemy battery on Purburell, battalion troops moved into the attack without a hitch. Where the tanks crushed the barbed wire, the Americans poured through. Where the wire still stood, they hurdled it. They went up and over the parapets, grenading and shooting their way into the trenches, while the remnants of the enemy fled down into the streets of the village.

Many stories are told of the assault. One rifle section was said to have shaved their heads, leaving only a scalp lock; with a few chicken feathers, a bit of paint, and bared bayonets, screaming Sioux war whoops, they were altogether too much for the enemy.

By 4:00 P.M. the Lincolns had all the strong points and the cemetery, and were fighting in the streets of the town. Rebel losses were heavy, their trenches filled with dead and wounded. There were fewer than ten American casualties— proof positive of what could be done with even a minimum of well-coordinated support.

On the morning of the second day, the Lincolns, joined by the greater part of the Americans of the brigade staff, moved directly to seize Quinto. The village swarmed with snipers, and the fighting became bitter. It was a struggle for each street, each building. Orders came down to protect the civilians at all costs. As the Americans advanced, they pounded on every door, yelling for the occupants to come out.

Robert Merriman, leading one of the bombing squads, advanced so rapidly that his group soon found themselves being grenaded by a section of the Dimitrov's Company 2, coming in from the north.

Carl Bradley writes of the taking of one strong point occupying a commanding position. Its walls were three feet thick. Machine guns bristled from every window. Bradley called for ten volunteers.

> We waited until our anti-tanks began to pound the building to keep the snipers away from the windows. Then we went armed with bottles of nitroglycerine to about

eight yards from it. Two men were wounded on our way to
the building; three had to carry them back. This left only
five of us to carry on. But five was enough!

We each picked a window, and BANG! Every bottle went
home, exploding with tremendous flames inside. It was
damn good pitching. Next, we rolled a drum of gasoline
inside with a fuse attached to it. That finished the job. The
building burned all night.

The fighting continued, sometimes hand-to-hand. At one
point the Lincolns discovered, after having advanced halfway
through the town, that the rebels were beginning to encircle
their attackers by weaving backward along the outlying buildings behind the American advance. Once the maneuver was
known, it was turned against its perpetrators.

Going through town, Charles Nussar, with Herman
"Gabby" Klein and a number of men from Company 1,
entered a grocery store and yelled for the owner. No one came,
so they filled their pockets with goods from the shelves—*and
left all their loose change on the counter.* Arthur Munday and
the machine gun company adjutant Nick Pappas paused in
the midst of battle to select new socks from a local variety
store.

A water tank was captured and driven over the plain to
be used to make nightly soup and coffee. This was done in
full view of the enemy on Purburell. On the previous night,
Lieutenants Larry O'Toole and Melvin Anderson, from
Esquanaba, Michigan, had led a foray between the village and
the Azaila-Zaragoza road to cut the pipeline carrying water to
the garrison.

The Dimitrovs captured the railroad station; then, with the
help of a section of the Lincoln Company 1, seized a cement
factory. A battery of 10.5s was captured intact, along with its
crew and the half-dozen heavy machine guns assigned to
protect it.

The church is invariably the major building in any Spanish
village, forever of massive proportions and situated to domi-
nate the surrounding terrain. Through all the years of the
Moorish wars, the church was *the* fortress, the planned center

for defense of the area. So it continued to be in this Spanish war—the reason, actually, why so many were destroyed. Both sides, but especially Spain's Fascist military, would convert these churches into fortresses.

All Lincoln survivors speak of Quinto's church. Nelson, for example, writes:

> Big action around the church. Lots of guys wounded. There were Fascist machine guns on all four sides. One could walk around it if he stayed close to the walls. I did, but I lost one runner wounded and two killed. Capt. Thomas Wintringham was wounded there too. The walls were ten feet thick and the windows were eighteen feet high. Some of the guys got ladders and climbed up and tossed grenades in. At one point a window opened and men began to climb out. They were pale and scared. They lined up without weapons against the wall.

And in the *Book of the 15th Brigade,* a Lincoln observer is quoted as follows:

> While we gave cover-fire the Dimitrovs broke the door down with a beam. The Fascists immediately opened fire from within, and started throwing grenades at us. We retaliated in kind. Next we got bundles of hay, threw them inside and pitched grenades on top of them, trying to set them afire. It took a long time before we succeeded.
>
> In the meantime a section of the Lincoln's Company 1. approached the side of the church where there was a small window. A few Fascists tried to escape through it. But realizing the hopelessness of their situation, they began to surrender. We took seventy-five prisoners through that window alone. One of the Fascists had his hand blown off above the wrist. He was bleeding profusely. We applied a tourniquet and gave him first aid.
>
> Soon all surrendered, excepting a few officers. Carlists, Falangists, Civil Guards, and young conscripts; they were lined up, many of them badly wounded, most of them terror stricken. The conscripts, however, were quite happy, shouting, "Viva la República!" and, "Viva el Frente Popular!"

Purburell hill was the final bastion. The British and the Fifty-ninth had been attacking it for two days without success. On the night of the twenty-fifth, a squad of desperate rebel soldiers had been captured attempting to infiltrate the British lines in the hope of getting water. Their information was that the hill, though strongly held, was completely without water and by siege could easily be forced to surrender. But Brigade headquarters would accept no delay.

On the twenty-sixth, with the aid of the 7.5s and 10.5s, plus the Fifteenth's three antitank guns commanded by the English captain, Hugh Slater, the assault began again. The time was high noon. It developed as a slow infiltration toward the hill by the British on the west, the Fifty-ninth on the east, and Company 3 of the Lincolns, led by Owen Smith, to the south.

Hour after hour passed as they inched ahead over the plain and up the base of the hill. Casualties were kept to a minimum. The memory of the insanity of Jarama was forever in the minds of men and officers alike. In the late afternoon, while the guns still pounded Purburell, hundreds of civilians appeared on the roads to the west of Quinto, climbed into trucks, and, in full view of the parched insurgents, were evacuated south. Suddenly, a roar of planes filled the skies. The artillery ceased. Men hugged the earth. Eighteen two-motored Capronis, sweeping in low from the north, then unloaded their bombs—on *Purburell!* Mussolini's pilots had erred.

All down the enemy line, through the haze of cordite and dust, white flags appeared. Rebel officers, however, rushed forward to haul in the flags and to unleash a murderous fire against both their attackers and their own troops who had attempted surrender.

Their effort was to no avail, however. Felix Kusman of Company 3 states:

> We saw additional white flags and the throwing down of rifles from the hill. We also heard terrific fire against these men. *Their officers are shooting them from behind.* The sun is going down. The first couple of positions we occupy with no opposition—lots of dead, lots of wounded—lots of

prisoners. We order the prisoners to take the wounded to the center of the hill. There we find a command bunker surrounded by machine gun nests. They are empty now as is the bunker. The officers have retreated to the northeast section of the hill and are putting up a last resistance against the 59th Battalion. They are wiped out! We continue in that direction. Then we see this White Russian officer. Larry O'Toole and I approach him. He screams in mixed Russian and Spanish: "Red Pigs! Red Pigs! If you come any closer, I'll shoot." He has a gun to his head. O'Toole yells back: "Go ahead! If you don't, I will." And so the guy blows his brains out, and I take his gun and sword and a Russian bible from his body.

Our small company had so many prisoners that we had to send for help to get them off the hill—too dark to count them. They were later taken to the cement factory.

A British report is more laconic:

Barbed-wire ahead, and the brown earth of the parapets. I remember Paddy O'Daire's yell: "Charge the trench!" As we ran up the last few yards the trench came alive. A mass of white faces, hands upstretched to the sky, and in cracked voices from parched throats, the cry *"Agua! Agua!"*

Shots rang out further down the trench. It was a group of Fascist officers who had committed suicide. One was German, another White Russian. His revolver was of the pre-war, Russian imperial pattern. . . .

Inspecting the fort we had captured, we felt proud of ourselves. Revolving gun turrets with overhead cover commanded the country for miles around. In deep dugouts were stacks of shells. To us it was an object lesson in fortification. And the garrison had been a big one; over half of whom were dead or wounded. *Our attacking force had been less than that of the defenders.* . . . The trenches stank with the smell of the dead.

The battle for Quinto was over. In the morning trucks arrived; by mid-afternoon the battalions of the Fifteenth were swimming in the Ebro, opposite Pina Station. The town of

Fuentes del Ebro was just a few kilometers to the north, and the roar of newly arrived guns against attacking units of the Republican Fifth Army was more than audible.

As of the twenty-seventh of August, the battle for Zaragoza had yet to be decided. While the Fifteenth fought for Quinto, Spanish troops drove twenty kilometers into enemy territory to seize the villages of Rodin and Mediana and to enter Fuentes—only to be driven out again. As at Brunete, Lister again made the farthest advance. Some of his units went another ten kilometers to within *three* kilometers of the suburbs of Zaragoza itself. But, as at Boadilla, he was forced to withdraw, lacking support.

To the west, the Republican Colonel Vivanco had stormed La Puebla de Albortón, Fuendetodos, and had surrounded the important bastion of Belchite. Closer to Quinto, the Thirty-second Brigade of the Thirty-fifth Division had driven through three concentric lines of fortifications to seize the village of Codo; while to the north and east, Colonel Trueba's Twenty-seventh Division had also driven twenty kilometers to cross the Gállego River and capture the town of Zuera, thus threatening Zaragoza from that direction.

In effect, the American bivouac at Pina was *not* a rest period. They awaited only the capture of Fuentes, after which they would drive through that town and beyond it to attack Burgos del Ebro, the last stronghold before Zaragoza from the south. At the same time, the Twenty-seventh Division would drive southwest from Zuera.

An information bulletin issued under the seal of the Fifth Army, Division B, and signed by its commanding general— known as Walter, but really the Polish General Karl Swierczewski, who in World War II would be the first to enter Poland in pursuit of the fleeing Nazis—describes the victory at Quinto del Ebro.

> During the night of the 23–24 of August we began our offensive on the Aragón Front. Two International Brigades received the order to operate jointly and to take Quinto de Ebro, an exceptionally important fortified position closing the Zaragoza road.

76

In the fight which lasted from the 24th to the 26th, both Brigades fullfilled their tasks to perfection.

| | |
|---|---|
| Losses of the enemy: | More than 1,000 prisoners—350 dead. |
| Armament captured: | Four 10.5 calibre guns; two damaged 7.5 guns; more than 60 automatic guns, some motars and much miscellaneous material. |
| Our losses: | In *both* Brigades: 269 wounded and 50 dead. |

WALTER

On the seventh day of the campaign, the Lincolns were ordered to the citadel of Belchite. Rebel counter-attacks were mounting in intensity, creating the possibility of a lifting of the siege of the town. The Anarchist press of Barcelona had already irresponsibly announced that their forces had captured Belchite. If the siege were now lifted, exposing the lie, the truly anti-Fascist rank-and-file of the Anarchist movement would be further demoralized.

Strategically situated, Belchite offered opportunities for both the isolation of the Aragón capital of Teruel to the south, and the investment of Zaragoza to the north. Historically, it was "the town that Napoleon himself couldn't conquer." As matters stood, Vivanco's Twenty-fifth had taken all outlying positions to the south and west, while the Thirty-second Brigade had driven to within 500 meters on the north and east. Supposedly, the Lincolns would now finish the job.

By nightfall, a forced march of some twenty kilometers brought them to Codo. They camped in defense formation on the plain, facing toward Mediana and Monte Sillero. Word had reached them that the situation was deteriorating rapidly, that a breakthrough had actually taken place. The Franco radio boasted that the siege of Belchite would be lifted within hours. General Walter then dispatched the British Battalion to bar the road, which it promptly did, meeting an enemy battalion head-on and driving it all the way back to Mediana and even retaking a portion of that village.

Arriving at Belchite in the late afternoon of the following day, the now-veteran Lincolns, with scarcely a halt in their forward movement, deployed through terraced vineyards and olive groves to advance to within 300 meters of the town. This, despite the fact that their arrival had coincided with a bombing run by a dozen or so Ju-52s.

Some Americans made it sufficiently close to the first houses to hear the Fascists talking. Two of these, Herman Klein and Saul Birnbaum, failed to receive a withdrawal order and awoke the next morning to find themselves pinned down by the rebel guns. Klein relates that prior to the ensuing Lincoln attack, a lone Republican tank came up the road and stopped at the ditch where he and Birnbaum were lying, to ask for the positions of the enemy. Klein could only wave weakly at the houses ahead—he'd had no food or water for twenty-four hours—and point to his mouth and croak, *"Agua! Agua!"* Upon which the T-26 commander, risking his life, popped out of the tank's depths with a loaf of bread and a can of marmalade—but no water! An example of the incongruity of war.

The brigade assault then began, but this time under the all-too-familiar circumstances of little or no support. Company 2 (Spanish) led off, suffered heavy casualties and was immediately pinned down. Its young adjutant, Lieutenant Howard Goddard from Los Angeles, fell with five bullets through his body (but survived). Its Socialist commissar, Aldo, rising to lead the men on, was instantly killed.

The First and Third Companies fared no better. The advance was over a series of terraces leading to the parallel Azaila Road, beyond which were the first houses. Each time the men sought to rise to make a run for the next supporting rock wall, they were cut down. At last they could go no further.

Orders came from Brigade to Hans Amlie: "Continue the advance, at once!" But neither Amlie, nor battalion Commissar Robbie, would ask the men to go forward.

William Wellman of San Francisco describes the situation:

> It was daylight and there was a heavy cross-fire. There were two or three terraces to cross before we came to the

road. We went over a couple of them and lost a lot of men. My squad leader [Company 1] was killed there. We then told them of our positions and that no man could make it; that we were under a heavy cross-fire. . . . But the orders kept coming and Captain Amlie kept pocketing the orders. . . . This one attack, when my platoon leader was killed, twenty-two men started out. None of them made it. Two of them survived.

That was the thing that led to the situation where Hans Amlie would not tell the men to continue the advance. When Amlie got the orders: "Either send your men and see that they go, or you face court-martial!" Amlie said to us: "What'll I do? Court-martial at the front means *shot!*" And we said, "Well, you just give us the order. You order us to go and then *we'll* refuse. Then you tell them to come down here and *lead* us, and we'll follow *them!*"

Brigade Commissar Nelson states that Robbie said to him on the phone: "We are being mowed down! It's insane to continue. What's more, *our own damned artillery is firing on us!*"

This last was unfortunately true. The *single* gun that had been brought into action was dropping its shells on Lincoln Company 1. The argument continued. Robert Merriman, his arm still in a sling, was now in a role analogous to Copic's or Gal's, insisting that Amlie do that which he, Merriman, had fought against in the disaster of February 27. It is to his credit that some flexibility prevailed. Steve Nelson was ordered forward to the Lincoln positions. Nelson writes:

Amlie's temper was fully as bad as Bob's. "What the hell is the matter with you guys?" he shouted at me. "Go forward? How can we go forward? The town's bristling with machine guns. You want to slaughter the whole damn battalion? Where's the artillery?"

"I don't know," I said. "But the guys can't stay where they are. And the anti-tanks can't hang around all day shooting snipers out of the window for us."

Then I left the command dug-out and went down the wash a 'ways and peeped cautiously at the town. The church had to be taken before the town could be taken. I took two or three boys with me and we worked our way around to that side of the town where we found a dry ditch leading toward the first buildings. It ran close to an olive-oil factory, a mill—which was right across the street from the church.

We didn't know what was inside the factory but it seemed quiet. We sent back for men and grenades. A dozen came up bringing two of the new light machine guns issued at Híjar.

We got set and, at a signal, lobbed grenades through the factory windows, waited an instant for the burst, then rushed in through an opening blasted by a previous shell. There was no one inside. Quickly the guns were set up, commanding the main approaches to the factory on the town side.

We had a foothold in the town. We were set!

No time was wasted. A section of Company 1 and a part of the battalion staff itself moved into the factory. Simultaneously, the Dimitrovs, with the aid of the shifting guns of the antitank battery, advanced to seize positions before the first houses on the northwest side of town.

By day's end, however, every company commander of the Lincoln Battalion had been hit. Charles Nussar of Company 1, tall, lanky, and possessed of a contagious courage, was wounded again, this time badly enough to warrant his withdrawal from any future action. His place was taken by Wallace Burton, a big, jovial midwesterner and, according to Herbert Matthews, a veteran of *five* wars. Burton, leading an attack against the church, received a bullet in the spine and died almost instantly. His commissar, David (Mooch) Engels, now took command.

Company 3 fared no better. Owen Smith, shot through the chest, was evacuated under heavy fire. Paul Block, commissar, took over.

Two days passed with no further advance. And, while Lister's brigades fought for Monte Sillero, fresh enemy battalions counter-attacked at La Puebla de Albortón; while Republican forces held tenaciously at Rodin and Fuentes, El Campesino's Forty-sixth Division drove to the very gates of Jaulin. The strange admixture of attack and counter-attack was writing a new and interesting page in warfare.

The Lincoln's probes continued. Henry Eaton was killed in one assault. Samuel Levenger, from the American Student Union at Ohio University, was killed in another. Captain Hans Amlie received a serious head wound. A courageous and concerned commander, Amlie was then repatriated to the United States, where he carried the cause of the Spanish Republic to American audiences across the land.

New orders came from Division. Belchite must be taken without delay! Merriman hastened to implement them. The entire brigade staff moved into the firing line to supplement the dwindling manpower of the battalions. Six tanks were given the brigade, and they, together with the antitank battery, began methodically to drive into the town's defenses. On the fourth day the church was captured. Manny Lancer, the Lincoln machine gun company commander, writes:

> The group on the right, a couple of dozen men led by Mooch Engels, charged from the trenches about forty yards from the church. They had first to cross a deep gulley that ran the length of the church wall. Once across they knocked down the fascist parapets. . . . As they entered the church from the rear, the enemy re-entered from the front. There was a quick, short, bloody battle of hand-grenades and bayonets—and the Americans were the masters of the church.
>
> Several men led by Lee Levick deployed in the open doorway and fired into the mass of fleeing fascists. Levick's squad, in turn, was being fired at from all sides by the fascists in the surrounding houses across the church plaza. One after the other of Levick's men were hit, but they hung on since this was the only entrance through which the fascists could rush the church and regain control.
>
> Sandbags were brought from the trenches, plus a heavy Maxim. A barricade was built across the doorway. The church was now ours.

Captain Carl Bradley then led sections of the First and Third Companies and members of the brigade cadre pool in an uphill charge of some 350 meters to seize positions in the town's main plaza. Bradley writes:

> We began to advance *through* the buildings by breaking holes in those thick Spanish walls. At one point we heard voices in a cellar and discovered a large number of enemy soldiers and civilians. A Spanish officer was sent to talk them into surrendering. He was successful. We also took a number of prisoners right by our last barricade.

The Spanish officer was from the Fifty-ninth Battalion. The remnants of two companies, scarcely more than sixty men, of this battalion had paralleled Bradley's advance. Both groups then deployed into the main plaza for an assault against the Falangist *Comandancia* on the Calle Joaquín Costa.

With the church and plaza captured, a bitter street-by-street battle began for control of the town. The Dimitrovs blasted their way toward the Calle Mayor. The Lincolns seized houses fronting this street and worked south to meet Bradley. It was a fight for every building; grenade against grenade; bayonet against bayonet. There was no doubting the courage and tenacity of the enemy and its determination to hold out.

Radio messages continued to insist that help was on the way. Planes flew over each night dropping food and ammunition; a lot of it fell into American hands. Strauss of the brigade medical staff saw blinking lights above on the fourth night and blinked back with a flashlight. Seconds later, he was "bombed" with a large burlap sack containing mail, ham, bread, and instruction from the rebels to the Belchite garrison. They were being told to hold out and to prepare to counter-attack; they had taken Quinto and were approaching Belchite from the north and east.

Herbert Matthews refers to this and to other communications from General Muguel Ponte's headquarters at Zaragoza as "a clever move, since they knew quite well that Belchite was doomed."

By the fifth night the town had become a charnel house of death, destruction, and raging fires. As Major Malcolm Dunbar writes:

Belchite presented a picture of the horrors of war which no Hollywood film could ever give. Many buildings were ablaze. Tongues of flame shot up into the black pall of smoke overhead. The summer breeze wafted across the countryside the stench, nauseating and strong, of dead bodies, human and animal. Above the crackling fires maniacal yells arose from some demented creatures whose nerves could no longer stand the strain. Through the night, the continuous explosions of grenades marked the relentless advance of our bombing squads. It was war shorn of all glamour, war cruel and bloody—but a war we had to win.

Merriman, Phil Detro, who had returned from hospital, Battalion Commander Lamb, Commissar Geiser, and almost every officer of Brigade staff was now on the firing line. Paul Bloch, veteran of Jarama and Brunete was felled by a sniper's bullet, as was Sidney Shosteck, aide to Merriman and a former president of a local of the Teamsters. Daniel Hunter, a former college track star, also fell victim to a sniper's fire.

On the morning of the siege's sixth day, the much-loved Brigade Commissar, Steve Nelson, was shot down in the plaza by a gunman hiding in the church tower. His life was saved, but like many another veteran, Nelson could see no more action. Instead, he returned to the United States, to raise money and his voice for the cause of Spain.

As the list of casualties to sniper fire grew, captured snipers were dealt with summarily. Herbert Matthews says of this:

> All through the town snipers held their positions gallantly until their last cartridge or their lives were lost. Those who surrendered were summarily shot—a stain on the otherwise admirable record of the Americans and other Loyalists. . . . The officers, for the most part, stuck to their posts until death.
>
> No officer or man to whom we spoke up there withheld his tribute to the fighting qualities of the Carlists who made Belchite such a hard won prize. The conscript troops, of course, did not do so well as the others; prisoners taken were almost all of this class.

No man slept. Individual stories tell only of fighting, bombing parties, and assaults. Eating, drinking, sleeping, and the like belonged to a past that no longer existed, that had no place in the inferno of bursting bombs, shells, grenades, and fire.

On the seventh day a deserter appeared and volunteered information as to the disposition of the garrison. Merriman sent him back to his fellows to convince them that further resistance was useless. A few hours later the deserter reappeared, leading some 300 men, all of whom laid down their arms before the Americans and surrendered. The bastion of Belchite was finally cracking!

There then occurred the event that brought all resistance to an end. The *Book of the 15th Brigade* describes it:

> The clinching of the victory required one final assault, the straining of every fiber, every ounce of strength for a supreme effort.
>
> Then Dave Doran, the new young Brigade Commissar, commandeered a "sound-truck" with a loud-speaker, which he had spotted on the road, got hold of an interpreter, wrote out a short speech, brought the truck up to the church and, with the fascists only a half a block away, launched his political attack. . . .
>
> He told the fascists that their radio was lying. Quinto was safely in Republican hands. Instead of fascist reenforcements it was the People's Army that was steadily pressing on to victory. Next he contrasted the status of the enemy rank-and-file with that of the men in the Republican Army. He ended bluntly by saying: "Take your choice!"
>
> "Further resistance means death! Death for each and every one of you! Come over to us and live. Drop your arms and come over the barricades one by one. All who come over will live."
>
> There the speech ended. Deathly silence followed from behind the barricades. Their machine guns had ceased firing; the *voice* had silenced them all. There was an unearthly hush. The word "death" seemed to have taken a shape, a living form, stark and grim, ghastly and enor-

mous, pressing down with an ever increasing weight on the fascist line. Then the break came.

The street behind the barricades suddenly began to swarm with men. Fascist soldiers, shouting *"Viva la República!"* and *"Viva el Frente Popular!"* came over the barricades, without arms—one by one.

Between 300 and 400 came over; the surrender of the rank-and-file was complete. Prisoners and war materiel taken surpassed that of Quinto. Belchite was again in Republican hands.

On September 9, 1937, the Mackenzie-Papineau (Canadian) Battalion, 625 strong and with the majority of its personnel American, left the training base at Tarazona de la Mancha to join the Abraham Lincoln Brigade, at rest in the olive groves outside the village of Azaila. Canadians had been fighting in all units of the brigade since the first days. Robert Kerr, Canadian commissar and a veteran of Jarama, had devoted his energies to the battalion's creation, and would now be its representative at Albacete.

The Canadian Battalion had more training and better firepower than any other International Brigade that had yet gone into action. It was quite a spirited outfit. The men had a bugler to awaken them, summon them to their meals, and signal them to bed at night; nevertheless, the baptism in battle would be much on a par with the Lincolns' experience at Jarama—a fiasco, ridiculously planned and tragically executed.

In the sand-blown olive groves outside Azaila, nicknamed "Windy Alley," the Lincoln survivors listened with something akin to horror to the bugle. On the second morning, the "Mac-Paps" were late in rising, since the bearded and hard-eyed Lincoln men had shoved their bugle beneath the tires of a food truck to render it silent.

The battalions reorganized. The Lincoln's Captain Leonard Lamb, wounded in the last days, was replaced by the newly-returned Phil Detro. Milton Wolff, also a section leader, took command of the Lincoln machine gun company from Lieutenant Lancer, who was returning home.

Ernest Hemingway, Sefton Delmar of the *London Times*, Herbert Matthews, and Martha Gellhorn (now writing for NBC as well as *Colliers*), took time to visit the brigade at Azaila. Gellhorn brought with her the French writers Genevieve Taggard and Simone Thery. This visit was the source for many stories about the deeds and valor of the Lincolns in Aragón. Hemingway wrote movingly:

> When we got up with the Americans, they were lying under some olive trees along a little stream. The yellow dust of Aragón was blowing over them, over their blanketed machine guns, over their automatic rifles and their anti-aircraft guns. It grew in blending clouds raised by the hooves of pack-animals and the wheels of motor transports, and in the gale of clouds of dust rolling over the bare hills, Aragón looked like a blizzard in Montana.
>
> But in the lee of the stream bank the men were slouching, fearful and grinning, their teeth flashing white slits in their yellow powdered faces. Since I saw them last spring, they have become soldiers.

This period also saw the departure from the ranks of the Fifteenth of the truly courageous Dimitrov Battalion and its commander, Prohaska. After fighting through the terrible years of World War II, Prohaska would become the Mayor of Prague, an honored member of the Central Committee of the Czech Communist Party—and one of those to stand with Czech Premier Dubchek during the tragic 1968 Soviet invasion of his country.

During this period of semi-rest, from September 20 to October 10, the four battalions maneuvered over much of the Aragón front, their first march taking them to Albalate and within a few kilometers of the American field hospital near Pueblo de Híjar. The hospital had its counterpart in a second medical unit serving the Córdoba front in the far south. Both were mobile. The Aragón unit was commanded by Dr. Irving Busch and staffed by some thirty doctors, nurses, drivers, technicians, and helpers. As at Brunete, these men and women had performed a yeoman service amidst constant air attacks.

Exactly two days were spent at Albalate, time enough for the Mac-Paps to get their rifles and machine guns, then back to Azaila, and from there east by truck to the town of Grañén, just south of the rebel-held citadel of Huesca. The brigade staff set up its command post in Grañén; the battalions moved into secondary positions.

Then the rains came, a torrential downpour. The Mac-Paps, who had settled themselves into comfortable *barrancas*, found themselves being literally washed down those same *barrancas* by flash floods that threatened to drown them. The Lincolns, given tents, had weathered the storm in great style.

The Canadians had joined the Fifteenth at a time when the rigors of the campaigns of Jarama, Brunete, and Aragón were having their effect on the men. The tactics at Belchite, like those of the other campaigns, had come under criticism. Why, the men wanted to know, had they not been given support, as they had at Quinto? Why the tragic orders to Amlie and Robbie, who knew far better than Copic and Merriman what could or could not be done? And why had the Fifteenth Brigade, depleted in manpower, worn out from the assaults on Quinto and Purburell, been forced to throw its remnants against the defenses of Belchite in the first place?

They dared to criticize and they dared to ask, for they were not ordinary soldiers. As Edwin Rolfe wrote, they were

> an army of articulate, thinking, reasoning human beings—young men who fought not as automatons, but as highly conscious anti-fascists. There was no officer-caste among them, and therefore none of the blind obedience normally exacted of soldiers. There was discipline, of course; no army unit can function without it. But the discipline was of a rare kind, far deeper than the usual surface discipline of military machines, with its outer formality and trappings.

In the midst of all this questioning and grumbling, a half-dozen of the men stole an ambulance, headed toward the

French border, and were captured. The brigade was instantly confronted with a unique problem. The men involved were, after all, *volunteers*. If they chose now to change their minds, even to the extent of stealing an ambulance, could they be treated as regular deserters? The final authority in such matters was the Commissariat. But could it really impose the kind of sentence mandatory in any other army?

Company meetings were held in all battalions. The desertions were discussed and action in the form of resolutions requested. The commissars spoke for the death penalty; the International Brigades were after all like other military units in time of war and could not countenance desertion. The rank-and-file, however, rejected the death penalty; in fact, no single company of any battalion would support it. The men were then simply reprimanded, returned to their units, and that was that. Certainly, this was a first in the annals of the American military.

Throughout all this, the fighting for Zaragoza had never ceased. On October 10, 1937, the Lincolns, alerted, were rushed back to Quinto by truck. Their orders: to attack and take the still-resisting bastion of Fuentes del Ebro. The plan was an intricate one. For the first time in the history of modern warfare, an attack would be launched in which a full battalion of men would *ride* tanks into battle.

Such a plan would normally merit careful preparation. But the Mac-Pap commander, Robert Thompson, states that not even a brief reconnaissance of the enemy positions by brigade officers was suggested. Instead, the Brigade Commissariat chose the very night before the attack to discuss charges leveled by the Canadians against their commissar, Joseph Dallet, that he was willful and arrogant. The discussion went on until after midnight, and the lengthiness of the meeting was in part responsible for a delay in moving the men into their assault positions.

Fuentes, like Quinto, lay west of the Ebro River, and also like Quinto it was below the plain. Unlike Quinto, however, the attack would also be from below the plain.

The British, being first to the trucks, were in their assigned trenches before sun-up. The Lincolns, arriving just as dawn pearled the first hills, left their Company 3 in the open and under heavy enfilading fire. Donald Thayer, assigned to bring them in, received his second wound, a bullet through the jaw which broke the bone and shattered seven teeth. In Quinto he was strapped in a dentist's chair, without ether, for needed repairs—ether was being reserved for the seriously wounded.

The Mac-Paps, the last to enter the trenches, were forced to march over the crest of a low hill and then cut their way back through their own barbed wire to reach the shallow positions prepared for them—this because there was no guide.

Time passed. What was to have been an assault in the first hour of daylight failed to materialize. Desultory firing from two Republican batteries began at approximately 10:00 A.M. After a number of salvos the "barrage" ceased. Two more hours passed, during which the enemy repaired what little damage the shells had caused. Government planes came over then, eighteen single-engined Rasantes. They flapped like great clumsy condors to the enemy lines and dropped their bombs.

After that, there was *nothing* until approximately 1:30 P.M., at which time the promised tanks appeared, forty of them— more than the Americans had ever seen before! On the sides of each T-26 were four to six men—Mexicans, Cubans, and other Latin Americans of the Fifty-ninth Battalion. The look in their eyes was stunned disbelief at what was about to happen. The tanks simply halted in a ragged line, fired a number of 47 millimeter shells, and *charged!*

The orders were: "Follow the tanks at twenty meters. Spread out. Don't bunch up. Continue on into Fuentes."

The tank charge wrecked whole trench sections. At one point, two young Spaniards were crushed. At another, a squad of Spaniards from Mac-Pap Company 2, poorly informed as to what was to happen, thought that the tanks were the enemy and fired on them. The tanks continued in a wide front toward the rebel positions.

The terrain fronting brigade positions was as follows: the Canadian line extended west from the road to climb the spur of a hill leading up to the plain. To its front was an open field, almost flat, ending at the crest of a ravine some 600 to 700 meters distant. Across the ravine, at an additional hundred or so meters, were the enemy fortifications. Behind these positions of cement, steel, railroad ties—all that the ingenuity of German engineers could muster—was the town of Fuentes del Ebro.

The Lincoln line extended from the Mac-Paps right flank to a canal, on the far side of which was the left flank of the British Battalion, whose line then continued to the river. The area to the front of both the Lincolns and British was sandy loam, grapevines, and gullies, all sloping up to the enemy fortifications about 400 meters distant.

The rifle companies of the three battalions arose to follow the tanks, which roared ahead at such speed that the men were immediately left behind. This was a cardinal error. The rebels, with machine gun nests that had in no way been destroyed, had a field day. The distance to be covered by the tanks also gave the enemy gunners ample time to zero in on the men clinging to the turrets. More than half the riders were killed before they ever reached the enemy trenches. At the rebel strong points the tanks destroyed the barbed wire, crushed the bunkers, and drove into the streets of Fuentes— another, this time final, error. The narrow streets afforded no room to maneuver. The tanks were trapped by antitank guns and the grenades of the defenders.

Fewer than half returned. Seventeen were reported captured, with another half-dozen destroyed. One rebel historian writes briefly that: "Our lines closed behind the tanks and our fire destroyed both men and tanks alike. Few escaped to return to their lines again."

A survivor, Nicolas Ramírez, a Mexican-American from Los Angeles, writes that those who dropped off the tanks behind the enemy lines made every effort to fight their way back. In most cases, they fought to the death, refusing surrender. Ramírez and three others, all that remained of a squad of ten, held out for two days and then, on the second night, made a run through the lines to safety.

The Lincolns had in some places made it to the wire. But Phil Detro, sensing disaster, ordered a halt and a withdrawal as soon as darkness fell. A Black volunteer, Joe Taylor, spent

Billy Alto, American guerrilla leader

An International's grave. Hidden from view, these graves were carefully tended by peasants throughout Franco's long reign

Yale Stuart, popular brigader, amputee

Mobile operating room, used near the front

**Sgt. Bob Thompson**
**Distinguished Service Cross**

**Capt. Larry Cane**
**Silver Star**

**Capt. Vincent Lossowski**
**Legion of Merit**

**Capt. Mike Jimenez**
**Legion of Merit**

**Capt. Irving Goff**
**Legion of Merit**

**Sgt. Neil Wesson**
**Legion of Merit**

Only a few of the veterans of the Abraham Lincoln Brigade who earned distinguished medals during World War II. Hundreds of medals were earned by the 600 Lincoln vets who fought in the later war. In addition, over 400 Lincoln vets served in the Merchant Marine.

Lincoln trenches, Jarama front, February–June 1937

Major Robert Merriman

(from left) Captain Oliver Law (American); Captain Fort (French); Captain Copeman (British); Major Allan Johnson (American); Chapaiev (Yugoslav). Captain Law, who was killed in action, was the first Black man to lead a mostly white unit in U.S. military history.

The Washington Battalion moves to the assault on Mosquito Crest

A group from Transport

Fifteenth Brigade
command post

The church at Quinto

(from left) "Jock" Cunningham, British Battalion Commander; Major George
Nathan, Brigade Chief of Staff; Ralph Campeau, Commissar

the greater part of the day in the protection of a burnt-out tank within *three yards* of an enemy bunker.

The British suffered grievously, losing both their new commander, Harold Fry, and their commissar, Eric Whaley, both killed in the first minutes of the attack.

It was the Mac-Paps, however, who had suffered the greatest losses. On the left, at the point of Company 1's advance, both its commander, William Neure, and its commissar, Jack Shifman, were killed. The men of the company fell back, and Battalion Commander Thompson sent Battalion Commissar Dallet to lead them out again. Dallet was immediately hit. Mortally wounded, he ordered all first-aid men from his exposed position. Moments later, he died. Everywhere it was the same. The bodies of men wounded and dead marked the advance to the crest of the ravine. Captain Thompson, accompanying them the full distance, ordered a heavy Maxim to be brought up on the right flank to cover a 300-yard gap between the Mac-Paps and the Lincolns. He later stated that the signs of a disaster were apparent. He feared a counter-attack. Sergeant Milton Herndon, brother to the young American Black leader, Angelo Herndon, was killed attempting to carry out Thompson's order, as were two-thirds of his crew. Ruby Kaufman, machine-gun company adjutant, was so seriously wounded that he lay for twenty-four hours among a row of dead before he was found and rushed to an evacuation station.

As night fell, the full measure of the tragedy became apparent. Except for its staff and the machine gun company, the Fifty-ninth Battalion had been destroyed. The Canadians had been brutally mauled, with sixty dead and over a hundred wounded. With the exception of the machine gun company, every Mac-Pap company commander was hit at Fuentes. Joseph Dougher, ex-Pennsylvania miner commanding Company 3, received a wound that retired him from any future action. On the third day Isidore Schrenzel, Company 2 commander, was mortally wounded and died on the hospital train to Valencia.

The Fifteenth remained on the lines for an additional ten days. On the fourth day it gave support to an attack by the Sixth, the Anarchist Brigade. Commissar Keller, who had taken the place of the wounded Carl Geiser, describes it as attacking *through* the Lincoln positions with less than 800 men.

"The Commander was an Anarchist," Keller says, "and he gave such an eloquent speech to his men, so moving and emotional, that a good part of the Lincoln Company 3, under John Tsanakis, went over with them."

This time, however, there were but a handful of guns in support, and *no* tanks or planes. Their failure was therefore almost preordained—raising the question, "Why?"

Why indeed had this unit been thrown against what was without a doubt the strongest of all hedge-hog redoubts protecting Zaragoza? Manuel Aznar states that in the instance of Fuentes, "The *Red* forces in the line of attack were confronted by no less than the effectives of *three Army Corps of the Nationalist Army.*"

Like the Lincolns before them, the Sixth Brigade was stopped at the enemy wire, where their commander was killed. Theirs was the last assault in the Zaragoza campaign.

The Fifteenth was then withdrawn to Quinto, and all the officers of the Fifth Army were summoned to the town of Lécera. Cresencio Bilbao, Socialist and Chief of the War Commissariat of the Army of the East, asked that all concentrate on one subject—why Fuentes del Ebro had not been taken.

When the turn came for the Fifteenth's commissars to speak, Saul Wellman for the Mac-Paps gave an emotional oration on the Canadian losses. Fred Keller of the Lincolns simply described the action as he saw it. Dave Doran, according to Keller, launched into a political diatribe, whereupon Bilbao insisted that he leave the rostrum and sent two guards to see that he did so.

The results of the meeting were never officially made known, though as Edwin Rolfe wrote later, "It was discovered that the failure of artillery and airplane preparations had been caused by the sabotage of the Tank Commander." In a sense, he echoed the rumors from the Albacete Commissariat that "*Tuckachevsky officers* loyal to a Soviet marshal by that name who was then on trial in Moscow had undermined the whole campaign." The charge was almost infantile. In no way could the tragedy of the attack at Fuentes be explained by such Comintern denunciations. Nor did the Lincoln Brigaders accept that explanation.

The Fascist and Republican high commands, were, throughout the conflict, obsessed with Madrid. Most of the campaigns described in the following pages were undertaken by the Republic to forestall an assumed Francoist attack against the capital. Most of the Republic's commanders had won their spurs and their promotions in the battles at the city's outskirts. For the Fascists the capture of Madrid meant the end of the war and their triumph.

The campaign in Aragón, the final massing of forty tanks at Fuentes from the Republic's meager store of weapons, could very well have resulted in the desired breakthrough. This tragedy then, the result of sabotage, stupidity, or both, was not just the destruction of the Fifty-ninth Battalion, or the heavy loss of men. It was a tragedy for Spain itself. For coincidental with the cessation of operations, mixed Italian and Spanish divisions of General Solchaga entered Gijón, the Asturian capital, and the north was irrevocably lost.

Three weeks prior to this, President Roosevelt had delivered a speech in Chicago in which he had spoken of the growing menace of Nazism and Fascism. At that time he asked the countries of Western Europe to join to "Quarantine the Aggressor!"

A week later, ex-Prime Minister David Lloyd George of England summed up the perfidy of England's "Frankenstein monster," the Committee of Non-intervention. "Bilbao, Santander, the Asturias," he thundered, speaking of the Republic's losses,

> were all defended by as brave men as ever went into battle—traditionally so, and racially so. But they had no munitions; they had no guns. Who is responsible for that? Non-intervention! Who is responsible for keeping Non-intervention alive? His Majesty's Government. If democracy is defeated in this battle, if Fascism is triumphant, His Majesty's Government can claim the victory for themselves.

So, as the Abraham Lincoln Brigade waited, deluged by rain in the blasted town of Quinto, the lowering mass of still-gathering clouds held something more ominous. The American officers, Merriman, Thompson, Wellman, Doran, Keller, Lamb, and Detro, like the commanders of the fledgling army corps of the Republic, were sharply aware of the new situation. A true storm was coming, a holocaust of steel and explosives. Added to the already prodigious mass of the rebel center armies, there would now be Solchaga's 150 battalions, the more than 300 pieces of artillery that had broken the Cinturón before Bilbao, the divisions of the Italian Corps of the CTV, and the clouds of fighters and bombers of the Condor Legion that had destroyed Durango, Tarna, Guernica, and a hundred other Spanish towns and villages.

The storm was truly coming. That it would be met and, in part, held back, would someday be a subject for song and saga. That the Lincoln Brigade was destined to be at the very heart of it would be history.

Two events took place during the brief stay at Quinto. The first was the appearance of young peasant boys from the surrounding countryside, asking to join the Republican forces. They had not done this when the Anarchists were in control; only now would they do so, when the laws of the Popular Front were being enforced. Upward of 500 of the young volunteers were in the Quinto area alone. Many asked to fight with Los Americanos of the Brigada Lincoln.

The second event was a surprise visit by Major General Stephen Fuqua, U.S. Military Attaché to the American Embassy in Spain. He had come, he said, with the permission of the Spanish government. His desire was to inspect the American volunteer units and to have a look at the fortifications of Quinto, Belchite, and Purburell Hill. Given every courtesy, he spoke but a few carefully chosen words to the men when they lined up for review. It was little enough, but the volunteers were cheered by his presence.

Fuqua had also visited the growing Anglo-American training base at Tarazona de la Mancha, where he spent a pleasant two days with Major Allen Johnson, base commander, whom

he had known personally in the United States Army. Johnson
gave Fuqua the red-carpet treatment, ignoring demands from
Albacete that this American major general be sent packing.
As a result, Johnson became the target of harsh criticism from
André Marty, head of the Brigade Commissariat.

Existing archives record that the Anglo-American training
base, under Johnson's tenure, was a model not just for the
International Brigades, but also for the fledgling Spanish army.
Well over 5,000 officers and men, a preponderance of them
Spaniards, passed through his hands.

The Fifteenth returned to its bases on the Madrid front: the
Lincolns to Albares; the British to Mondéjar; the brigade staff
to Ambite; the remnants of the Fifty-ninth to Loranca de
Tajuña; and the Mac-Paps, first to a drafty, *hacienda*-like
house overlooking a nameless village, then to an equally
drafty castle called Pezuela de las Torres, on the Madrid
Highway.

Delousing showers, hot food, clean clothes, relaxation, and
leaves were sorely needed. The brigade as a whole had been in
action for nine long months. American casualties at that
point were 600 killed and more than 1,300 wounded.

New drafts of recruits arrived from Tarazona—Americans,
Canadians, British, and Spaniards. A group of Finns, disliking
their status with the German Eleventh Brigade and hearing
that there were Finns in the Mac-Paps, joined the Canadians.

Blockade and piracy on the high seas had by now taken a
prodigious toll. Madrid especially was hungry. The government program to evacuate unneeded personnel had failed in
part. The streets still thronged with *Madrileños* who stubbornly, and in the face of ever-present death, clung to their
city.

The Hotel Florida's silverware, as the Americans soon
found, was still polished to a luster; the table linen remained
magnificent. But the menu, though served with the usual
flourish, had changed considerably. It was now a slice of
bread, garbanzos cooked in olive oil with onions, and possibly
an orange. The coffee was burned barley water. The liquor,
too, was gone from the little sidewalk cafes and the night-
clubs. Table wine, anisette, *aguardiente,* and a vile, soul-

searing brand of cognac was all there was to be had. The Marx Brothers were by now an institution at the Capital cinema, and a five-year-old Buck Jones movie could be seen at a smaller house. The Paramount, however, now played to capacity audiences—in spite of the shelling. Its new bill was "Tiempos Modernos," *Modern Times*, starring "Carlos" Chaplin. It was still Madrid, the soul of the Republic, where even the barley water tasted like ambrosia.

Moreover, when all else failed there was always Hemingway. No visiting American brigader was ever denied the pleasure of his company. As the last commander of the Lincoln Battalion, Milton Wolff, observed, "I got a vague impression at the time that Hemingway's rooms at the Florida were headquarters for Phil Detro and Freddie Keller."

War-torn Madrid was still host to the international press and to the many prominent Americans making the long journey to Spain. Among them were the writers Dorothy Parker, Lillian Hellman, and Langston Hughes; the Black actor-singer Paul Robeson; Jerry O'Connell, congressman from Montana; and John T. Bernard, Farmer-Laborite from Minnesota. Granted the facilities of the Government radio, Bernard spoke bluntly to Spaniards and Americans alike:

> We sincerely hope that those democratic nations that have thus far refused to accord the legally and democratically elected government the right to purchase arms and ammunition will soon realize that such a policy directly aids the aggressor forces. On our return to the United States we shall do everything within our power to inform our congressional colleagues and the American people of the urgent necessity of granting the Spanish people the aid they are so justly entitled to by international law.

Bernard and O'Connell added their pleas to those of the "man on the spot," the American Ambassador to Spain, Claude G. Bowers, who, throughout the war never ceased in his protestations to the State Department and to his personal friend Franklin Roosevelt, to break with the disastrous British policy of defeat and appeasement, and to grant the Spanish Republic its human and legal rights.

In the United States the Friends of the Abraham Lincoln Brigade continued its fund raising. Coupled with the publication of its new magazine, *Among Friends*, was the release of the films *Heart of Spain* and *Spanish Earth*, the latter a documentary written by Hemingway and directed by Joris Ivens. Both played to packed houses and union halls across America.

While the first repatriated wounded were being given medical care, the Friends scheduled such activities as the All Union National Conference to aid in the rehabilitation of those who had yet to come home, as early as June 1937. The list of major participating unions was indicative of the solid, grass-roots support enjoyed by the volunteers.

In Spain the very atmosphere was now alive with the ominous portent of the not-so-distant drums. Fighting was reduced to a minimum while each side girded itself for the coming Armageddon. Despite the German batteries on Monte Garabitas, however, celebrations marking the first anniversary of the defense of Madrid went off without a hitch. Tens of thousands of *Madrileños* marched and sang their defiance beneath the noses of the omnipresent enemy.

It was just then that an unfortunate change took place within the office of the Fifteenth's Commissariat. The new Brigade Commissar, Dave Doran, was given a deliberate build-up. This had never been done before, at least in the English-speaking units. Commissars had generally come up through the ranks, and had earned their star and circle without benefit of fanfare. Jean Barthel, the Fifteenth's first commander, and George Aiken, and especially Nelson, had all been outstanding personalities, and outstanding commissars. All had had a singular human ability to relate to their men— to lead them and to learn from them. Not so, Doran. Although said by some to be courageous and able, to the men he seemed arrogant and elitist—and he had had no previous military experience at all. His almost immediate appointment, therefore, to the highest office within the brigade other than commander over the heads of all other battle-tested battalion and company commissars was, understandably, the cause for some concern. As one source explained:

> It was he, Doran, who in the spirit of the Government decree incorporating the International Brigades into the formal ranks of the Spanish Republican Army, undertook the retraining of the men after the Aragón offensive.

To suggest, however, that the newly-arrived Doran—whose only meaningful credential was influence in the Communist Party at Albacete—was *the* instrument for the reorganization of the veteran, war-tested battalions of the Fifteenth International Lincoln Brigade is nonsense, demeaning to those men best fitted to do the job; and there were many competent commanders in those ranks. Whatever the brigade had become, it was these officers, working closely with the men, who had made it so. Whatever it would become, it would be their responsibility. (Doran, it must be mentioned, lived and died as courageously as a man could.)

Other changes were in the offing. William Lawrence, American base commissar, was returning to the United States. His place would be taken by the youthful John Gates, who came to the base with excellent recommendations. Lieutenant Colonel Morandi of the Eighty-sixth Mixed Brigade wrote:

> He [John Gates] took a leading part in the reconstruction and organization of the Twentieth Battalion after suffering heavy losses in the many battles in which it was engaged. . . . As a special honor he was proposed as Brigade Commissar and designated as Adjutant Commissar. All of the missions imposed upon him were satisfactorily carried out. He has gained a high reputation, not only among his constituents of the Twentieth Battalion, but in the Brigade H.Q., and in the Brigade itself.

The American mobile hospital unit was also withdrawn from the southern front. Its original founder, Edward Barsky, had returned to Spain from a four-month speaking tour in the United States, during which he had also helped in the creation of a new, west-coast medical unit for Spain, under the leadership of Leo Eloesser, professor of surgery at Stanford University Medical School.

The quiet persisted along the 1,800 kilometers of trenches. The weeks of peace even produced some false hopes of stalemate. In Madrid, with the icy winds of the encircling Sierra de Guadarrama gripping the city, some American newsmen spoke of the coming Franco offensive as being delayed until spring. But the grim needs of the Rome-Berlin Axis in its ongoing climb to power brooked no delays.

Madrid would be the target! So said the world. The strident *pronunciamientos* from Burgos, Salamanca, and Seville promised it!

The ongoing struggle for Madrid, begun in the first days of the rising, had never ceased. All roads north, from the Franco-held ports of Cádiz and Seville to Badajoz, to the valley of the Tagus and to Madrid's famed Casa de Campo and University City, were marked by destroyed villages and towns, burned-out tanks, pitiful blasted attempts at fortifications—and the countless dead of the People's Militia.

In the first months the militia, courageous to a fault, but lacking every requirement needed for a modern army, had simply been bombed into the ground or cut to pieces by the new, advancing juggernaut.

And then, at a terrible cost, the drive was slowed. Indeed, the true saga perhaps of the defense of Madrid began after the fall of Toledo and the stubborn, step-by-bloody-step retreat through the last peripheral towns to the Manzanares, the small river separating the city proper from the famed rolling parkland of the Casa de Campo and the Parque del Este. It was there that the militia's remnants held out for a full ten days and against all odds, true to their promise "that they would hold shut the gates or die"; this, until newly organized brigades could reach them, including the International Brigade then mustering in the center town of Albacete.

November drew to its end. Rain, high winds, and snowstorms blanketed all central Spain. Again the Lincolns received their marching orders, not toward Guadalajara as expected, but, by train again, to Aragón!

Now for the last time the battalions moved eastward. And for the last time they said goodbye to the villagers, who were more like their families now. At midnight, December 11, 1937, they passed through Albacete. During a brief halt for coal and water, they were joined by "recruits," Lincoln men deserting *to* the front. Among these were Benjamin (Butch) Goldstein, an ex-boxer from New York, and Frank Alexander, a young Black from Los Angeles. Butch was deserting Officer's Training School because, in his words, "Even my own mother couldn't make me go to school!" Both had fought with the Mac-Paps at Fuentes.

Two days later they detrained at the division center of Caspe—a name they would hear again soon. From Caspe, they marched an additional two days to the villages in which they would bivouac—all within 100 kilometers of the rebel-held Aragón capital of Teruel!

Brigade headquarters was set up in the town of Alcorisa. Edward Barsky's mobile first aid unit joined them there. It consisted of Doctors Norman Rintz, Oscar Weissman, and Albert Byrne. The nurses included such front-line veterans as Anne Taft, Rose Weiner, Norah Temple, Toby Jensky, Sana Goldblatt, and Selma Chadwick. As a mobile operating and front-line medical outfit, the unit had no equal.

The Lincoln Battalion billeted in Agua Viva, on an arm of the Guadalope River, the British and Canadians in Mas de las Matas, and the Fifty-ninth, in Alcorisa.

The march from Caspe had passed through some of the most beautiful areas of that section of Spain. There was an almost New England-like texture to the stands of oaks, pines, and aspens, all in the myriad colors of the season. The air lay still. It was bitterly cold. Vineyards were blackened, leafless, locked in the grip of winter. The hills were dark, foreboding, starkly outlined against constantly lowering clouds. The rushing waters of the Guadalope were already turbulent with a spate of late rains and early snows.

In the last village where the battalions paused to refresh themselves, they found an electrified population, exuberant and shouting their joy. The streets and small plaza were filled with a celebrating mob shouting to the marchers that the city of Teruel had fallen to the new People's Army!

The volunteers joined in the festivities to such a degree that much later the still-celebrating Mac-Paps were ordered into the freezing night to continue the march as the only means of sobering them up.

All Spain was aroused. On the very eve of the long-heralded great Fascist offensive, the Government of the Republic had dared to strike first in a gamble that had succeeded. It was an all-Spanish victory. No international troops were involved. Divisions of the Republic had smashed through the salient from east and west to cut off Teruel and to then storm its peripheral villages and fortifications. And they had done this without planes, without artillery, and through heavily falling snow in below-zero temperatures.

Spain's Fascist military were stunned; so were the Nazi and Italian Fascist advisers. They were now off-balance, fixed as the bull is fixed by the skill of the bullfighter. Like it or not, they were now forced to fight on ground chosen by the Republic. Madrid had again been saved.

The spirit of victory was contagious. Each night in the little villages of the Lincoln Brigade, the men would join with the peasants in the small cafes for news from the local radio. The ensuing days of Christmas were a gala celebration. Trucks of the brigade Auto Park, with Lou Secundy in charge and Frank Chesler as expediter, went as far afield as Valencia, Barcelona, and Lérida in search of scarce toys and candy for the children of the villages. Secundy even discovered good cognac and champagne in out of the way places. An almost endless round of brigade and battalion fiestas followed, which the villagers joined. Dances were held, songfests encouraged. The fleeting days were easily the most pleasant ever experienced by the men. Some brigade staff parties were held jointly with Barsky's medical unit, with many of the battalion and company commanders and commissars attending.

Dispatches from the front then began to report massive counter-attacks by enemy divisions of the corps of Galicia and Castille. By December 29, the villages of Concud, San

Blas, and Campillo had been retaken. Blood now poured in an endless stream in the valley of the Turia.

In the early hours of New Year's Eve, with small celebrations still under way, dispatch riders appeared in every village. The orders were: "Fifteenth Brigade. Prepare to move out!"

By noon of January 1, they were being driven through blinding snow over winding mountain roads that took a heavy toll of trucks and men. George Foucek, from California, tells of seeing American Diamond-Ts, driven by Barcelona cab drivers with little knowledge of snow and ice slicks, wrecked in the precipitous ravines below.

Dr. Barsky, following the convoy, also describes trucks plunging from cliffs, and icy winds blowing snow in swirling clouds, reducing visibility to zero. Anne Taft, Barksy's assistant, recalls that the medical contingent was snowbound. She, with nurses Goldblatt and Jensky, climbed down a mountain to a small village and enlisted the peasants to dig them out.

The Canadians went directly to the bombed-out village of Argente; the Lincolns, British, and the Fifty-ninth went to Cuevas Labradas, instantly named the "North Pole" for its below-zero temperatures. The Lincolns deployed in the frozen hills to the north of the rebel-held village of Altas de Celades. New enemy divisions were streaming into the salient, and a simultaneous thrust against several points could quite possibly destroy the Republican front.

On January 3, a giant armada of some 200 bombers and fighters swept in a low and tight formation over the snowbound Mac-Pap positions. The entire battalion held its breath. "They came in just over the hills," one man recalled, "so low you could hit the sons-of-bitches with a shovel. They looked right down at us—and didn't see us." This phenomenon was discussed for days.

The assignment given the Lincoln Battalion was to protect the right flank of a Spanish brigade. The British and the Fifty-ninth, to the north of the Lincolns, had a similar task with Republican troops on their right. To the front of the Americans there was nothing except a more or less flat plain upon which, in the distance, was the important Zaragoza-Teruel

Highway. To the south the village of Celades was a center of intense activity.

At Teruel the very air thrummed with the vibrations of ongoing barrages. Not for an instant was the sky free of aircraft. The sight and sound of exploding bombs on all the horizons was incessant.

On the second day the Lincolns were given an object lesson in what to expect from the new People's Army. Under cover of an intense barrage from many batteries, fully four battalions of the rebel General Aranda's Corps of Galicia hurled themselves at the troops on their flank. By day's end the field was covered with rebel dead. Nowhere had the lines been breached.

On the following day the assault continued, with the same results. At midday it was broken off, at which point Captain Detro received a hurried note, saying that large numbers of the enemy were infiltrating the *barrancas* between the American and Spanish positions. Lieutenant Levine was already contesting this attempt with the concentrated rifle fire of the few men deployed. He requested that Detro send Company 1 onto the plateau together with the machine gun crews of Joe Bianca and Al Kaufman. Captain Lamb led the men out. Rolfe writes:

> They deployed beautifully, spread like a fan across the plateau under heavy fire, and after only thirty minutes of brisk fighting routed the enemy, drove them off the plateau, and established a line only a few meters from the down slope leading into the valley.

That night a runner from the embattled troops on the Lincoln's flank brought the Spanish commander's thanks for the American's swift action in smashing the rebel attempt to flank their lines. That night the Mac-Paps arrived and were positioned in the *barrancas* directly behind these same Spanish troops—just in case.

Each day saw a new barrage, a new wave of attacking men and planes, and still the Spaniards held. The British and Fifty-ninth on the right sustained the weight of two consecutive attempts, but held their positions. Mac-Pap observers who moved directly into the Spanish lines told of smashed bunkers, trenches destroyed, and heavy casualties.

Of the many tales told of the North Pole, none fail to mention the misery of dirt, lice, frozen food, and forever-zero temperatures. Because of the open nature of the front, there were often wide stretches between strong points. On one occasion Lieutenants Wolff and Levine, and the Company 3 commander, Bill Titus, went on night reconnaissance. They passed through the enemy lines to the very outskirts of Celades. Laying belly-flat against the snow, they evaluated the situation. Wolff and Levine were forced to bring Titus back almost bodily. He had wanted to grenade what he insisted was the rebel command post for the area.

Captain Cecil Smith, the Mac-Pap commander, and Captain Nilo Makela of the machine gun company, and this writer, repeated the maneuver, albeit accidentally. On a nocturnal visit to the Spanish positions, we unknowingly went through the lines to within a few meters of the rebel wire, where we were challenged by hysterical screams of *"Rojos! Rojos!"* and the instant roar of several machine guns. We made it back unscathed, but others were not so lucky. Yorki Burton from Vancouver, who had hiked into northern British Columbia on snowshoes to deliver its first copies of *The Worker*, alone with a second communications man, were lost on a trip to the lines. On the same night, the young artist Clyde Taylor, a Mac-Pap topographer, was also lost. Rebel prisoners, taken on the next night in that flat area of snow and ice, hinted that Taylor, Burton, and the second Canadian had been questioned and summarily executed.

To the rear, in the frozen village of Cuevas Labradas, Dr. Barsky's mobile unit and Dr. Mark Strauss's first-aid unit underwent one vicious bombardment after another. The village became a cemetery of collapsed buildings through which shrapnel-pierced ambulances threaded their way to the *autochirs* (mobile operating units). Barsky states that their surgery was generally for chest and abdominal cases, wounds that otherwise might not survive the trip to the rear. His unit tended not just the wounded of the brigade, but all line troops in the area.

"They stood alone," declared General Walter, who visited Barsky in the company of Herbert Matthews and a number of other newsmen. "There was no medical unit in all Spain operating closer to the front than they, or possessing their technical equipment and skill."

Dr. Eloesser had set up a 200-bed evacuation hospital on the very perimeter of the Teruel fighting. This world-famous neurosurgeon, who spoke six languages and was to become a veteran of both World Wars, had many of his original contingent with him, including his assistant, Ave Bruzzichesi, Doctors Van Zandt from Texas, Weissfield from Washington, and Leonard Larsen from San Francisco. Also serving in the Republican medical corps was Johannes Muller, from the University of Texas. He later went on the win the Nobel Prize in medicine, for his work on X-ray-induced genetic mutations. Alfambra, the site of the hospital, was a bombed-out ghost town, a blackened, steel-point etching against the surrounding fields of snow.

There was no let up in the Franco counter-offensive. News dispatches from Hendaye quoted Francoist sources as saying that they had committed 150,000 men to the cauldron. A rebel Salamanca dispatch, dated January 1, claimed recapture of Teruel. On the very same day, however, Matthews, reporting from inside Teruel, described the surrender of some 350 Civil Guards from a hold-out building inside the city.

Journalists seeking to acertain the truth of the matter were taken under escort directly into the line of fire on the Concud-Teruel Road. Their vehicle was promptly hit by Republican artillery, proof positive of who controlled the city. The following dispatch describes the tragedy:

> Eleven correspondents were in automobiles proceeding to the city and had come within a few kilometers of Teruel without being warned of the peril, when a shell struck the car containing the victims. These were Sheepshanks of the British Reuters Agency; Johnson, of the American magazine *Spur*; Neil, an American member of the Associ-

ated Press; and Philby, of the *London Times*. The latter survives, while the bodies of the others are being shipped home to relatives.

On January 5, the Eleventh International Thaelmann Brigade (except for the Thaelmanns and the Lincolns, all other Internationals had remained on the center or southern fronts), together with Spanish battalions, launched local attacks around the threatened perimeter of the city. Vital positions on La Muela, an escarpment separated from Teruel by the confluence of the Turia and the Alfambra Rivers, were recaptured, with the Eleventh taking more than 250 of the Navarese prisoners, at bayonet point.

On January 14, the Abraham Lincoln Brigade was ordered to the defense of the city. The brigade would move, according to General Walter, "to a post of honor!"

The Mac-Paps, preceding the Lincolns and British, passed in the dead of night between the hills of El Muletón and Santa Bárbara, crossing the narrow but swift-flowing Alfambra to take positions along the eastern face of La Muela. Company 1 occupied a seventy-foot cliff edge, with its back to the valley. Enemy positions were within a scant fifty meters, the intervening space dotted with the unburied bodies of the Navarese whom the Thaelmanns had killed. Company 2 extended into La Muela, close to the Zaragoza Road. Company 3's lines swung east in a wide arc and were flanked by a Spanish marine battalion occupying three small chalk hills between La Muela and El Muletón. The railroad to Zaragoza ran along the base of the cliff edge, into Company 3's hill, and on into enemy territory. Across the narrow valley of the Alfambra was Teruel and its outlying cemetery on the hill of Santa Bárbara. This hill, too, was precipitous. Around a thousand-foot arc at its top, facing both west and north, was the British Battalion. Its guns were trained on the insurgent positions, over the heads of the Mac-Paps and the *Marineros*.

The Lincoln companies were positioned in the first outlying buildings of Teruel proper, among them an insane asylum belonging to the Dominican Order. The still-decimated Fifty-ninth was across the valley and facing the southern tip of La Muela.

To the Americans, the panorama of Teruel was like no other in Spain. Here was no village of stone houses and massive churches, no olive groves or wheat fields. Here, instead, was a hellish Goya etching, stark, frozen, surrounded by bomb-blasted, blackened hills. Its reputation of being the coldest spot in all of Spain appeared true. Now it lay half-destroyed, its fields plowed by shells and seeded with the frozen bodies of Carlists and Moroccans, of Republicans and Communists.

A lull set in. The skies cleared. The sun shone on patches of sparkling snow—and on the wings of black *tau* crosses (the Francoist insignia) on the dozens of Italian and German planes which bombed without let-up. According to most Americans, the planes did less damage than the incessant mortar shells and the constant sniping.

In this last respect, the Americans and British always gave more than they got. Their training forms, plus their excellent marksmanship, were almost certain guarantees that whenever they relieved line troops anywhere, the ensuing few days would be veritable turkey shoots. At Teruel hardly a day passed in which the Mac-Pap snipers, led by Americans Leonard Levenson and Jack Penrod, did not turn in formidable scores of "hits."

This was also true of the machine gun crews. The British, firing across the valley and over the heads of the Mac-Pap companies, had an absolute field day. They swept the exposed and startled Navarese trenches with an accurate hail of fire from a distance of 1,000 meters. Their accuracy at this incredible distance was attested to by the stream of stretcher bearers moving in and out of the enemy lines.

The Lincoln Battalion, its back to the city, still faced the problem of the Dominican asylum in its midst. No one knew with certainty that the occupants were all really "inmates." Commissar Fred Keller, a non-Communist with a Catholic background, had long conversations with the Mother Superior. She had with her as helpers, six nuns and a dozen acolytes. All had feared rape and general mayhem at the hands of the "bloody bolsheviks." When they saw that their fears were not only unfounded, but that they and the inmates received the best in food, clothing, and medical care that the Americans and the Spaniards could offer, they settled quietly to the care of their charges.

Brigade, however, still wanted them out, so they were finally coaxed onto trucks with the promise of oranges and sunshine and sent down the road to Valencia.

On the third day, lanky Phil Detro, the eighth man to command the Abraham Lincoln Battalion, was mortally wounded by a sniper's bullet. Captain Leonard Lamb, competent, unassuming, and efficient, was again the battalion commander.

On January 17, the rebel assault was renewed. Francoist archives tell of thousands of shells sweeping like a tempest over Celades, El Muletón, Las Pedrizas, and El Mansueto. By 9:00 A.M. that day, Aranda's Corps of Galicia, some 65,000 assault troops in five divisions, auxiliaries of 600 heavy guns and an equal number of planes, moved to the attack. The few Republican guns were silenced. Still, whole brigades were shattered by defending Republican machine guns. At day's end but two minor hills in the area of Las Pedrizas had been taken.

In the sector of the Fifteenth and Eleventh Brigades, the main thrust was against the Thaelmann remnants on El Muletón, with only a holding attempt against the Lincolns. Even this, however, was met by the British antitank battery dug in on Santa Bárbara. While El Muletón disappeared in clouds of smoke and cordite, the antitanks sent salvo after salvo into the trenches of the First Navarese facing Canadian-American Company 1, knocking out one machine gun nest after the other.

Wave after wave of the enemy hit El Muletón, and died there. By 3:00 P.M. the Fascist troops were retreating back over the plain to Concud, at which point the rebel guns switched wholly to the Mac-Pap's Company 3, commanded by Lionel Edwards, and the *Marineros* on their chalk hills. These last disappeared instantly under the pounding of a sea of explosives—and the enemy battalions, thrown back from El Muletón, wheeled round to drive directly south.

The Canadian and Spanish guns inflicted terrible losses. Still, the waves of attackers carrying standards denoting their battalions came on under the threats of their officers. The British then switched the rapid-fire antitanks toward the north, and literally hosed them with over a hundred shells in the space of minutes. This, plus the withering fire of the defenders' Maxims, stopped them dead. Their ensuing rout became a slaughter.

But then, thinking perhaps that the *Marineros* had still retreated, and hoping to roll up the flank of the American-Canadian line, the insurgent command sent a number of squadrons of Moroccan cavalry in a wide arc around the chalk hills and into the narrow valley of the Alfambra. The charge had artillery protection, a rolling barrage to the mouth of the valley. Driving between the chalk hills and the British gunners on Santa Bárbara, they then wheeled and struck directly toward the line of the railroad and a tunnel protecting the Mac-Pap command post.

Captain E. Cecil Smith, a Toronto veteran of Brunete and the new Canadian commander, simply met them head-on with two machine guns and the rifles of his hastily mobilized staff. It was direct fire at close quarters, with many visible casualties. Fleeing back up the valley, their remnants came under the guns of Company 3, the *Marineros*, and the British. Few escaped. The Alfambra River ran slow with the frozen bodies of horses and men.

At the crack of dawn the fighting began anew. Again the rebels concentrated their strongest effort against El Muletón. All morning the hill was pulverized by the shells of a hundred guns and continuous flights of Ju-52s raining bombs into the inferno. At noon the anti-Nazi Germans still held the hill, but not for long. Once again the enemy moved to the attack. The distance between the Fifteenth and Eleventh Brigades precluded support of any kind. The English-speaking battalions were forced, therefore, to watch the remnants of the German anti-Nazi Thaelmanns being destroyed before their eyes. Throughout the afternoon, they made a fighting retreat along the spine of El Muletón. Neither artillery nor aircraft came to their aid, nor were there, apparently, any reserves. By nightfall the strategic height was lost, with less than a quarter of the Eleventh Brigade surviving to reach the lee of Santa Bárbara and the protection of the British guns.

All down the line of the Fifteenth the word came to stand firm, to be worthy of the sacrifice of the Thaelmanns. For there was nothing now between the enemy and the city, except the four battalions of the Abraham Lincoln Brigade.

William Carney, a *New York Times* reporter in the rebel zone at the time, wrote that all of La Muela was now in Franco's hands, that he personally had viewed Teruel from the tip of that position while being briefed by Colonel García Valiño of the First Division of Navarre, facing the Fifteenth Lincoln Brigade. Valiño reputedly said: "When we cross the river, it will then require no great effort to capture Santa Bárbara hill, dominating Teruel on the northeast."

This was an error: Carney did *not* stand on the tip of La Muela—simply because it was *occupied* by the Lincoln Brigade. Moreover the river had yet to be crossed, and the Fifteenth barred the way!

The key to the valley was the chalk hills and the positions of the Mac-Pap's Company 3, now heavily reinforced. The opening barrage came at 8:00 A.M., from guns lined hub to hub before Concud. They fired at point-blank range, since Republican artillery had ceased to exist as a counter-threat. As on El Muletón, the Canadian and Spanish positions disappeared in clouds of dust and cordite. By noon they had beaten back every assault. At 1:00 P.M., in the midst of the second attack of the day, reinforcements from all companies were thrown into the line of Company 3 by Captain Smith. The rebel infantry came on again—and the shattered and decimated marine battalion broke, abandoning the three hills.

Lieutenant Ricardo Díaz, a young Spaniard attached to the Mac-Pap staff, then made his way alone through the barrage to rally what remnants he could. With these, he hastily formed a line just south of the abandoned hills. But for this weak defense, the entire mouth of the valley now lay open, with the Mac-Pap's Company 3 bearing the full weight of the insurgent onslaught. Their guns at no time ceased firing. The slaughter of insurgent troops before their positions was horrible. The enemy, according to American and Canadian survivors, came on in *column*, banners waving, coerced and threatened by their officers. They sought to seize the abandoned chalk hills. But again the British on Santa Bárbara, under the command of George Fletcher and at a distance of a thousand meters, cut down all who attempted to enter those hills.

Thus the fruits of victory were denied to the Corps of Galicia.

Lieutenant Edwards, noting the work of the English gunners, extended his flank to encompass one of the hills. John Field of Arkansas dashed forward with two sections of men and a number of light Tuckeroff machine guns. Within seconds they were pouring flank fire into the attackers.

There now began a whirlwind of action and counter-action. The situation was fast becoming desperate. The sea of shells now ranged over every square yard of the valley. Merriman, chief of operations, ordered the British rifle companies down into the valley to block any further attempt.

The British were positioned on Santa Bárbara in an inverted L, at a right angle to a long gulley splitting the face of the cliff. Down this precipitate *barranca* the rifle companies came. The first was Company 3 under Sam Wilde, then Company 4, which was spotted and heavily shelled. Major Attlee Company (the first company, named for British Labour Party leader Clement Attlee) brought up the rear, and came under even heavier fire. Many were killed before they reached the valley floor.

The three companies then deployed with fixed bayonets and moved forward, a thin line of English and Spanish troops, advancing through the roar of exploding shells. They were forced finally to dig in on a rising slope facing the two lost hills, with the Mac-Paps to their left and Díaz's handful to their immediate right. As night fell, a veritable curtain of fire played over every open space in the valley.

William Rust, the British historian, vividly records the action of the following day:

As the sun arose and the barrage began again, the Fascists advanced in great force from Concud against the Canadians. Their firm stand prevented the British from being encircled, and these, in turn, performed a similar service for the Canadians. Then the Fascist artillery directed its fire against the Major Attlee Company, who were all too poorly protected by their hurriedly dug trenches. The British machine gunners who had remained on the cliff top suffered the anguish of seeing their comrades being slaughtered in the valley below. But the M.G.'s were able to cover the retreat of the remaining members of the Attlee Company. Revenge came when the enemy infantry sought to occupy the vacated trenches. They were again mown down by the British on the cliff's top.

Heavy shell fire on our Number 3 and 4 Companies on the right flank had also compelled them to retreat. It was not a rout, however, but a consolidation of the positions; a tribute to steady nerves and cool judgement.

Positions had been lost and some of the best men killed, but the command had no intention of giving up the valley to the Fascists. On the contrary, all three companies moved to a fortified blockhouse controlling the valley's entrance. That night the blockhouse was feverishly fortified, and fresh trenches were dug in commanding positions around it. A consolidation was effected the next day under the protection of the M.G.'s on the hill-top. The Fascists, naturally, directed a terrific artillery bombardment against Fletcher's gunners. The M.G. Company's trenches were reduced to rubble, but the gunners stood nobly to their posts. These last were strongly built, in one case resisting *five direct hits*. . . . Fletcher kept sighting his guns so that they killed the maximum of Fascists and gave the line in the valley time to reform.

A heavy Fascist attack against the blockhouse was then defeated, and in the end the attempt to drive into Teruel through the Fifteenth Brigade was completely repulsed.

Simultaneously with the first retreat of the British, the Canadians lost their captured hill. Of the thirty men who had occupied it and held it to prevent the British from being flanked and overrun, almost all were casualties. Among the dead was young John Field. A singular reflection on personal tragedy is that at the moment of his death, Ralph Field, his father, who had tried to pass as John's older brother in order to be accepted as a combat soldier, was at work in the Mac-Pap kitchen to the rear. It was difficult to inform him of the death of his only son.

Lional Edwards writes of this position, which he, too, helped to defend before ordering the withdrawal:

> It was an advanced post on the Mac-Pap's right flank. We had occupied it with about thirty men and four machine guns. The Fascists blasted hell out of us with heavy artillery, and in between barrages sent their troops over to attack. But their men were too scared to get anywhere. We could see them sneaking up, with their officers threatening them with their revolvers. We'd let them get into short range and murder them. After two days of constant artillery, however, all our machine guns were blown up by direct hits and there were just four of us holding the position. Every other man was dead or wounded.

Much had transpired on the day of the British retreat. Mac-Pap Company 3 had not only been driven from the chalk hill, but had also, since its flank was now exposed, lost its original line and two-thirds of its men—well over a hundred. It had retreated as much as a hundred meters or so to new positions.

On January 22, a last frontal attack was made against all Lincoln Brigade positions. The enemy was stopped dead, so thoroughly beaten that by early afternoon all contact was broken off. Only the littered field remained as proof of the attempt.

Casualties had been severe. Canadian losses were estimated at over 250 men. The British claimed 150, a third of their strength. The Lincolns lost perhaps 80 all told, as did the Fifty-ninth. Among the dead were such outstanding men as Larry Kleidman, fortifications officer, Pablo Carbonel, Cuban machine gun commander, killed with all his gun crew, Norman Lisberg, a well-liked young Black from Los Angeles, Carl N. Kelly of Ohio, Charles Ashley from San Francisco, Nelson

Fishelson from New York, Matti Haukkale from Minnesota, Walter Swiderski from Toronto, and dozens of other brave men whose loss would be deeply felt.

On the evening of January 20, Juan Modesto, Commander-in-Chief of the Fifth Army Corps, especially commended the Canadian and British battalions for their stand. Battlefield promotions were issued: Captain E. Cecil Smith to major, Lieutenant Ricardo Díaz to captain, Lieutenant William Alexander, of the British Battalion, to captain. Commissars Saul Wellman and Wally Tapsall of the Mac-Paps and British, respectively, were singled out for special commendations by the army command. All in all, the Lincoln Brigade won the praise of not just the Spanish army, but also of the many war correspondents and military observers from both Britain and the United States.

Herbert Matthews sent the following dispatch:

> In the midst of the battle one must be sparing of details, but the American and Canadian Volunteers are writing an impressive page in the history of the International Brigades in Spain. . . .
>
> For the first time an artillery barrage comparable with those of World War One was laid down. At the American H.Q. it was estimated that in the sector of its battalions there was not five feet of ground that did not receive shells. No fewer than ten waves of men surged forward, brigade after brigade, fresh troops and more fresh troops, until human endurance could bear no more.

A last communiqué on the Teruel campaign from rebel sources underlines the total lack of respect for fact often shown by the high command of Franco's Fascist military:

> Associated Press, Hendaye, France, January 27, 1938. Official Spanish Insurgent dispatches from Salamanca said today that two American Volunteer Brigades, the "Lincoln" and "Washington" Brigades, had been destroyed in Saturday's fighting on the Teruel Front. The Insurgents said that a third International Brigade, the "Walter" Brigade, had been decimated.

On February 3, after having held its "post of honor" before Teruel for twenty days, the Fifteenth International Lincoln Brigade was relieved by men from El Campesino's Forty-fifth Division, and so retired from the lines.

The four battalions, hungry, ragged, and weary, looking like anything but the elite shock troops they now were, marched south to Puerto Escandrón. They rested for twenty-four hours. On the fifth they boarded a train composed of boxcars only, traveled for a few kilometers, and were then joined by a French artillery unit. They were minus the Mac-Paps and Fifty-ninth, who would wait until the following day for their train.

Word somehow preceded the Lincolns, so that when they reached Valencia they were met by thousands of relatives and friends of their young Spanish comrades. This welcoming crowd brought fish, bread, fruit, and many other things, which they gave out to Spaniard and American alike. Many wept to see the hunger, the ragged uniforms, and the war weariness of the Americans. That night the men camped in the bull ring. A great part of the next day was spent in rounding up the Spaniards who had fanned out to their homes all over the city. It was dusk when they left Valencia, on the long journey to the Madrid front.

Major Humberto Galleani was in charge of the train. At one point he protested vehemently to Lamb and Keller that the men were tapping huge tuns of cognac at a railroad siding where the train had stopped for fuel. Visiting the scene of the "crime," Lamb and Keller concluded that this was a proper syphoning off of much-needed "antifreeze" for the water-cooled machine guns. Each man then lined up for a full canteen against future need.

At a final stop in the hours of darkness, a telegram was handed to Lamb, ordering the Abraham Lincoln Brigade to return immediately to Teruel. Similar orders were given the other battalions.

On the very day of the Fifteenth's departure from the lines, two new rebel army corps had struck directly east from the Zaragoza-Teruel Highway to seize Perales, Argente, Alfambra (the site of Dr. Eloesser's hospital), and Fuentes Caliente. A breach of over thirty kilometers had been opened through the eastern front of the salient.

A diversionary attack was needed at once, to allow the Republican army of the Levante and its weary troops to close that monstrous gap. Just why the exhausted Fifteenth and Eleventh Brigades of the Thirty-fifth Division were chosen for the task was one of the many small mysteries of the war.

Troop movements are at best chaotic, and the reassembling of the battalions of the Fifteenth was no exception. One American, Lawrence Cane, describes but a single phase of it:

> We marched twenty kilometers, got on a freight train, rattled, started and stopped, marched again for a couple of days, sometimes on trucks; came to one last town. No place to sleep and nothing to eat. Snow and cold. We stood in the freezing wind and sang "Always fucking well waiting" in the dark. A Spanish officer passing saw us shivering there and broke into tears. His had been one of the units to break, and he felt responsible for these poor, bedraggled men—who still had the guts to sing.

The site was the picture-postcard village of Seguro de los Baños. The Canadians had arrived first. There was no food, and no place to sleep had been assigned to them. The Lincolns and British then came marching through light swirls of snow, drew up in the plaza, and were almost instantly assigned billets. The Mac-Paps had been ignored—or forgotten.

Ex-boxer Butch Goldstein took exception to this. Butch, a very colorful and courageous soldier, reputedly had the loudest mouth, the most caustic tongue, and the strongest rank-and-file sentiments of any man in the brigade. He went straight to brigade headquarters to tell a frowning Dave Doran that the Mac-Paps were freezing in the snow, and demanded that something be done. Doran coldly told Butch to mind his own damn business, to which Butch replied, "Go fuck yourself." He was promptly arrested. Afterward, others on the staff demanded his release, and Butch was allowed to return to the Mac-Paps. Time passed, with still no action, no food, no billets. The temperature continued to drop. Finally,

Butch again went to brigade, arriving just in time to hear Doran say to men of the headquarters company, "I want you to go out and to bring back mattresses and blankets for the *Estado Mayor* [headquarters], and I don't care how you get them."

As Butch recalls:

> I assumed right away that he meant to take this stuff from the peasants, and I said, "You mean to say you're going to take mattresses and blankets from the peasants for the Brigade staff? And on top of that the Mac-Paps are still out there freezing, with no houses?" And Doran says: "You keep the hell out of this, Butch!" And I said, "You can go fuck yourself again, Dave!" And he had me arrested again.
>
> He did that because he thought he was a big-shot, and no one should talk like that to a big-shot. So they put me in a room under armed guard, and I was there all night and until almost noon of the next day. Then Merriman came in and said, "Butch, I think you should apologize. I don't want to keep you here. You shouldn't *be* here. But you should apologize. After all, this is the Spanish Army and Dave Doran *is* Brigade Commissar, and discipline has got to be maintained."
>
> I said: "In the first place, I will not apologize. Second, if you go [to] any bourgeois jail—any jail—they feed the prisoners. I have been here all this time and no food."
>
> So food was sent in, but I still wouldn't apologize. Then Milt Wolff came and after him George Watt, and then Saul Wellman. And they all wanted me to apologize for the sake of discipline, and I said that I believed in conscious discipline, not imposed discipline, and that I wouldn't apologize.

A Party meeting was held in Butch's cell, and members argued all afternoon. Then, after every non-party officer on the staff had had his personal session with Butch, he agreed, as he put it, "to apologize for the sake of Spain." He then went to Doran's quarters and said briefly to the somewhat chastened officer, "I apologize," and abruptly marched back to the cheering veterans of the Mac-Paps.

On the night of February 16, the battalions moved west from Seguro to attack rebel-held positions on Monte Atalaya and Sierra de Pedigrosso. Spanish peasants, familiar with the terrain, acted as guides. The Canadians went first, moving off into a darkness of bone-piercing wind and hail of icy sleet. They were silent ghosts flitting across a broad valley, a frozen stream, on to the slopes of Atalaya. No man spoke. Machine gunners with their heavy burdens kept their grunts muffled. After what seemed hours, they were in position. The Lincolns passed them in the darkness, going still further south, toward Pedigrosso. Lawrence Cane describes the Mac-Pap assault:

> The hill was well fortified and ringed with a double line of barbed wire. Our wire cutters went forward and Rudy Haber was the first to cut a path through the wire. We'd caught the Fascists by surprise, going through the wire simultaneously in a number of places. When they were aware of what was happening, it was too late. They opened up with machine guns and the works, but we blasted the M.G.'s and the trenches with grenades and charged in after them. Other than minor resistance by officers, which was quickly overcome, they soon surrendered. They were mostly young kids, a hundred or so of them. We captured a number of machine guns, mortars, blankets, cigarettes, and canned sardines.

The Lincoln Battalion reached its attack positions just before daylight and took its first hill from an already alerted enemy. The hill was lightly held by a corporal's guard with two machine guns. There were no casualties. When the Lincoln's moved on their prime target, Pedigrosso, it was daylight and they were in full view of the enemy.

Pedigrosso was protected by two companies of infantry with four heavy and eight light machine guns, plus a number of eighty-one millimeter mortars. Like the Mac-Paps, the Lincoln staff—Keller, Wolff, David Reiss, the new battalion commander—all were on the line fighting their way upward through the sweeping fire of the enemy guns. Reiss yelled to the enemy, *"Camaradas! Somos hermanos!* ['Comrades! We are brothers!'] Surrender, you sons of bitches!" He cheered the men around him as they moved ever closer to the parapets. The moment came. They moved in from all sides, beating down the wire and hurling grenades into the bunkers.

Bill Titus, Company 3 commander, hurdled the wire with a grenade in either hand and met his death on the insurgent bayonets. Seconds later it was all over. Only a handful of officers attempted further resistance. They were instantly subdued. Wolff states of the young commander of the Fascists: "He was a real snob, arrogant as hell. He actually demanded special treatment as apart from his men. I gave it to him. I booted his ass down the side of that hill in full view of his troops. I'm sure they appreciated it."

That night the Canadians tried for a third hill, and failed. A number of dead were abandoned on the wire. Butch Goldstein, the first to cut through the wire, was wounded. Unarmed, he went down the hill looking for a first-aid post. Since no consolidation had taken place, troops of both sides were everywhere. Butch, challenged by a young *Gallego* on the road, knocked him flat with his good arm, took the man's gun, shoved his fist in his mouth so he couldn't cry out, and wandered around with him until he heard the welcome sound of English-speaking voices.

Prisoners taken by both battalions numbered more than 300. Arms captured included a dozen eighty-one millimeter mortars and over twenty machine guns. And, too, they now had Portuguese cigars, bread, side arms, and cases of canned sardines and octopus. This last was sampled with great gusto.

The expected counter-attack came at dawn of the following day, and continued for two days. But the Fifteenth held on to its captured hills; indeed, the British and Fifty-ninth Battalions chased a vastly superior number of rebels down a valley toward the village of Vivel del Río and could have taken it had they any reserve help at all.

The next day, the Fifteenth was again withdrawn. The action as a whole is referred to in brigade archives as "the perfect maneuver," an example of what could be accomplished with good leadership, trained men, and certain dedication.

What the Americans did not know at the time was that at a

distance of just twenty kilometers to the west was the entire corps of the Italian CTV—50,000 men, 300 field guns, and some 250 tanks. That they had not made their presence known was a measure of both their strength and their confidence. For the time of the great offensive was truly at hand, and they were but a small part of that which the Lincolns would call "The pressure no man can withstand!"

# PART III

# the storm

No man knows war or its meaning who has not stumbled
from tree to tree, desperate for cover, or dug his face deep
in the earth, felt the ground pulse with the ear-breaking
fall of death. No man knows war who never has crouched
in his foxhole, hearing the bullets an inch from his head,
or the zoom of planes like a ferris-wheel, strafing the
trenches.

EDWIN ROLFE 1909–1954

TERUEL WAS LOST to the Republic. Casualties on both sides had been the greatest since the war began. Material losses were enormous. For the Republic, they were disastrous. The mounting flow of Nazi and Fascist planes, tanks, guns, and men to Spain was now well known. Soviet aid, on the other hand, had long ceased being delivered to Republican ports but was instead being unloaded in France, where it was instantly impounded!

Even as the Republic fought for Teruel, whole new army corps of Franco's Fascist military had moved into position. The true offensive, the one the Republic had sought to throw off-balance, would now be unleashed. The Negrín Cabinet and the War Ministry, though fully aware of what was happening, were powerless to do anything other than maneuver its limited forces in the hope that the onslaught could be held back, that time could still be bought with which to reorganize its armies and rear guard, and to tap its resources. In Anarchist-dominated Catalonia, for example, a meaningful arms industry had yet to be mobilized owing to mismanagement and sabotage.

The Thirty-fifth Division now moved to the towns of La Puebla de Híjar and Azaila, in Aragón, where it would rest and reorganize as a part of the active reserve. Leaves, however, were restricted to officers only, and to those who were sick and in need of hospitalization.

Some 800 men then arrived from the Tarazona Base. The levy included many veteran officers from the training school. The base itself had literally been stripped of its personnel. With David Reiss now in command, and Eric Dewitt Parker from the training school as his commissar, the battalion was again at a healthy figure of 500 or so men, the other battalions likewise.

The Fifteenth moved closer to the front; the Americans toward the scene of their earlier conquest, Belchite; the English to nearby Lécera; the Fifty-ninth and Mac-Paps to Letucs.

"At the beginning of March," wrote Frank Bonetti of Los Angeles, "we moved again. The front was quiet. We were not expecting anything serious."

On March 9, however, an air of uneasiness swept the Lincoln encampment. In the distance, a sudden and prolonged thunder of artillery, plus the labored thrumming of Ju-52s and Caproni bombers, was sufficient cause for alarm.

As dusk fell, troops appeared on all the roads in what was obviously a disorganized retreat. Lawrence Cane, with a squad on the Letucs Road, states that they were suddenly confronted with dozens of soldiers without weapons or equipment. They had received orders, they said, to retreat. Their officers had fled; some mentioned treason. Artillerymen, surprised by the enemy, had destroyed their guns or had fled with the locks of those they had not had time to blow up.

On the evening of the tenth, motorcycles arrived at all headquarters with orders from Merriman: the Canadians were to proceed by forced march to Azuara, southwest of Belchite, to reinforce any Spanish troops they might find in the area. The Lincolns were ordered directly to the defense of Belchite; the Fifty-ninth and British to hasten to the aid of the Lincolns.

In the interest of history, and to explain what later ensued, it is necessary to know the strength of the opposing forces and the intent and direction of the rebel onslaught. Information is derived mainly from *Franco* archives.

The breakthrough area would be enormous; beginning at the town of Fuentes del Ebro and extending to Pancrudo below Vivel del Río—over 100 kilometers. The objective was a shattering of the Republican front in the first phase of a drive to the Mediterranean. If successful, Republican Spain would be cut into two parts, its armies destroyed, and the war ended quickly in Franco's favor.

Franco's Corps of Galicia, approximately 40,000 men, attacked directly east from Pancrudo and Vivel, and in the direction of Montalbán-Alcorisa, the Christmas headquarters of the Fifteenth Brigade.

The Italian CTV, comprised of the Littorio Division and the Black, Green, and Blue Arrow divisions, approximately 50,000 men in all, motorized and armored, attacked directly east from Fonbria and Badenas in the direction of Rudilla-Córtez de Aragón.

The beefed-up Corps of Morocco, under the command of General Yagüe, with six divisions and auxiliaries, approximately 60,000 men including 30,000 Moroccans and Foreign Legionnaires, struck east-southeast in the direction of Fuendetodos-Azuara-Belchite, toward Azaila, Castelnou, and Escatrón.

Artillery attached to the three breakthrough corps was as follows: Corps of Galicia, 192 guns; CTV, 232 guns; Corps of Morocco, 188 guns. To this was added the Italian air squadrons of no less than 350 planes, the Condor Legion of 300 planes, and the Spanish rebel air force with 300 planes. The CTV reputedly possessed no fewer than 250 Fiat-Ansaldo tanks, likewise the Corps of Galicia and Morocco. In addition, the Eastern army command had been given the use of the German tank corps under Colonel Ritter Wilhelm Von Thoma—a total of 180 PZKI tanks together with four battalions of 180 antitank guns.

Added to the above were engineer battalions, Monasterio's cavalry divisions, anti-air units, and transport battalions replete with fleets of new American trucks, shipped to Spain from wholly-owned GM plants in Italy.

From Zaragoza to the French border, the fresh Corps of Navarre, under General Solchaga, and the Corps of Aragón, under General Moscardo, were also moving into position.

There were greater concentrations of guns and men in World War I. But in terms of actual fire power plus massive mobility of arms, the forces Franco unleashed on March 9, 1938, were by far the most formidable array of armaments and men ever amassed for any battle.

To oppose this juggernaut, the Republic had but sixty available planes and an equal number of tanks. It is also doubtful whether even 100 guns had survived the rout at Teruel. Moreover, facing four-fifths of the front of the three rebel corps and the CTV was a single Republican corps of the line, the Twelfth.

To compare this corps with any one of the aforementioned rebel corps in terms of arms would be ridiculous. It is doubtful, for example, whether its 25,000 men possessed the equivalent in machine guns of *a single Italian division*. The corps's reserves were nine brigades of recruits, mostly unarmed, stationed at a distance of fifty kilometers to the rear.

The only effective forces—and this will forever be cause for strong conjecture—were the Eleventh and Fifteenth International Brigades of the Thirty-fifth Division. In the first days of decisive battle, they, together with the Twelfth Corps, totaling but 30,000 men, would face alone the motorized onslaught of over 160,000 superbly trained and well-equipped troops. Manuel Aznar, the Francoist historian, writes

> A profound silence greeted "H" hour. The waiting was agonizingly tense on that morning at 6:30 A.M., March 9, 1938. Each of the Army Corps had communicated its readiness for battle. The gigantic din of the vast concentrations of artillery would begin shortly. A great emotion crossed the heavens of National Spain. The plan of maneuver of Franco would shortly take the flight of an eagle.

The barrages began as planned—massive, sustained, shattering. In a matter of hours the front from Fuentes to Herrera de los Navarros, a distance of sixty kilometers, was irrevocably broken.

To the southwest, other brigades of the Twelfth fought courageously and doggedly, blunting the steel tip of the oncoming hordes of Italian Legionnaires. Still further south, the depleted battalions of the Twenty-first Corps of Lieutenant Colonel Cardón hurled themselves magnificently and desperately against the avalanche of armor of the Corps of Galicia.

The alerted Fifteenth Brigade moved up in the early dawn into an almost complete vacuum of space, except for the now-advancing enemy. The immediate deployment was as follows: the brigade staff, including the American officers Merriman, Peter Hampkins, James Bourne, and Eli Biegelman, and the Lincoln commissar John Gates, established a command post in Belchite. Ahead just a few kilometers and to the immediate left of the Belchite Hermitage, the Lincoln Battalion had established its line: Company 3 on the left flank, Company 2 (Spanish) to the center, Company 1 anchored on the Fuende-Todos Road, and machine gun company Commander Al Kaufman, distributing his guns along the length of the line. Battalion headquarters was in a tunnel to the rear.

Almost immediately, enemy artillery ranged the American positions. Overhead, shrapnel burst in well-directed salvos. Skirmish lines and solid columns of enemy troops deployed in the far distance. Tanks and armored cars preceded them. On the horizon, too, were many units of mobile artillery. The barrage became heavy, smashing the meager Lincoln parapets. Squadrons of Heinkels and Me-109s swarmed against the American positions, strafing the trenches in a series of giant pinwheels. At 10:00 A.M., with the Lincoln's heavy guns attempting a long-range fire against the now-advancing enemy, the battalion command post sustained a direct hit. Killed instantly were the commissar, Eric Dewitt Parker, and three of the staff. Wounded were Al Prago, Yale Stuart, and Frank Rogers, adjutant commissar. David Reiss was mortally wounded. Stuart describes the event:

> I was ordered forward. Our main observation post required a personal visit since there were no phone connections. The post was deserted. Beyond the range of lower hills to the front, all I could see was a road covered with hundreds of trucks, tanks, and batteries of guns. The tanks were very close to the gap through which the road ran to Fuendetodos. I immediately returned to report to H.Q. More planes; we were bombed again. I took shelter with Company 1, whose commander, wounded by strafing, accompanied me to the rear.
>
> I gave my report to Reiss. The staff, with Reiss in the lead, then moved out of the tunnel. Reiss looked up to the nearby company positions; some of the men were already

beginning to fall back. A shell zeroed in on the tunnel mouth. The blast was terrible. When I came to, I saw that Parker was dead. Frank Rogers and Al Prago were wounded; Dave Reiss was dying. Others of the H.Q. Company were also dead and dying. Sid Rosenblatt, the battalion clerk, came from the mouth of the tunnel. I told him to stay with Reiss while we tried to get an ambulance.

With all American senior officers killed or wounded, Maxim, the only Russian ever attached to the Fifteenth Brigade, then asked the wounded Stuart to go instantly to brigade and inform them that on his own, he, Maxim, was ordering an evacuation of the positions.

Sid Rosenblatt, who would die in World War II, stayed on with Reiss, despite the dying man's pleas to leave, as there was nothing to be done. Rosenblatt was captured shortly after, still trying to keep Reiss's intestines from bursting through the shrapnel wound in his stomach.

Coming up fast, the British and Fifty-ninth advanced to a flanking position to the right-rear of the Lincolns. Simultaneously, the brigade machine gun company, issued rifles to replace the guns they had given to a Spanish battalion, were thrown into the maelstrom.

To the east the Thaelmanns were also heavily engaged. Like the Americans, they had found that they were the first line since the enemy had reached the Ebro River, below Quinto. By noon they were falling back before a whirlwind of attacks by *tabors* of the Corps of Morocco. The original defending elements of the Twelfth had been effectively destroyed.

The Lincoln disaster is best seen through the eyes of those who fought there. Harold Smith, Brunete veteran, describes the action:

> Things began to happen. A heavy movment of troops to the left; ours falling back. A sporadic shelling, flat trajectories, German 88s. Heavy bombings to the rear and on both flanks. Brigade anti-air battery [three Oerlikons] knocked out. Artillery now zeroing in on Lincoln trenches. Heavy damage. Heavy casualties! Flights of fighter-bombers over Lincoln trenches. Strafing runs.

They come in slow, slipping from side to side to cut speed. They make a run first and then come back with a shower of small bombs. They repeat this over and over. Blaine Owen of my squad is wounded. Lincoln ammo dump is blown up. I send Owen to first-aid post. He returns. The Company is gone! Battalion has received orders to fall back on Belchite. In the excitement, my squad and Bianca's gun crew are forgotten.

I go quickly to Company and Battalion H.Q. Only wounded and dead there. My Company commander, Bonetti, is there with his leg blown off. I return to my squad, signal Bianca's crew and we begin to pull out.

Twenty Fascist tanks spread out in each valley to the right and left of our positions and advance toward us. They open fire. Lincolns fall back from ridge, carrying wounded, seeking cover, firing back, retreating. . . . We cross an open plain to olive groves under constant tank fire. On Belchite's outskirts, we take cover—in the same factory through which Nelson led the attack many months before. Two of our armored cars and some heavy M.G.'s using armor-piercing bullets hold the tanks at bay.

With the greater part of the battalion intact, we get new instructions from Merriman. Aaron Lopoff now commands Company 3. Al Kaufman commands the battalion. Heavy enemy movement is observed on the right flank and to the rear—in trucks! Small groups of enemy advancing in skirmish line.

The machine guns of the British and Fifty-ninth also directed armor-piercing bullets into the advancing Ansaldos, punching holes in their light armor, destroying some, keeping others at bay, and allowing the Lincolns to fall back beyond Belchite. There were those who, surrounded, fought to the last on the far chain of hills, men such as Paul MacEachron, who had left Oberlin College to volunteer for the Republic, and Jack Corrigan, a leader of the National Maritime Union. One gun crew, that of Henry Giler, a veteran of the Aragón and Teruel campaigns, was captured and survived the execution squads of Franco's Fascist military.

Utilizing the dry streamed of the Aguasvivas River to escape the profusion of shells, the Fifteenth, with steelly efficiency, then created a new line of defense. Orders by Merriman were to "hold it against frontal assault at all costs." They did, but were flanked again. At dusk, the order came to retreat.

The British withdrew to the southeast. By dawn of March 11, they had occupied another length of ridge, which they held until nightfall, and were then forced to retreat again, carrying their wounded with them.

Twice the Lincolns attempted to re-form east of Belchite. Each time the speed of the enemy advance ruined their efforts. A last attempt, wherein they were literally inundated by a wave of explosions, saw a further retreat during which confused orders resulted in the battalion being split into two parts. A platoon of the first part stumbled into a large enemy force; a few were captured, but most were killed. The other, led by John Gates, pushed on to Azaila. Major Merriman, leading the remnants of the first units, was forced into a running battle, with the enemy on all sides. Breaking through, they fell back on Lécera along with the brigade staff, units of the Fifty-ninth, and Spanish troops of the 135th and Sixth Anarchist brigades who, with the disappearance of their officers, now attached themselves to the Lincolns.

Everywhere the situation was the same. Spanish brigades, decimated by the onslaught, were thrown insanely into counter-attacks that effectively destroyed what little remained of their units.

The Canadians arrived at Azuara just as two battalions of the 140th Brigade of the Twelfth Corps were destroyed by advancing brigades of the Navarese Fifth Division. Elements of the Thirteenth International Dombrowski Brigade were slated to join the Mac-Paps. They never arrived. By late evening the Canadians, bombed and shelled for six solid hours, had still beaten back all attacks. But the remnants of the 140th were now retreating—and in total disarray.

The Mac-Paps had no choice. They fell hastily back across the Aguasvivas to new positions on cliffs to the south. The situation was precarious. Commissar Joseph Gibbons, a steelworker from Chicago, was sent to find brigade headquarters—at all costs! Instead, he found General Walter in his staff car on the Belchite-Letucs highway. Walter's objective? To see to it that *all* units of the Thirty-fifth evacuated the Azuara sector without delay. It was dawn before Gibbons reached the Mac-Paps with this information.

The withdrawal began immediately, except for two machine gun crews led by Leo Gordon of Brooklyn. His guns on the cliff face, though they dominated the terrain, could not be reached in daylight without running a gauntlet of impossible fire. Still the Canadian captain, Nilo Makela, and the American commissar, Saul Wellman, tried.

Wellman states:

> We yelled, fired our pistols, everything, but were unsuccessful. Two men tried to crawl along the ledge to reach them, but were instantly cut down. Seeing it was hopeless, we left. The two crews held up the enemy for hours. At some distance away, we could still see the shells bursting against the cliffs.

One man, Perry Hilton of British Columbia, did survive to tell the story. Victor Hoar, author of *The Mackenzie-Papineau Battalion*, writes the following:

> According to Hilton, twenty-eight men were entrenched on the ledge of the cliff-face sending a withering fire into the approaching fascists. Hours later they climbed back over the cliff to discover that they had been left behind and were being rushed by fascist soldiers. Frank Whitfield, a Canadian veteran, a man named Rose from Regina, and an American officer, probably Leo Gordon, fell dead. The survivors, Hilton among them, were lined up twice and threatened with summary execution. The majority of the prisoners were Canadian Finns whose blond hair meant only one thing to their captors: Russians. They were quickly shot. As Hilton was about to be dispatched, an angry officer walked up, brushed aside the Canadian's would-be executioner and placed the startled Hilton under personal arrest. A few hours later, Hilton was led across the crest of a nearby hill from which he saw the vast array of men and vehicles stretching to the horizon.

The Mac-Paps, arriving at Lécera, were assigned the task of covering the retreat of the remnants of the Thirty-fifth Division. Information sent to the Fifteenth by the Twelfth Corps was that the Italians had seized Muniesa and Oliete to their rear, and were heading for Alcañiz. The Thirty-fifth Division was to fall back upon that city immediately and to prepare for its defense.

Lécera, as of that moment, was under attack and partially destroyed by artillery and aviation. Throughout the night of the eleventh, the Canadians held the rearguard while American, German, British, and Spanish troops filed by toward Alcañiz.

The next morning, the Canadians, in the wake of the others, found Merriman awaiting them on the road. The enemy, he said, had broken the Fifteenth's marching order. A number of the staff, including Pete Hampkins, had been captured. He had escaped by driving over an open field and had stayed to warn them.

The two sections of the Lincolns were then rejoined at Albalate, and threw up a line outside that village. No sooner had the Mac-Paps arrived, than the enemy, mobile and traveling fast, again attacked. Artillery covered the hills and roads. No ridge escaped the bombs or bullets of strafing aircraft. The order remained: Get to Alcañiz! The Americans moved out again, this time directly over the hills toward the next town— La Puebla de Híjar.

Híjar was in the hands of the Corps of Morocco. The banners of the *tabors* of Ifni, Mehil-la, and Tetuán were plainly visible. The by now mixed companies of Spanish, Americans, and Canadians quick-marched south to more hills, formed a half-circle, and set up their machine guns. They were joined almost at once by the British, infiltrating over the hills from Vinaceite. Some say they were playing mouth organs as they came.

The Fifteenth Lincolns then broke all precedent. They chose on their own to rest and reorganize on the spot, ignoring the *tabors* of Mehil-la. For two full days and a night they did just that—while partly encircled and fighting off tank and infantry probes.

Híjar itself was in ruins. The once beautiful Anarchist hospital was a pile of rubble, glass, and twisted steel. The American mobile unit had escaped but a few hours before the entry of the Moroccans. It had been brutally bombed. Located on the outskirts of the town, its ambulances were wrecked, the drivers killed. Helen Freeman, a young nurse who had served with Dr. Barsky from the first days, was badly wounded, almost losing an arm. The tents of the *auto-chir* were holed like sieves. Through it all Doctors Barsky and Friedman, who had also served at Córdoba, continued operating.

At the end of the second day the battalions were joined by Wolff and other officers who had hastened back at news of the great breakthrough. The march to Alcañiz began again, grim, silent, exhausting. Again the enemy, having access to the roads, had outpaced them. The city was under artillery fire. Ansaldo tanks were in its streets. The goal now was Caspe— at a distance of thirty kilometers.

Luigi Longo, inspector general of the International Brigades, was now at Caspe, as was Dave Doran. Longo had hurriedly come up to take the place of General Walter, who, like Robert Merriman, was now missing, lost in the chaos of night marches, battles, and skirmishes. It would be for Longo and Doran to collect the remnants of the Fifteenth and use them in one final gesture of defiance.

It is no accident of history that the great Fascist offensive to win the war in Spain coincided exactly with the Nazi takeover of Austria; the same day the Lincolns were breaking free of Francoist encirclement, Hitler was speaking to hundreds of thousands in Vienna. In France, the rightist Chautemps government had collapsed before the wrath of the French people, and Leon Blum, the new Socialist prime minister, had formed a second Popular Front government—but without the Communists, as yet one more attempt to appease Britain. Virtually no punitive action was taken against the Germans for their actions in Austria, except that the long-impounded Soviet arms, intended for the Spanish Loyalists, were finally released. This belated act of friendship by France toward Spain stemmed directly from Blum's growing fear of the power of the Axis.

The reaction of England's Prime Minister even to this small act of decency was to announce to the world that the new French Government was one "wherein we cannot have the slightest confidence." Meanwhile, Chamberlain openly boasted of his new "pact" with Mussolini. According to its terms, Italian divisions fighting in Spain were recognized, "legalized"—*their evacuation to take place only after Franco's victory!* Thus was the British government's previous position, that there were no Axis troops in Spain, publicly contradicted by its own leader. So, too, did Chamberlain sound the death-knell of the Spanish Republic.

Alcañiz had fallen to Italian divisions. As of March 15, according to the Republican General Enrique Rojo,

> A front of more than sixty kilometers was open to the enemy, offering a veritable highway to the Mediterranean. Still, within three days and on the initiative of spirited officers and handfuls of men, a "front" was established. Calanda was the one anchor. Caspe was the other.

The brigade remnants arrived at Caspe at dusk on March 15, 1938, with the British fighting a rearguard action on the road. Of the original 550 men at Belchite, the Lincoln Battalion now had but 150 effectives, the British and Spanish Fifty-ninth the same, and the Mac-Paps, 200. Brigade strength was fewer than 700 men, the standard roster of one battalion. With these they would hold the converging units of two insurgent divisions.

The first act of the staff, now joined by the impeccable Britisher Malcolm Dunbar, and the English captain, Sam Wilde, was to set up strong points around the city's perimeter. Lincoln remnants were then thrown in a defense line across the Alcañiz Highway. The Canadians, British, and Fifty-ninth were used similarly to the north and west. Patrols were mounted within the city, using many of the Spanish stragglers who had attached themselves to the Lincolns.

Rebel archives tell of "a torrent of fire from all arms unleashed on March 16, against the *five* International Brigades defending Caspe during the 15th, 16th, and 17th of March, 1938." Only the 700 men of the decimated Fifteenth Lincoln Brigade, with perhaps a hundred or more Spaniards of the destroyed Anarchist Sixth Brigade, defended Caspe during those three days of decision, with some tank and armored car support. The Eleventh and Thirteenth were in action in the area of Sierra Vizcuerna, to the south of the Alcañiz Road. The Twelfth and Fourteenth International Brigades had yet to arrive from the center and southern fronts.

The Mac-Pap commanders, Nilo Makela, Henry Mack, Saul Wellman, and the newly-returned Cecil Smith were among those to organize the day-long defense of the high ground on the western edge of the city. By noon, enemy tanks, with the aid of artillery, broke through to either side of the defense positions. Simultaneously, a large body of infantry burst in upon the defenders in the trenches. It was driven back by well-organized grenade and bayonet attacks—only to come on again and yet again. A final assault at dusk drove the exhausted Canadian-American units from the hill.

Luigi Longo and Doran then demanded and got all the Republican tanks in the area—eight of them. Every rifleman and machine gunner, everyone available, was mustered to retake the hill. The attack was launched under the white light of a brilliant moon. The tanks fired high to simulate supporting artillery, then concentrated on the enemy firing points to cover the brigade advance.

The assault was made with less than 250 men. Rolfe writes: "They rushed furiously and impetuously forward, hurling grenades and dislodging the enemy from their positions." Lawrence Cane, who led a section of men, says that the action was utterly insane. "Some of us, I believe, were actually unarmed. All we could really do was to throw rocks and yell at them." *But the height was taken!* Indeed, the Canadians captured three heavy Fiat machine guns, fifty to sixty rifles, thirty prisoners, and *ten mules.* The British also took a number of prisoners and many guns. Larry Cane would survive, and more. He landed with the first wave of U.S. troops on Omaha Beach, June 6, 1944.

On that same night, enemy infantry and some tanks did

enter Caspe, leading to hand-to-hand fighting. Rebel archives report: "Heavy fighting around the railroad station with the *arma blanca* [the bayonet]." This could only have taken place against Sixth Brigade Anarchist and Lincoln Battalion units. In one rather brutal incident, a rifle section led by Captain Wolff ran into a number of Italian tanks. Not knowing whether they were friend or foe, the men stayed in the shadows while Wolff, with Sam Grant and John Martinelli, went to speak with the foremost tankist. "As soon as we got close," Wolff relates,

> I knew I had made a mistake—It was a Fiat. We weren't sure about the next step—there were more tanks coming up behind this one. The tank's machine gunner opened his turret-top and asked in bad Spanish, "From what part of Spain you?" I said, "Salamanca" [Franco territory], then turned and shouted to the men to take cover. The tankist cursed in Italian and started to close the turret. Grant had time to take just one shot at him. I ducked. The tank opened fire. He succeeded in catching some of the guys who had not heard my warning. The rest of us spread out and ran for cover. I looked back to see the tank run over the prostrate bodies of our wounded.

The British captain, Sam Wilde, was actually captured with three of his staff. But, in a particularly vicious free-for-all, they escaped, leaving a few broken Fascist heads behind.

The remnants of the Fifteenth held all the next day against repeated attacks from tanks, planes, and infantry. The artillery was particularly accurate. Again at dusk, and with their line almost surrounded, they were forced to withdraw—across a single railroad trestle, the only escape exit. In this withdrawal, Captain Makela, already a legend in the brigade, saw that the wounded were taken out first and cautioned against any disorganization. He actually stood out upon the hillside directing the retreat until he was hit by a mortar round. Makela survived evacuation only to die in an emergency operating tent.

The brigade was driven back into Caspe. Fighting went on all that night and through the next day. "By five the next night," relates Joseph Gibbons, "we had been driven out of Caspe. By seven that evening, we had fought our way back in again!"

But this time not without help. The Twelfth and Fourteenth International Brigades had finally arrived. However, both they and the Lincoln remnants would move that same night to prepared positions south of the Guadalope River.

A *Wehrmacht* military journal of the time describes the Fifteenth's defense of Caspe as "having permitted the first stabilization of Republican secondary lines, enabling other units of the army to prepare for continued battle."

Arriving at the rest village of Corbera on March 19, the American Battalion numbered less than 100 men. Many, lost in the chaos, had yet to reach the bivouac area. Most officers had now rejoined the battalion: Lamb, Merriman, Keller, Copic. Fred Keller had used his authority as a battalion commissar to drive the *Times*'s Herbert Matthews, George Soria from *L'Humanité*, and Joe North of the *Daily Worker* through Carabinero roadblocks to the very outskirts of Caspe, a thing absolutely forbidden. The word was that the War Ministry had a warrant posted for Keller's arrest. He lost no time, therefore, in seeking refuge with the brigade staff.

The brigade base at Albacete was being evacuated to Barcelona. So, too, was the Government of the Spanish Republic. The American base at Tarazona was cleaned out; all English-speaking trainees entraining for the Fifteenth Brigade—wherever it was. Walking wounded from all the hospitals were hastening too, to rejoin their units.

It has often been said by psychologists that those who volunteer for war do so mostly out of emotionalism and excessive ignorance. It is thus axiomatic with them that men who have been in combat seldom volunteer for anything again. Not so with the volunteers of the International Brigades, nor with the Spanish soldiers of the People's Army.

On March 9, the armored divisions of European Fascism had destroyed the Republican front in Aragón. On March 11, commissars of the People's Army went to every hospital and rest home to outline the peril and to plead for all who would defend the Republic to return, now, to the front.

Internationals and Spaniards alike left their hospitals with wounds unhealed, with arms still in slings, with hastily mustered canes in lieu of crutches. For the Americans coming up from hospitals at Villa Paz, Benicasim, Murcia, Denia, and Orihuela, the sky above would offer no canopy of protective planes bearing white American stars—the wings would show only the black insignias of the enemy. This would be true, too, of the artillery and tanks. There is no parallel, no record exists anywhere, of any American unit having faced such odds over such a protracted period of time.

The Abraham Lincoln Brigade would go again into "the valley of the shadow" with rifles, grenades, and a few automatic weapons against an enemy with an overwhelming preponderance of arms. An eyewitness account of the departure of volunteers from one hospital captures it all:

> Fourteen Americans joined with some thirty-seven men of other nationalities in three ambulances, and together with an ambulance of Spaniards, drove north from Orihuela toward Albacete. The ambulances went slowly. It had started to rain and their sides were strung with crutches and wire-slings with shreds of plaster-of-paris still attached. They were followed, despite the downpour and the quick-falling darkness, by a goodly portion of the townspeople and the doctors and nurses from the hospital. These last were chanting: *"No! No! No Pasarán! No! No! No Pasarán!"* the defiant cry of the battle for Madrid. Then after awhile they stopped and we left them there on the road. Some of the women were crying. The older men kept waving until we were out of sight.

The terror bombings began then, at Valencia, Lérida, Gerona, and Barcelona. There was flight after flight of Ju-52s, Capronis, Savoias—seventeen flights in three days over Barcelona alone. The center of the city was destroyed, with 3,000 dead, 6,000 wounded. Claude Bowers, the American ambassador, writes with a typical racism and misrepresentation of history:

> Nothing on such an appalling scale involving the white race had ever been seen before. The bombs were not aimed

at military objectives; they were dropped designedly in the middle of the city. Men, women, and children were mangled corpses, blown in many cases to bits, disemboweled. . . . And Neville Chamberlain, whose policy had so righteously denied the Government the right to buy anti-aircraft guns for the protection of the people, expressed himself as "horrified." I had no doubt at the time that the Axis was in training for London and Warsaw—*as we now know it was!*

The Abraham Lincoln Battalion would be commanded now, and for the remainder of its days in Spain, by Milton Wolff, the young Brooklyn art student. Wolff, tall, gaunt, and described by some as "ruggedly Lincolnesque," had fought in every battle since Brunete, and had risen slowly through the ranks.

John Gates became battalion commissar. Nick Pappas, also a Brunete veteran, was made machine gun company commander; his adjutant was Bill Bailey, the West Coast seaman who had fought in the Aragón and Teruel campaigns. Company 1 was now led by Melvin Offsink, with Irving Keith as his commissar, Company 2 by "Blackie" Maphralian, with Aaron Lopoff as his adjutant.

Time passes differently for the combat soldier than it does for civilians. To be in battle quickens the awareness of life. Periods of inactivity after the excitement of battle, for instance, seem to drag on endlessly; hours seem like days, days like weeks. Many of the American veterans, looking back on these dire days many years later, remember the period of time spent in the rest area as several weeks long; in fact, the Lincolns only got twelve days of recuperation time. On March 30, the Fifteenth was ordered to stand by. Hours later, after picking up new rifles and ammunition, the men were once again on the march.

On March 18, Republican Colonel Lister issued word to his Eleventh Division that the enemy it now confronted—the Italian CTV—was the same it had beaten at Guadalajara. The battle enjoined, and the Italians were again stopped dead. Again they tried. The fighting became brutal and bloody. Again they were stopped. According to Francoist historians, they attacked again on the twenty-seventh and twenty-eighth, to break through the now-exhausted Republican line, but to no avail. The Navarese of García Valiño, however, advanced below Caspe, maneuvering rapidly through holes punched in the lines, against desperate resistance by the Fourteenth, Twelfth, and a part of the Eleventh International Brigades. Then, on the morning of March 29, the Italians launched one last great assault—and Lister broke!

In effect, what was actually happening on the morning of the Lincoln's reentry into battle, was a general Fascist offensive along the entire front. And again, as at Belchite, the Lincolns were marching directly into it, and with no knowledge of that fact.

The British were the first to contact the enemy. With no information at all on the breakthrough, and while still moving toward their assigned positions at Calaceite, beyond the town of Gandesa, they rounded a bend in the road to stumble into the very midst of a tank column of the Italian Twenty-third of March Division.

The British commander, Captain Fletcher, instantly aware of the error, shouted for the men to "Break off. Head for the ridge!" He referred to a promontory to the southeast. William Rust writes: "Machine guns were mounted under great difficulties, and several of the tanks were put out of action, while many a hand-to-hand combat took place."

The encounter became a bloody, vicious tangle of individual fighting and isolated groups defending themselves while trying to break away. Commissar Wally Tapsall, challenging the tank commander, was killed in the first exchange of fire. Captain Fletcher, hit with four bullets, was rescued from the chaos and lived to fight again. Chief of Operations Malcolm Dunbar, marching with Tapsall, was shot through the neck and leg, but also managed to escape. The British, safely on their ridge, held against all comers. By day's end, however, they had lost over 150 killed and wounded, with another 100 captured. Among these last was the famed IRA Commander Frank Ryan, who had fought with the first *centuria* at Madrid in November 1937.

At dusk they fell back over the hills toward Gandesa. Rust

writes: "They had not given up. Carrying the parts of their machine guns, ammo, and rifles, they went on through the mountains until they were able to link with the command again."

It is axiomatic that weak defensive units dependent upon a parallel road are in serious trouble. The Italian corps, advancing over the hills from Mazaleon, had the Gandesa Road under artillery fire and were preparing to cut it along its entire length. Indeed, as dusk fell, the new Canadian commander, Ricardo Díaz, and his commissar, Carl Geiser, were met and warned by brigade officers that the now visible, bumper-to-bumper headlights of trucks coming toward them were Fascist.

At the first pearling of dawn, orders were received from Copic for the Mac-Paps to occupy two hills to the north of the road. Geiser, at the head of a section from Company 1 led by Lawrence Cane, moved out through a wooded valley, then, together with a light machine gun squad headed by Ed Hodge of Kentucky, broke away from the main group to scout a parallel ridge to the north. The ridge quickly fanned to an open slope upon which were hundreds of men leisurely eating their breakfasts. Geiser's first thought, that these were the Thaelmanns, was instantly dissipated when an officer called in a perfect Brooklyn accent, "Hey! Come on over. We're your friends." Geiser, walking warily, stopped when he saw the insignia *"23 de Marzo"* on the officer's tunic. Three machine guns were now zeroed in on Geiser and his six companions.

Unarmed, Geiser ordered his squad not to resist, hoping that they at least might be taken alive even though he would not be. The Italian officer asked his rank. Geiser replied, *"Comisario de Guerra"* (War Commissar). Whereupon a revolver was placed at his back and he was ordered to call the others up from the valley. He refused, saying simply, "As an officer, I cannot do that."

Cane, seeing what had happened, immediately opened fire, driving the Italian infantry to cover. Once beyond the ridge, Geiser's group saw troops of the Twenty-third of March Division literally covering the slopes and valleys. The road itself was jammed with battalion after marching battalion, interspersed with tanks and artillery.

At a farm building some three kilometers from the front, a squad of friendly Italian troops were set to guard them. A runner approached, calling for *El Comisario*. The guards grinned, pointed their fingers to their temples, and said, "Boom!" Geiser gave away his things, shook hands with the others, and followed the runner.

In a small room he was invited to share a breakfast of wine, bread, and smoked fish with a young Italian officer, who then politely inquired about the duties of a commissar. Satisfied with Geiser's explanation, he then described in detail the plans for the immediate offensive. It was to begin, he smiled, at 8:00 A.M. sharp—in exactly *ten minutes*. The Twenty-third of March Division, along with other divisions of the CTV, would attack directly east on the Alcañiz-Gandesa road, together with the Corps of García Escámez on the Italians' right, plus the Navarese of García Valiño on the left. All in all, according to the captain, some 80,000 troops were on the move. They expected, he said, to be in Gandesa by noon, Tortosa by evening, and to arrive at the Mediterranean within forty-eight hours. The war, he explained, would soon be over. Geiser was then sent back to join the others.

At 10:00 A.M., the sixteen prisoners were lined up against a concrete wall. A priest walked back and forth in front of them, his bible open in his hands. A uniformed medic stood in the background. A firing squad waited a short distance away. Several officers, starting at one end of the line, asked questions of each man: "What is your nationality?" "Are you a Communist?" "How many men in your brigade?" "How many machine guns?" "How many tanks?" The prisoners replied that they were American or Canadian, that they had volunteered to defend Spain's democratic government, that they were anti-Fascists, that they were familiar only with the weapons of their own unit. They had known what the questions would be and had agreed on the answers beforehand.

Two large command cars then stopped along the roadside, and several high-ranking Italian officers stepped out to dismiss the firing squad. The prisoners learned later that orders

Belchite after its capture

Joe Dallet, Mackenzie-Papineau
Battalion Commander, killed in action
at Fuentes del Ebro

At the American hospital at Tarancón: (from left) Dr. Irving Busch (American); Dr. Langer (Australian); Dr. Edward Barsky (American); Dr. David Krause (Polish)

Milton Herndon, killed in action at Fuentes

American nurses with mobile unit at the Teruel front, 1938: (from left) Rose Weiner; Norah Temple; Toby Jensky; Anne Taft; Sana Goldblatt; Selma Chadwick; Andrea and Leoncia (Spanish nurse's aides)

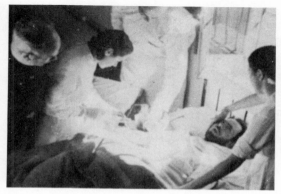

At Villa Paz: Dr. Norman Bethune, Nurse Anne Taft, and Dr. Pitts administer a blood transfusion. Dr. Bethune originated the "blood bank" and Spain was its first area of practical application.

British Battalion at Mondéjar, addressed by Copic, Captain Fred Copeman, Commissar Dave Doran, and Harry Pollit

Fortifications at Celades

Lincoln Brigaders moving into
Teruel

Italian Fiat downed in dogfight
(Aragón, 1938)

American flyers with the LaCalle Squadron, Republic Air Corps.
Standing (from left): Tinker, a mechanic; Riverola; Gil Castenda;
Captain LaCalle; Velasco. Seated (from left): Bastodo; Whitey Dahl;
Chang Selles; Lecha.

Fiats escorting Junker bombers on Teruel front, 1938

Lincoln Brigaders meeting across the Ebro (from left): Commissar John Gates; Lieutenant Donald Thayer; Captain Malcolm Dunbar; Lieutenant Colonel Copic.

Lincolns crossing the Ebro (July 1938)

Lincoln wounded at first-aid post immediately behind the lines

Mac-Pap command post, Sierra Pandols (from left): Frank Rogers, Lieutenant Harry Schoenberg; Major Cecil Smith.

Last parade of the Fifteenth Brigade. Arms are being handed over by the International volunteers to the Spanish troops who will be taking their places

The last parade of the Abraham Lincoln Brigade (November 1938)

Wounded American veterans returning home

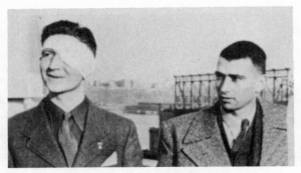

Repatriated prisoners of war: Charles Barr and
Maurice Conway

Lincoln Brigade veterans on parade in
New York City, 1938

had been issued to take Internationals alive between April first and April ninth, for exchange for captured German and Italian officers or flyers. Nevertheless, only in rare instances were captured Internationals not executed during the Spanish war. Carl Geiser, commissar of both the Abraham Lincoln Battalion and the Mackenzie-Papineau Battalion, was the highest-ranking American officer to be captured and escape execution.

Sergeant Cane, who would reach the rank of captain in World War II and win the Silver Star, the Croix de Guerre, and several other citations, had no intention of allowing Mussolini's troops to reach the Mediterranean through his platoon, which had now been joined by another from Company 1. His guns crews and riflemen had dug in well, beneath huge boulders. The Italians, contemptuous, attempted a frontal assault and were stopped dead. They tried it again with the same result. Mortar shells rained upon the Mac-Pap positions, but there were few casualties. As Cane put it, "It was the best defensive position I was ever in." A last attempt by the Italians was now beaten back, and the ammunition was getting low, so Cane sent a young Spaniard back for more. The boy returned to report that the battalion had disappeared!

The Italian forward movement had forced the Canadians back, split up the companies, and cut the highway between the Mac-Paps and the Fifty-ninth Battalion to the east. Tanks were everywhere, on the roads, in the valleys, and on the hills. The act of pulling out became all too quickly a confused movement of fragmented units, each fighting its own small battle.

Nickolas Meyers, ex-Canadian logger and combine operator, commanded a section of Company 3 situated on a small hill and completely surrounded by the enemy. He had but one defective Maxim. According to the *Book of the 15th Brigade*:

> Six Fascist tanks and over two hundred infantrymen repeatedly assaulted the hilltop. As dusk fell, and realizing that the Battalion had withdrawn, he ordered his men to escape through the enemy positions. *Every* man was able to make it.

Other men, lying prone in shell holes to the side of the road, attacked a tank column with grenades. A number of tanks were destroyed. Just three of the twenty-eight men involved survived.

Lawrence Cane had withdrawn rapidly toward the heavily wooded area of the brigade command post. He recalls:

> We finally ended up at a point where a guy was yelling and waving a *dictoryev*. It was Copic. We had reached the Brigade C.P. and Merriman and a number of other staff officers were there. Copic was yelling: "Who gave you orders to retreat? Where are you coming from?" I told him that the Battalion was no longer in front of him. He said: "What do you mean? No one has given orders to withdraw. Who gave the order?" I said, "Why ask me? All I know is that we got out with a whole ass!" Then, while Copic is yelling, "Why didn't you stay there and fight?" a Fiat-Ansaldo opens up on us, which answers his question. There were a few moments of a particularly vicious fire-fight with the tanks, and it was then every man for himself.

Most of the Canadians, like the British, managed to retreat in some order, making it over the hills to the south of Gandesa and thereby avoiding the total encirclement that was to overtake the Abraham Lincoln Battalion.

The disaster affecting the first three battalions of the Fifteenth had not immediately involved the Lincolns. To the contrary, Captain Wolff had pushed ahead more than a kilometer from the positions assigned him, to seize a series of hills which, until that moment, had been swarming with units of the First Navarese Division. Prisoners and a water truck were captured. By nightfall, the battalion had dug in solidly, little dreaming that the insurgent breakthrough had taken place already on both its flanks. The next few days would witness the swiftest and most confusing action in the war, action in which three-quarters of the battalion's cadres would be lost or killed.

Driving in the positions of the exhausted Fourteenth and Twelfth International Brigades on the Thaelmanns' and Lincolns' right flank, whole battalions of the Navarese First Division struck through the night to encircle the French Brigade in the area of Pobla de Masaluca, and to head for a juncture with the Italians at Gandesa. The lack of communications was such that the Twelfth Garibaldis, falling back toward Gandesa on the Batea Road, had passed within a few hundred meters of the Lincolns with neither of the two units being aware of the other's presence.

By dawn's light the Fourteenth Franco-Belge Brigade had been effectively dispersed and destroyed. The remnants of the Garibaldis were under attack at Gandesa by battalions of the Third Regiment of the Navarese.

Lieutenant William Carroll of the Lincoln armory was the first to bring news of the enemy's proximity to Gandesa:

> Since my ammo dump was short of armor-piercing, small arms ammo, I commandeered a truck and headed toward the Brigade armory. Approaching Gandesa, we found enemy planes attacking our positions outside the town; and this combined with *ground assualts* on our defenses. Passing through the town, and for several kilometers to the rear, we too were subjected to strafing runs.
>
> Brigade armory having no armor-piercing, we loaded up with antitank inflammable bottles and other munitions. Returning through Gandesa we ran the gauntlet of planes again and were forced to hit the ditch several times to escape them. The battle raged nearer to Gandesa now and, more serious, closer to the only escape road for the Eleventh and Fifteenth Brigades.
>
> Instead of going directly to the battalion, I went first to Brigade H.Q. [which had been shifted since the running fight of the previous day to a kilometer or so from the cross-roads], where I informed Merriman of the danger to our rear.

Communications had so deteriorated by that time that Carroll's was the *only* information the Fifteenth's staff received on the breakthrough by the Navarese. Checking the situation out—Copic in a staff car, Merriman in an armored car—Copic returned to headquarters to order the evacuation of the area.

His proposed line of retreat: east-northeast—*right into the midst of the advancing Navarese!*

Merriman headed with all speed to the Lincoln positions, where he, too, issued an order, on his own recognizance, for all units of the Thirty-fifth Division to evacuate the pocket without delay. It was now noon.

Wolff states that Merriman insisted that the crossroads had not yet been taken and that the road to Gandesa remained open. In essence, Merriman was still unaware of the full extent of the disaster, namely, that the threat to Gandesa was not just from infiltrating advance units of the CTV, but from the Navarese who had plunged to Gandesa's very gates. At that precise moment, a dispatch rider, coming over the open fields, brought the information that the enemy now held both the crossroads *and* the village of Batea to their immediate rear.

Divergent opinions then arose as to what to do. Merriman insisted that the road was still open to Corbera, if they could just get past Batea and into the hills above Gandesa. Wolff states that Dave Doran did not want to do this: "He wanted to fortify and to stand and fight to the last man, where they were."

Merriman's thinking won out. The Lincolns prepared to march. The battalions of the Eleventh had already passed to the south and east, including six tanks which made it to the Ebro. The Edgar Andrés, the last battalion of the Eleventh Brigade, would bring up the rear.

The Lincolns then began their march through what was already enemy territory. With the battalion were Brigade Commissar Doran, Chief of Brigade staff, Merriman, Captain Milton Wolff, Captain Leonard Lamb, Commissar Fred Keller, and most of the other remaining brigade and battalion officers. They skirted Batea in the dead of night, were discovered and subjected to a sporadic shelling and overhead high explosives fired blind. Dawn found them on the heights overlooking Gandesa. Ed Rolfe writes:

> The Fascists had advanced rapidly. From their vantage
> points the Americans could see their troop concentra-

tions, tanks and ambulances at the western end of the town. From the northeast troops were marching from Corbera. Their motorized columns had swept through Villalba de los Arcos and had taken Corbera during the night. The road from Villalba to Gandesa, a kilometer to the Lincolns' left, was filled with enemy concentrations pouring down from the north.

That Gandesa was still occupied by Republican troops was apparent, for intermittent fire played between the town and the forces surrounding it on three sides. The Battalion officers believed that the Tortosa road, leading southeast, was still open. They could see bursts of enemy artillery ranging the lines of communications. The Americans' only salvation appeared to be in breaking through from behind the ring of besieging troops to gain entrance to the town and join the defending troops. They watched the fascist tanks, artillery and truckloads of troops rolling into the outskirts of Gandesa. And then the decision—to attack and cut their way through—was made.

The attack got underway at ten o'clock in the morning. Company 1 advanced on the right flank, engaged the enemy in a running combat, and melted toward the town. The commander and commissar, Melvin Offsink and Irving Keith, were killed, and Fred Keller, the Lincoln staff commissar, was wounded.

The remainder of the company, center and left flank, was stopped dead, as was the battalion itself. The enemy, having observed their movement, was ready for them. They then retired to two small hills further north, where they hoped to wait until nightfall. They planned, under cover of darkness, to make their way across the stretch of road between Corbera and Gandesa, to the highway leading to Tortosa.

Milton Wolff states that this withdrawal was not made without casualties; that he sent men ahead to set up guns on the hills to give cover fire for the main body of the battalion. Al Kaufman, the seaman who had commanded the Lincolns briefly after the deaths of Reiss and Parker at Belchite, brought up the rear.

Cavalry swept in on the flanks, driving between Kaufman's

men and the other units of the battalion. Kaufman's gun crew, caught in the open, was mercilessly cut down.

Now there was a period of perhaps a half-hour's silence on the hill. Then, at a distance from the Lincoln hill, the cavalry formed a line. Simultaneously, sporadic bursts of overhead shrapnel began to range the Lincoln positions.

The cavalry, between 400 and 500 of them, drove quickly between the two hills. Fred Keller states that they were Italians, not Moroccans, and that an officer first rode out before them to exhort them to action. He then stood in his stirrups and shouted to the Americans to surrender.

The men lay quietly behind their guns, hardly daring to hope that this commander would persist in his insanity. *He did!* With banners waving and sabers to the fore, the whole line charged in classic style. The ensuing slaughter, according to Keller, was something to witness. Joseph Brandt, wounded in the engagement, tells of horses and men cut down by the Lincoln heavy guns so that the slope of the hill was covered with the dead and dying.

What was left of the Italians fell back and then, according to Wolff, they just as insanely charged the Spanish Company 2 on the second hill, with the same results. It was a fitting revenge, indeed, for the butchered bodies of Kaufman's gun crew!

The shelling continued all that day. With dusk, scouts brought back news of a way through the enemy concentrations. The men filed off the hill in silence, literally feeling their way through bivouacs of enemy troops. They crossed the Villalba Road and climbed the heights to the west of Corbera. The hills were aflame with bonfires, each denoting an enemy troop's encampment. Wolff comments:

> It would be useless to describe my feelings or the feelings of the men as we made our way through the dark in hostile, unknown territory. But this I believe: there wasn't a man who made that trip who didn't feel that death walked by his side.

Rolfe writes of the break-up of the battalion and of the beginning of the end:

Toward midnight they approached Corbera. The groves which the Americans had occupied a few days before were filled now with enemy soldiers. As the men crossed the vineyards in darkness they could hear the stirrings, coughs, snores, and whispered conversations of the Fascist troops. In the scramble to cross the Villalba road, and in scaling the cliffs on the opposite side, many men found themselves wandering, thoroughly out of touch with the vanguard.

When the road was crossed, Doran, Merriman, Lamb, Wolff, Keller, Joe Brandt, and a Chicagoan named Ivan were together, followed by a group of perhaps thirty-five men; this, as they approached Corbera. Ivan was in the lead, followed by Lamb and Brandt, with Merriman and Doran following. What happened was so sudden and startling that few of the survivors' stories afterward jibed. Unwittingly they had marched into a large force of rebel troops. These were instantly alerted by a terrified guard screaming hysterically: "*Cabo de Guardia! Rojos! Rojos!*" [Corporal of the Guard! Reds! Reds!]. The group broke, running to the right. Ivan and Brandt ran straight ahead. Lamb called out to Merriman, "I'm cutting directly across!" There was a steep embankment about twenty feet in height, down which Lamb slid, followed by two other Americans; then all three made a mad break for a hill opposite. Merriman and Doran took a different direction rushing, whether they knew it or not, toward the Insurgents. Brandt and Ivan heard a series of shots ring out of the darkness into which the two highest ranking Americans of the Brigade had disappeared. Then finally the order "*Manos arriba!*" [Hands up!]. That was the last ever seen of them.

The consensus on that far time is that both Merriman and Doran were summarily executed on the very night they were captured. At a later date, when the Republicans recrossed the Ebro, villagers of the area told them of the executions of many Americans, and spoke of how courageously they died.

One tragic reminder of that time of disaster and death is the haunting conviction that had there been any meaningful liaison at all between the brigade and the battalions, it need not have happened. The rebel commander, García Valiño, writes that his advance was so rapid, and his occupation of Villalba and Corbera so tenuous, that it was hard to tell who was surrounding whom.

> The houses of Villalba are filled with troops and prisoners. Munitions have not reached us. Communications with the rear are nonexistent. The overflow of the river Algas has prevented transport reaching us from the interior—and the 55th division has not yet come through to meet us. Who actually are the prisoners? We or they?

Be that as it may, for the French of the Fourteenth Brigade and the Americans of the Fifteenth, the results of the breakthrough were disastrous—far worse than the long and brutal retreat from Belchite and Híjar.

Men wandered for days, individually and in groups, behind the rebel lines. They were without food and, in most cases, without weapons. The hills swarmed with Mussolini's Black, Blue, and Green Arrows, as well as with Moroccan and Navarese infantry. These last were the only dedicated troops in Franco's army with any real ties to the peasantry in the largely agricultural provinces of Navarre. Paradoxically, their allegiance was not to Franco but rather to the Church, as they saw it, and to the Carlist pretender to the throne of Spain. Were it not for their hatred of that which they did not understand—republicanism, socialism, and the great Spanish unions—they would essentially have been anti-Franco. Their *true* nationalism, however, with its natural courage and steadfastness, was such that wherever the Lincolns fought, there, sooner or later, would be the Navarese.

Many stories are told of escapes made by the narrowest of margins. Harry Fisher, veteran of Brunete and Aragón, gives a very graphic description of one escape:

> At about one in the morning we sat down for a rest. There were nine of us left, although about fifty had started from the road in the evening. The others had had their own ideas about how to get through these hills. Cookson

was the leader. He seemed to be the only one who knew what to do. He was as calm as though we were a bunch of boy scouts on a hike. It was unbelievable.

We took inventory. All of us were from *Transmisiones* and everyone carried a phone or a spool of wire. Just one man had a rifle. The only names I can remember are Cookson, Sullivan, and Berkowitz.

Cookson did the talking: "From now on we walk in single file, in silence. We're heading north and east until we contact our side again. So, we'll keep going all night and at dawn we'll decide what to do.

The night was dark. No moon. The stars seemed extra brilliant. My poncho retained little warmth. I wanted to walk quicker but I was too tired. I had had two hours sleep the night before; none the night before that. All day I had been digging in hard ground. I remembered a speech Johnny Gates made about the League of Nations meeting the previous day. I also remembered watching our troops on another hill defending themselves against two cavalry attacks, with the Fascists suffering heavy losses.

Sullivan shook me: "Come on, we're moving."

"Sit down and keep quiet," Cookson whispered. We heard movement and it was coming in our direction. Soon a line, single-file, passed only a few feet from us. They looked at us as they passed. No one said a word. We sat. They walked. We waited ten minutes until they were a good distance from us. "They were as scared as we were," Cookson said.

Within a few minutes we again found ourselves facing a road on which marched soldiers in three columns. There were burros drawing light artillery pieces. We looked at them in amazement, and they looked back at us. Cookson turned his beret inside-out to hide his officers stripe. He told us to keep silent. If any questions were asked, he'd say "*Transmisiones*," and that was all. We knew that we'd stumbled upon a large body of the enemy. They were in good spirits, good order, and their officers were on horses.

A mounted officer stopped near us, looked us over, trying to make out who we were. As the end of the column passed, and with the mounted officer watching, we fell in behind and joined in the march. After awhile the column stopped and we all had a smoke. In a few minutes we were on our feet again. . . . So here we were bringing up the rear of the advancing Fascists who were supposed to be chasing us.

I looked at Marty Sullivan, who was marching next to me. He whispered, "God, but I'm hungry. I sure wish these bitches would stop and dish out some food." I kept watching both sides of the road for a good place to run if it became necessary. The officer had galloped up ahead.

It's difficult to say at this late date how much time we spent in the Fascist column. It was at least one or two hours. Anyway, we were going around a sharp curve in the road when we heard horses coming toward us from the front of the column. Cookson stopped, held up his hand, and without a word sat down on the side of the road. We joined him, hardly daring to breathe. The mounted officers reached the end of the column and stopped just a few yards from us. They carried on a conversation in subdued voices, looking at us from time to time. The only words we could make out were—"*Como Rojos*" [Like reds]. Then they galloped away again.

Apparently they had been afraid to challenge us. Which was all right where we were concerned. We got up immediately and crossed the road and went into the woods.

Captain Lamb, who had barely escaped capture with Merriman, comments:

I read the North Star as conscientiously as I ever read a shirt for lice. I headed for the river. For four days I travelled, sleeping in the hills; fed sometimes by friendly peasants. At other times I ate berries and the still-green almonds on the trees.

During the breakthrough attempt at Gandesa, they were overrun by enemy cavalry. Some of the men were killed, and some escaped. Among those captured were Keller and Kenneth Staker, who was to become a captain in the U.S. Army in World War II. In the village of Flix, Keller stunned his guard with a blow to the jaw. His companion grabbed the man's gun and brought the butt of it down on the top of his head. The two made it back to the river. Keller swam the river, despite the hip wound he's received at Gandesa. Staker's escape across the Ebro rivals Keller's in daring.

There were some, though, who never made it across the Ebro, who drowned in the attempt. Among these was the Company 3 commander, Blackie Maphralian. Norman Pearlman, of Los Angeles, recalls that he swam to within fifteen yards of the far bank, became exhausted, and could go no further. He gave up, allowed himself to sink to the bottom, and prepared to take a deep breath and end it all. Instead, his feet touched sand and clay, and, still underwater, he walked the rest of the way to shore.

Milton Wolff, the Lincoln commander, says, "For nine days I watched Italian Legions marching along Catalonian highways, accompanied as always by their scores of artillery pieces and tanks, and in the air by their planes." He describes being fed by peasants, eating olives and roots, lying in the plowed furrow of a field all day while enemy troops and motorized columns passed within twenty yards of him. Approaching the river banks of Asco, he gambled that the rebels were not in occupation of the far side and swam across.

Wolff was the last American officer to return to his command.

While the Lincolns and the Eleventh and Fourteenth Internationals were being shattered and destroyed, remnants of the other battalions of the Fifteenth were being rallied by such men as Dunbar and Cooney of the British, and by Henry Mack and Leonard Levenson of the Mac-Paps. They moved south from Gandesa.

Valiño's Navarese also drove south and east from captured Corbera, and the rebel colonel, Escámez, smashed through the Maestrago toward Vinaroz on the Mediterranean. It was left for the Italian CTV to continue down the Gandesa-Tortosa Highway. Along the way it was met with a ferocious and wholly unexpected resistance. This occurred at a point ten kilometers to the southeast of Gandesa, just short of the village of Pinell, where there is a highway junction. One branch of the highway continues south to Cherta, the other to the Ebro River and the town of Mora de Ebro. Any force dominating that junction could deny an advance to the enemy. In this case, it would mean that if such a point could be held, even for just hours, valuable war materiel and troops could still escape across the one remaining bridge at Mora— and new Republican forces now moving up from Tortosa would be given time to dig in.

The terrain at the junction, a series of serrated hills, was admirably suited for defense. Fewer than 300 men, British, Americans, Spaniards, Germans, and Canadians, had occupied the dominating hill of this group. They had rifles, hand grenades, a half-dozen machine guns, and that was all. Still, under the command of Dunbar, Sol Rose, Levenson, and Mack, they proposed to deny the road to the Italians for a full twenty-four hours.

The Fifteenth's guns on the hill were zeroed in on the road. Men with boxes of grenades dug in at the hill's base. Their position was protected by a sharp bend in the road. Their intent was to stop any tank column headed for Cherta. In the final hours of the first afternoon, all probing units of the CTV were driven off.

The clear dawn of April 3 disclosed to the defending 300 men a sight that, as one man put it, "if we lived to be a hundred we would never forget." The road to the north and west was one solid mass of tanks, trucks, artillery, and marching men. It seemed that all the military might of the entire sector had converged upon this one point. And there it sat— awaiting their destruction.

The attack began with a thunder of artillery. Fascist archives state that the ensuing defense gave evidence of a decision by the Reds to resist violently and at all costs. "During forty-eight hours," writes the Francoist Manuel Aznar,

> they held the heights beneath artillery fire that theoretically was absolutely unsupportable. It was finally necessary for the Seventh Regiment of the 23rd of March Division to take by surprise a dominant flanking hill which made the Red positions untenable.

Rolfe writes:

> Long trains of enemy supplies were stalled on the road while the small group held the strategic heights. Planes

and artillery rained bombs and shells upon them, tanks advanced against them but were turned back; a cavalry detachment sent against them was decimated by the fire of their last cartridge pans.

And William Rust recalls: "The hills they occupied were an explosive inferno, and there were miraculous escapes from death. But not a man left his post. Again and again the tanks were forced to withdraw."

In the dark of that night, to the rumble of encircling tanks and mobile artillery, the men slipped off the hill. For the most part their units, too, became fragmented and lost. The greater part of the British section reached Cherta, where it crossed the Ebro by boat. Others crossed at Benifallet. Dunbar, with a handful of his staff, reached Mora de Ebro before the bridge was blown. Most, like Wolff, Keller, Lamb, and Carroll, spent many days behind the insurgent lines.

The defense of the junction by the Fifteenth's 300, however, had enabled the remnants of the Republican Fifth Corps to dig in and to hold at Cherta, Tortosa, and Amposta. And though the rebel armies reached the sea at Vinaroz on April 15, Catalonia was safe. Along the length of the Ebro and Segre Rivers new lines had been created, and the Franco advance was halted.

April 15 also marked the end of the appearance of Lincoln Brigade stragglers from across the river. All who had not made it were either dead of wounds, alive but captured, or executed by the firing squads of Franco's Fascist military.

# PART IV

# WiNTER'S SOLDIERS

Dead in the sun, in the cold
In the bitter rain, the frost
Beside the great torn holes which
The guns have broken,
Under the drip of your blood, like
Harp strings, the fine grass
Sings again in the wind, your song,
Unsung, unspoken.

RAFAEL ALBERTI 1938

ON APRIL 15, 1938, the Navarese reached the Mediterranean at Vinaroz. On April 16, William Carney, a *Times* reporter assigned to the Franco side (the same man who had claimed La Muela—at Teruel—for Franco while the Mac-Paps still held it), wrote that the end of the war was but a matter of days, that

> all Republican forces will be forced to flee toward Barcelona before next Tuesday; that Madrid will be abandoned for lack of food and munitions, and that within a fortnight Franco's fleet will have two Mediterranean bases—Tortosa and Valencia.

Carney would again be wrong—this time, *by almost a year.*

The final phase of the Spanish war was indeed at hand, however. History reveals that in the Western world, the leaders of the Spanish Republic—and as of this date there was but one Communist in the Negrín cabinet—stood alone in their awareness of the true menace of the Axis powers.

Fascist Italy and Nazi Germany were at war now, not just on the battlefields of Spain, but in Ethiopia, the Saar, and Austria. Further, their arrogant demands on Danzig, Czechoslovakia, Poland, and France could lead only to either a servile surrender of sovereignty—or to war. Axis positions allowed for no alternatives.

The leadership of the Republic was both patriotic and realistic. In the rebellion's first phase, it had fought the Fascist military and won. In the second, that of the massive introduction of foreign arms and men, it had held grimly to a full half of Spain. The third phase witnessed a limited infusion of

Soviet weapons, the creation of an army, albeit poorly trained, poorly led, and poorly armed, and the introduction of that army to a series of tactical offensives.

The position of the Negrín Government was now quite simple. It reasoned that appeasement of the Fascist powers by the governments of Britain, France, and the United States was being perpetuated without the consent of their peoples, and that internal pressure to reverse these policies were mounting by the day. The Government's perspective, therefore, would continue to be to hold and fight for every inch of Spanish earth until such time as such a Western policy reversal took place.

But Spain had yet to experience the depths of betrayal to which England was prepared to sink. Just one day after Spain was cut into two parts, England and Italy signed the Mediterranean Pact, which provided, among other things, that the Mediterranean would be defended jointly by their two navies. It is history that in the six weeks following its signing—beginning on April 17, before the ink was dry—dozens of ships of the Western powers, including twenty-two of the British merchant marine, were attacked on the high seas. The attackers were Italian submarines and German and Italian bombers based on Sicily and Mallorca. Eleven English ships were sunk and some two dozen British sailors drowned—as were a half-dozen trusting observers from England's Non-intervention Committee. To the shame of all England, some of these ships were sunk within a short distance of cruising squadrons of the Royal Navy. No orders were received from the Admiralty either to attack or to rescue.

In contradistinction to the British policy of appeasement, the Axis program for world conquest was bold and cynical. The success of its first steps, however, was realistically predicated upon a quite basic truth: A Republican victory in Spain would not just seriously endanger its drive for power, it might also be *the* catalyst for its destruction. Whatever the cost, therefore, the Axis would continue to supply whatever was needed for the Republic's defeat.

Pressures to reverse England's avowed pro-Axis policy burst out anew with the Republic's defeat in Aragón. There was no city, town, or village in all of France that did not see its pro-Republican rally. People marched in the hundreds of thousands. So, too, in England. Voices in the House of Commons and the House of Lords gave evidence in swelling chorus of where true English sympathy lay. Churchill, too, came to the fore to denounce the Mediterranean Pact and the entire policy of the Chamberlain government.

Sympathy for Spain in the United States paralleled that in Western Europe. Unions, Democratic clubs, Masonic lodges, churches, and political independents—millions demanded that American policy be reversed, and that the Spanish Republic be given arms for its defense.

Sixty members of the United States Senate and House sent words of greeting and support to the Spanish Government in Barcelona. The time for a change in policy was ripe. Drew Pearson's column of April 12, 1938, discussed this possibility, and how it was sabotaged:

An amazing story has just leaked out telling how State Department "career" men blocked a last minute move to lift the embargo on arms to Spain, a move which was under consideration by the President.

The background of the story is a growing conviction on the part of the President, Secretary Hull, and several powerful Congressional leaders, including Senator Pittman, Chairman of the Foreign Relations Committee, and Senator Borah, that the embargo on arms to Spain *was one of the most tragic mistakes of American Foreign Policy* [emphasis added].

Its effect has been to deny war weapons to the Spanish Government while Franco's Fascists have been equipped with the most modern tanks, airplanes and artillery that Germany and Italy could offer. Of late the Spanish Army has been fighting literally with its bare fists, while Spanish gold reserves remain in New York banks, ample to purchase arms were it not for the embargo.

Roosevelt and Hull have both deplored the situation privately and felt that the United States was merely playing into the hands of Mussolini and Hitler. But until recently they did nothing. Then, just before he went to

Warm Springs two weeks ago, the President had a talk with Breckinridge Long, former Assistant Secretary of State, who as Ambassador to Italy was thoroughly familiar with Fascist aims. Long pointed out that there were provisions in the Neutrality Act permitting Roosevelt to lift the Spanish embargo, and argued that he do so. Roosevelt then arranged a personal appointment for Long with Secretary of State Cordell Hull.

Long arrived the next morning at the State Department to be confronted with a letter which Hull had supposedly written to Raymond Leslie Buell of the Foreign Policy Association, outlining reasons why he could *not* lift the embargo.

The letter had been released to the press by Hull just after he had received the President's telephone call.

Naturally Ambassador Long asked for an explanation.

"Oh, that was just a letter that Hackworth gave me to sign," replied the Secretary of State, implying that he had not paid much attention to it. [Green H. Hackworth was the legal advisor of the State Department.] Ambassador Long then pointed out that the United States was playing into the hands of European Fascists, and that if the Loyalists [the Republic] were defeated, Germany planned to move into Czechoslovakia, that it was not too late now to save the Spanish Republic if the United States lifted the embargo.

Hull then referred the matter to James Dunn, the State Department's solidly pro-Franco political relations advisor, who, along with dignitaries such as William C. Bullit, Joseph Kennedy, Pierrepont Moffat, and Judge Walton Moore, had *all* been long committed to England's pro-Axis policy.

With this cabal, Ambassador Long got nowhere. He returned to Hull, who then asked for "overwhelming proof" that the situation in Spain had changed since the government's application of its embargo.

He got the proof. On the following day, the Spanish ambassador, acting on Long's suggestion, personally delivered to Hull a formal note listing in detail the names of ships and the dates of arrival, and the munitions received by Franco from

Italy and Germany. "It was a most impressive mass of statistics," according to Drew Pearson.

> It clearly showed that since the time the American embargo was clamped down upon Spain, Franco had become nothing more than a vassal of Hitler and Il Duce.
> The day after the delivery of the note Ambassador Long went back to see Hull. The Secretary of State had not even seen the Spanish Ambassador's presentation. His "career" boys had taken the letter "to be translated," *and had kept it!*
> Once again Long told Hull that it was not too late to save Spain; that the Spanish Government had ample funds to buy arms; that it would buy from private dealers and arrange for delivery.
> Meanwhile also, several prominent Senators, including Borah, Nye, and Clark, the chief authors of the Neutrality Act, and Thomas and King of Utah, had given private pledges that they *would support the Administration if it lifted the arms embargo.*

But the inept and aging Hull simply turned the plea down, telling Long that it was now "much too late." And, too, President Roosevelt, coming up from Warm Springs to have a hand in the matter, was confronted by the conservative Catholic-bloc spokesmen—headed by Joseph Kennedy—with dire warnings as to the internal consequences if any assistance was given to "Bolshevists and Atheists."

Franklin Roosevelt's tentative decision to end the embargo was thus reversed.

In retrospect, those closest to the Spanish tragedy have little doubt that had Roosevelt rescinded the embargo, thereby freeing France, too, from the yoke of British policy, the ensuing guarantee of arms from both America *and* France to the Spanish Republic would have altered the course of history. Indeed, it is not at all inconceivable that the next world war, which the American volunteers were fighting so hard to prevent, would have ended precisely there, on Spanish soil—where it had begun.

*   *   *

The miracle had been accomplished. A Catalan front had been established. The rebel armies had been halted, turned so that they now faced west, for the drive toward Valencia and the Mediterranean littoral.

The Internationals, who on April 15 were but fragmented sections and squads of men, were given time, like the fabled phoenix, to rise again from the ashes of their own destruction.

For the Lincoln Brigade, this would be no easy accomplishment. Lieutenant Aaron Lopoff, adjutant to the drowned Maphralian, became the commander of the American stragglers, his authority being derived from the skeleton brigade staff now forming around Malcolm Dunbar, Hugh Slater, and the young Spanish Brigade Commissar José María Sastre. Lopoff set up his *Estado Mayor* in the open fields adjoining Mora la Nueva, commandeered new weapons, and sent trucks north and south in search of Lincoln cadres. Many arrived singly or in pairs, dirty, with bleeding feet, and half-naked.

Among the first motley collection was Alvah Bessie, newspaperman, novelist, and future screenwriter. Bessie, traveling in one of the search trucks, found George Watt, John Gates, and Joe Hecht on a hillside near the village of Rasquera. "They were lying on the ground," Bessie writes, "wrapped in blankets; under the blankets they were naked. They told us they had swum the Ebro that morning; that other men had tried to swim and drowned."

Just then a Matford roadster drove around the hill and two men got out. They were Herbert Matthews and Ernest Hemingway. "They were just as relieved to see us," Bessie relates, "as we were to see them."

John Gates also describes the incident:

> Suddenly a car drove up, stopped, and out stepped two men. Nobody ever looked better to me in all my life. . . . We hugged one another and shook hands. They told us everything they knew—Hemingway tall and husky, speaking in explosives; Matthews just as tall, but thin, and talking in his reserved way. . . . The writers gave us the good news of the many men who were safe, and we told them the bad news of some who were not. Facing the other side of the river, Hemingway shook his burly fist.

"You Fascist bastards haven't won yet," he shouted. "We'll show you!"

And so they came back. The little villages, from García north of Mora and south to Ginestar, became the gathering depots. As the men returned, scenes occurred that were emotional to a degree never before known among the Americans. Many wept unashamedly. The affection and fellowship loosely spread over 500 men became intense when concentrated on a few dozen. *Hundreds were missing,* and those who remained were precious beyond possessions, beyond any friendship. Never before had the dead and the missing reached such a terrifying total. Never before had so few faces reappeared.

More came to join them from the hospitals and from the brigade service units, now moved to Catalonia. Among these were the indefatigable Captain Lamb, who immediately became commander of Company 1, Lieutenant Howard Goddard, who had survived five bullets through his body at Belchite, Yale Stuart, and a host of others.

Edwin Rolfe quit his post as editor of *The Volunteer* to join the Lincoln Battalion. Courageous, dedicated, a living example of Thomas Paine's "Winter's Soldier," Rolfe exuded no aura of romanticism. Bessie says of him,

> He was frail; he resembled a bird; he had a fine delicate bone structure and he did not look as though he could be in any army. I do not think I have ever met a gentler guy, a less pugnacious guy, less of a soldier. But he had the iron conviction in him just the same.

With the British, Spanish, and Canadians arrived by foot and truck from Benifallet and Rasquera, the brigade was now complete. The Fifteenth then occupied a hidden valley a short distance from the river. In the daytime, the men would fortify the hills above the sandy loam of the river bank. At night they would descend to the river to occupy listening posts, machine gun nests, and rifle pits.

Floats were made by the Americans with various provocative slogans. At daybreak, these were floated down the river. The enemy would then open fire upon them, and the Americans would spot their firing points and blast them in return, deeming this a fitting way to celebrate May Day 1938.

Lieutenant Louis Secundy's brigade transport unit, the American section of the Albacete Auto Park, and the almost all-American Second *Esquadrón* of the First *Regimiento de Tren,* Fifth Army Corps, had also made it across the Ebro—but not without heavy losses in men, both killed and captured, and in rolling stock.

The original Auto Park, now in the area of Falset, functioned as usual, servicing all the International Brigades. Prior to Aragón the American section could boast of, at best, fifteen to twenty vehicles. At Quinto and Belchite American drivers advanced with the troops to seize all captured rolling stock, damaged or otherwise. American drivers, working closely with Secundy's unit, salvaged twenty trucks and a water tanker. At Teruel, they seized an equal number, plus tools, parts, and a mountain of accessories.

One such reclamation, involving the rear guard, became known as the "Barcelona scandal." For the Americans, masters at hijacking rolling stock from other units, had, in their enthusiasm, appropriated the personal car of the famed Dolores Ibarruri (*La Pasionaria*), a leader of Spain's Communist Party. They were forced, of course, amid humorous exchanges, to give it back.

The original brigade transport unit was disbanded, with the men incorporated into the Lincoln Battalion. Lieutenant Secundy was offered an infantry command. His military knowledge was scanty, at best, he said, so he would serve in the lines with the rest of the men. He insisted upon this, as did others such as Frank Chesler. They gave up their commissions without complaint and accepted a rifle for the last great battle.

American medical units, arriving in Catalonia from the center front—they had been given ninety-six hours in which to evacuate—were relocated specifically at Vich, Mataró, and S'Agaró. Doctor Eloesser headed the main unit at Vich—a deserted monastery with as many as 1,500 beds.

Eloesser was both administrator and head surgeon; under him was a most competent American, Spanish, and International staff.

The seaside town of Mataró was given a 500-bed hospital. Mildred Rackley, a member of Dr. Barsky's first group, became head of the administrative staff. The problems were similar to those of the first American medical unit at Romeral—a desperate need for more beds and equipment. At first, all supplies sent from America, France, England, and other countries were administered by Barsky, now in command of all International hospitals in Spain. Later, based upon a decision made by himself and others, these supplies were reissued equitably to *all* hospitals in the Catalan zone.

Except for a military hospital in Barcelona's Tibidabo area (*Las Planas*), where a few American doctors and nurses served, the last completely American hospital was at S'Agaró, a seacoast town on the Costa Brava. It was a transition unit, really; in it, men recuperating from wounds that had made them *inútil*, unfit for further duty, awaited repatriation to their homelands.

The last group of Americans to climb the mountains into Spain, some thirty or so with an equal number of Canadians and British, arrived at brigade headquarters on June 30, 1938. Volunteers were no longer being accepted into the International Brigades. Among the Americans was Wilfred Mendelson, group leader of twenty men who had arrived at Le Havre on the U.S.S. *Manhattan*, Sam Nahman (also known as Manny Harriman), who had made it to France on his own, and Duncan Kier, an ex-signal corps sergeant recently discharged from duty in Panama. Archie Brown, also of this group, was a west coast longshoreman who, for some unexplained reason, had stowed away on the *Manhattan*. Mendelson, his twenty volunteers, and a sympathetic ship's crew, had seen to it that Brown had the best of everything.

Eight more Americans were to join the battalion. Seven of them had already seen service in Spain, been wounded, sent home, and were now returning for a second hitch. The seven were Joseph Rehill, William Wheeler, Walter Kowalski, Joseph Cuban, Joseph Gordon, Al Tanz, and Joseph Cobert.

Wheeler, explaining why he returned, says: "I was quite miserable in the U.S. I had read about the big retreats and I had only one thing in mind—to get back to Spain at the earliest opportunity."

The *last* volunteer was James Lardner, son of the famed writer Ring Lardner. He had arrived in Barcelona with Hemingway and Vincent Sheean, with credentials from the Paris edition of the *New York Herald Tribune*, which was also Sheean's paper.

Sheean describes Lardner:

> A pleasant-looking youth, not particularly robust, with brown hair and eyes protected by horn-rimmed glasses; he had long legs and the slight awkwardness and ready laugh which belonged to his age and type. He was twenty-three: Andover, Harvard, and the Herald Tribune in New York. . . . He had taken the liveliest interest in Spain, and knew a good deal more about the geography of the war and some of its leading characters than I did.

Disappointed at what amounted to an outright censorship of his articles by the *Tribune,* Lardner announced to his friends in Barcelona that he had decided to volunteer for the Lincoln Brigade. "I am told," writes his brother, Ring Lardner, Jr.,

> that they all tried to dissuade him. But I don't think their hearts were in it. You couldn't know Jim and expect to win an argument like that.
>
> Spain was the beginning of his life and the end of it. Anti-Fascism derived from a simple process of logic; it only remained to get close enough to the conflict in order to see the necessity of taking an active part in it, of engaging, for the first time in his life, in purposeful, directed effort toward a tangible goal. Pacifism, evolved by a previous mental process, was abandoned because its logic no longer obtained.

Lardner arrived at battalion headquarters in the first week of May. He had a new uniform, a new pack, and a number of books among his possessions. The men, who were playing baseball outside the *Estado Mayor*, examined him curiously while he waited to be interviewed by Wolff. Rolfe writes:

> Wolff, informed of Lardner's arrival, didn't answer. George Watt repeated his words, adding, "You know who he is— Ring Lardner's son." Wolff looked up for a moment, then shouted in the voice he used when he was either pleased or angry, or embarrassed: "Yeah, I know. What do you expect me to do about it?" Then more softly, "Put him in Company 3." The message was quickly delivered to Lardner, who got his big pack together, walked off toward Abad's dirt cave, and was immediately assigned to his platoon and squad.

Wolff himself says:

> I was opposed to Lardner serving at the front. That's what I was shouting about. I did not think he would be of much help at this stage. His role as a writer sympathizing with the Republic was more important. But Lardner insisted.

Lardner's own reasons for joining the Lincolns were to the point. "The cause is so plainly a worthy one," he wrote, "that the question which the young men of the world should be putting to themselves is what justification they have for staying out of this struggle."

Spring turned into summer, days and nights of sticky heat and much rain. Amidst training, baseball, Spanish classes, and the development of a new activist movement within the ranks of the battalions, life soon became routine. It was a new situation for the Americans. Until now there had been but a week or two of rest—then back to the vortex of battle.

On June 13, the French border was again closed. The failure of the United States to lift the embargo had thrown France back into the lap of England's appeasers. The great mass of the insurgent armies ground slowly toward the Republican seaports of Castellón, Sagunto, and Valencia, with progress made at an enormous cost of blood and men.

On July 4, the Abraham Lincoln Battalion paraded with flags flying to the town of Marsa, then to the soccer field for a display of close-order drill to the townspeople. The other battalions followed, and a fiesta ensued with wine, food, and cigarettes.

Colonel Copic had been replaced by Major José Antonio Valledor, who then addressed the gathering. Valledor was an Asturian with an outstanding war record. With the Fascist rising, he had become a company and then a battalion commander in the People's Army. His record, especially his brilliant resistance at Trubia and Oviedo, earned him special tribute. When Santander fell, he directed his troops of the Army of the North in a furious forty-six-day battle in western Asturias. When the north itself fell, he switched to guerrilla warfare, ranging the Cantabrian Mountains with a hardy group of fighters. Directed by the Republic to make his way to the center zone, he was wounded and captured in a running gun battle on the French border, but was able to cheat the firing squad by giving a false name. After five months of prison labor, he made his escape, this time to Barcelona. Valledor was a fitting commander indeed to lead the Abraham Lincoln Brigade in its final campaign.

Republican General Rojo lists the Franco campaign against Valencia as a victory for the Republic. Under the command of the loyal Colonel Menéndez, the Twelfth, Seventeenth, Twenty-first, and Twenty-second corps, led by Colonels Gallego, Vallejo, Cristóbal, and Ibarrola, respectively, put up an absolutely magnificent defense in the battle of movement to save Valencia. None of these officers were identified with the burgeoning clique of capitulationists in the High Command; nor could they be listed as "lackeys of the Spanish Communist Party." They were loyal Republican officers of the new People's Army. *The retreats of Aragón were simply not repeated.* Indeed, the corps of the Fascist military paid in rivers of blood for each foot of terrain.

What had begun in March as an "end the war offensive" had been contained. Moreover, a growing disaffection now plagued young enemy officers in newly constituted units. The terrain they had entered was a desert of abandoned villages.

News of the destruction of Republican cities by fleets of German and Italian aircraft evoked a smoldering anger directed toward the *extranjero*. Officers of insurgent units fought with their German and Italian counterparts in the barrooms and streets of rear-line garrison towns.

The Falange General Yagüe, impressed by the Republic's stubborn defense, openly praised their courage and ability. At a dinner commemorating the anniversary of the founding of the United Carlist-Falangist Party, he denounced the Germans and Italians as "beasts of prey." Moreover, he suggested that it was time for the Fascist Falange to extend the hand of reconciliation to the "Reds." At this, he was summarily dismissed from his command by General Franco himself.

War weariness was such that in the month of June a wave of sentiment swept all Francoist Spain for an end to the conflict. The German ambassador, Eberhard von Stohrer, warned Hitler that "Voices are being raised in favor of ending the war. Even in the highest ranks of the army objections are made." Reactions by the Fascist military to this remark were quick and severe.

Acutely aware of the contradictions at work in the Franco zone, Juan Negrín, the Republican premier, addressed a meeting in Madrid on June 18, 1938, saying, "Not one more second of war should be tolerated, if Spain's existence as a free country is to be preserved."

Seizing the initiative, he attempted to negotiate an end to hostilities. He met in Paris with the German ambassador, Count Welczeck, but to no avail. Other contacts through a relative of Serano Suñer, Franco's brother-in-law, also failed. Having exhausted all channels, Negrín could only conclude that the cabal of Spain's Fascist military, together with Nazi Germany and Fascist Italy, would accept nothing short of unconditional surrender. The already 200,000 executions in Fascist territory clearly indicated what such a surrender would bring.

The Government of the Spanish Republic chose to demonstrate once again its ability to attack as well as to defend. A victory now would silence the defeatists, give strength to the clamor for peace in rebel ranks, and give heart to those who, come what may, would fight to the end.

The month-long resistance of the Republic's divisions falling back on Valencia had bought sufficient time for the organization of just such an offensive. Republican General Vicente Rojo, who, together with Colonels Modesto, Sarabia, Cordón, and Galán, had drawn up the plan, writes of its intent:

> We had arrived at a moment of military crises. Our troops had retreated to the line chosen and organized by the general staff of the group of armies defending Valencia and Sagunto. The last reserves from the fronts of Madrid, Andalusia, and Estremadura had been placed in this line. If they failed in their mission of defense, Valencia and Sagunto would be lost. And, if the Valencian region fell—it was the richest, agriculturally, in all Spain, the most highly industrialized—we would indeed have no choice but to regard the war as in the process of being lost, and to assume that we had reached its decisive stage.
>
> We were then given that rare and strategic opportunity wherein a menaced front is indirectly aided by acting offensively in a theatre far from it.
>
> On the 23rd of July the enemy was halted, *smashed* before Viver and the fortifications covering Valencia. The rebel armies moved instantly to regroup, to bring up fresh troops and greater masses of equipment.
>
> It was precisely *then* that we launched our offensive on the Ebro!

As early as mid-July, the little Catalan villages near the Ebro had begun to fill with troops. The nights, especially, were alive with marching men; lines of blacked-out trucks carrying pontoons, munitions, and boats, and pulling pieces of light artillery. It was as though each dusk brought a sudden wave of movement, pushing silently but inexorably toward the sandy loam of the riverfront. But for the first time since Jarama, all five of the International Brigades were together on a single front.

Although it has often been said that during the Spanish war

the Soviets dictated which units would receive Russian arms, generally speaking, the limited supply of arms simply went where the fighting was. Beyond that, of course, much was wasted in the hands of untrained troops, or lost in the retreats of poorly-led units. Certainly, the International Brigades fought the greater part of their battles with a minimum of support of any kind—often surviving solely on their incredible élan. Materiel shipped from France at the time of the reopening of the border, for example, went almost in its entirety to the center front, to be used by the altogether heroic—and certainly non-Communist-led—divisions of General López Menéndez, for the defense of Valencia and the Levante. Those arms were rushed to Menéndez at the very hour when the divisions of Lister and the Eleventh, Fourteenth, and Fifteenth International Brigades were holding shut the passage to the sea with their bodies and little else.

On the eve of the Battle of Ebro, the disparity in arms between the forces of the Spanish Republic and the Fascist enemy was truly awful. The International Brigades, it should be noted, were shock divisions. The estimated strength of the Thirty-fifth Division (which included the Eleventh, Thirteenth, and Fifteenth brigades) was approximately 12,000 men, two-thirds of them Spanish; 6,000 rifles, 162 light and 69 heavy machine guns, 38 mortars, and four antitank guns. This, for a full shock division! During World War II, by contrast, most Allied divisions had upward of 800 light and heavy machine guns alone, plus a preponderance of all other arms and artillery. Certainly, all divisions of Spain's Fascist military were now armed in this manner.

The Lincoln Brigade left the village of Marsa on July 21. On July 23, it was in the *barrancas* of the Río de la Torre, in the proximity of the village of Torre del Español.

"We were in good shape," Captain Wolff says, "mentally and physically, and our morale was high." Many attest to this excellent morale. Yale Stuart of the Lincoln Headquarters Company writes:

> The men knew there was little chance for a total defeat
> of the enemy. They thought specifically in terms of seiz-

ing territory, then entrenching and holding it. They knew that the only real hope for victory lay in a significant change in the international situation. They *knew* the score, as it were. No mechanical attempt at an infusion of morale from the top would have made any difference. For their morale was the meaningful kind; derived of their own convictions and of their personal understanding of the Spanish struggle.

It is history that three Republican army corps, the Fifth, Twelfth, and Fifteenth, known as *El Ejército del Ebro* (The Army of the Ebro), crossed the river at 1:00 A.M., July 25, 1938, on a front of forty kilometers. Within three days they penetrated to a depth of twenty-five kilometers, seized eleven villages, captured more than 6,000 prisoners, plus war materiel to almost equal that of Guadalajara, and stopped the insurgent attack against Valencia dead in its tracks.

The Thirty-fifth Division crossed the Ebro near the town of Ascó on the opposite bank. Their zero hour had been 0015. The first to go over were scouts and *guerrilleros*, peasants from the opposite shore who were familiar with the terrain. The crossings were made with muffled oars. An echelon of the Thirteenth Brigade, moving out in their wake, was discovered in mid-stream and fired upon. But those already ashore stormed the machine guns and dispersed the defenders. Within minutes, the first bridgehead was established.

Enemy fire had sunk a number of boats. Two infantry companies of the Thirteenth were forced to swim the river in full pack. By 0400, engineers of the Thirty-fifth had spanned the 300-foot river with the first single-planked foot bridge, this, at the confluence of the Río de la Torre. At exactly 0440, the entire Thirteenth Brigade was across the river and heading inland.

At 0510, the Thaelmanns began their crossing and, although the element of surprise had been lost, they quickly moved to attack the village of Ascó against a desperate enemy resistance. Almost simultaneously with the Thaelmanns' crossing, the Fifteenth arrived at the Ebro's banks to the south of Ascó. The Canadians were the first to go over, the men in boats, the machine gun company swimming their gun-laden mules. On the far shore the Mac-Paps, followed by the Fifty-ninth Battalion, moved to the aid of the Eleventh Brigade at Ascó. The river, the hills, and the town were now sharply outlined against a fast-breaking dawn. Enemy artillery fire ranged the *barrancas* through which they advanced.

Among the first casualties was the Company 1 commander, Lionel Edwards, and his commissar, Nick Meyers. Edwards had led the famed Company 3 at Teruel. With enemy fire decreasing in direct proportion to mounting pressure by the Thaelmanns from the north, it was apparent that the enemy was attempting a pull-back. They were not to be allowed to do this. The Fifty-ninth, in an enveloping skirmish, took thirty prisoners; the Canadians likewise. Ascó was then surrounded, and units of both battalions moved into its streets. Meanwhile, the Eleventh drove forward to seize the church and capture some 300 prisoners and much booty in the form of small arms and machine guns. The men then, like the Dombrowskis before them, moved quickly inland.

The Mac-Paps and Fifty-ninth made a clean sweep of the remainder of the town, accepting in the process the surrender of an additional battalion of the Fiftieth Division of Yagüe's Corps of Morocco, plus a complete company of cavalry and an impressive number of rifles, mortars, machine guns, and small arms ammunition.

There then began one of the most startling small-scale maneuvers every attempted by a unit of the Fifteenth Brigade. The Mac-Paps had cavalry! Since their original orders were to fight through to Corbera, they mounted twenty of the horses, added two mules and one full section of the machine gun company, and headed straight into enemy territory.

The British Battalion was already driving toward Corbera in the wake of the Thirteenth Brigade. The Canadians hoped to arrive in time to aid in its capture.

The 59th, under the American Captain, Mark Millman, set off through the mountains of Fatarella in a race to invest the town of Villalba de los Arcos. The Canadians swept south and west toward Corbera in open, artillery formation.

The experiences of the Mac-Paps' Company 4 were similar to those of the battalion as a whole. Lieutenant George Carbonel and his commissar, Irving Weissman, led the men out. Samuel Nahman, a nineteen-year-old New Yorker, and one of the last recruits to join this company, states that the advance led through a wheat field. He suddenly saw a boot sticking out of a clump of vines, and then:

> The whole field seemed to erupt with enemy troops, hands raised and surrendering. They were mixed Moors and Spaniards. They were anything but hostile. Actually, they were terrified. Carbonel lined them up and Weissman, lean, tough, hardened by a full year of battle, went from man to man, asking bluntly, "Who are the officers? Who is the commander?" One look at Weissman was enough. Within minutes all the officers were identified, including the C.O., who had tried to disguise himself. There were prisoners all over the place, well over 250 men.

The prisoners were sent to the river; the advance continued. In the early afternoon waves of planes came in low over the hills. They were subjected to three bombing runs. And something new had been added. Along with the familiar Ju-52s and Capronis was the quite startling German Stuka dive bomber, the same that would later strike such terror to the hearts of early Allied troops in World War II. To the veteran International and Spanish battalions, however, it was just another plane that bombed in a different way. Their steadiness calmed the recruits. They simply glanced curiously up, lit their cigarettes, hugged the earth and cursed.

Dusk found them in the sector of Venta de los Camposines, where they threw up defensive positions and settled for the night.

The Lincoln and British battalions crossed the river immediately after the Canadians. An example of the élan of the Lincolns in the first moments before the crossing is described by Alvah Bessie:

> Aaron [Lopoff] appeared from around a stand of cane. "Bess," he said, "come look at this." His face was bright, like the face of a happy child, and we went around the cane and stood looking at the water. Broad and placid in the

sun, it was filled with little boats, little rowboats full of men, moving sedately back and forth across the river, drifting somewhat with the swift current.

"It's Prospect Park in the summertime!" he said. "It's wonderful!"

Shells ranged both banks, and Captain Wolff personally directed the men to the boats. Captain Lamb, leading the first eighteen men of Company 1, crossed in a boat with the reassuring name of *All Right*. Wolff was the last to cross. The British, always more formal than the other battalions, hoisted Republican and Catalan flags to head their advance. The American goal was Fatarella, some fifteen kilometers inland. The march began, against an enemy who even now had more guns of all calibers, more planes overhead, more of everything than the attacking force.

There wasn't a single *Chato* or Mosca in the sky. *All* were on the Levante front. It would be at least two days before artillery could cross the river, likewise tanks and transport, and even ambulances for the wounded. In effect, the Republican Army of the Ebro was advancing on a forty-kilometer front with no weapons except the rifle, the machine gun, the grenade—and its own incomparable courage. Bessie writes:

> You could see the flankers moving up and down the hills far to our right and left, watching for the possibility of ambush; for we had no way of knowing where the enemy might be. He might have retreated kilometers, or he might be planning to stand us off at any point on our march toward Fatarella.

By twilight, the Lincolns were in possession of a dozen or so prisoners from scattered skirmishes. The five companies then mounted the last ridge before Fatarella, dug in, fortified their positions as best they could, and waited through the night.

The British Battalion, advancing rapidly, linked up with the Thirteenth Dombrowski Brigade at approximately three in the afternoon, just a short distance from the village of Corbera. Captain Sam Wilde, meeting with Polish liaison officers, was told that the Thirteenth was preparing to attack it, that Moroccan troops had been sighted in the foothills to the south, threatening its flanks. The British then assigned themselves the double task of protecting the Polish flank while routing the Moroccans.

Moving immediately out, they began a running fire fight through hills covered with brush, scrub oak, and olive groves, which would last through the night. It would end with the *tabors* of Morocco breaking contact, with the British taking a number of prisoners, and with the listing of the first British casualties of the campaign.

The Thirteenth, moving to the assault of Corbera, was met outside the town by a newly-arrived rebel column—a fresh battalion of 800 men and a full *tabor* of *Regulares*.

Having previously captured seven mobile 7.5s, mounted on tractors, the Dombrowskis put them to instant use—while the anti-Fascist Poles impetuously charged the enemy line. Within minutes, they had smashed the rebel positions, accounted for at least 100 enemy dead, and over 200 prisoners. The Fascists fled back through Corbera, with the Thirteenth in hot pursuit.

By dusk the Dombrowskis were within grenade distance of the first houses to the north of the town of Gandesa; indeed, they could have entered it were they not now confronted by heavily fortified strong points, fresh troops, clusters of machine gun nests and concentric lines of barbed wire.

In terms of military feats, the Thirteenth International Brigade had forced the crossing of a swift river; stormed a series of fortified points; seized the town of Venta de los Camposines and the command post of the First Media Brigade of the rebel Fiftieth Division—with a lieutenant-colonel and all his staff; captured two batteries of guns, hundreds of prisoners, and much war materiel; moved on to the assault of Corbera (with the subsequent defeat of more than 1,000 entrenched troops); and then laid siege to Gandesa. There, at a distance of twenty-five kilometers from its starting point, the brigade halted for the night. All this had been done on foot, and within the space of eighteen hours!

From north to south the offensive went well. Penetration

everywhere was at least ten to fifteen kilometers. In the arc of the Ebro itself, the Third Division, operating to the north of the Thirty-fifth, had crossed the river to storm the towns of Ribarroja and Flix, and had captured many prisoners and much war material. To the south, Lister's Fifth Corps had penetrated at least ten kilometers to seize Pinell, Miravet, Mora de Ebro, and the southern slopes of the Sierra de Pandols and Sierra de Caballs.

The response of the Fascist military to the Republican challenge was instantaneous. General Yagüe, sector commander, called for massive air support. He got it. The shifting of air strength from the Levante front accompanied the rapid dispatch of shock divisions previously intended for the final assault on Valencia. The picture was of eight fresh insurgent divisions rushing to join those already committed to action. Within a span of days, the forty-kilometer front linking the two arms of the arc of the Ebro would be witness to two armies, over 200,000 men, locked in mortal combat. It was this limited theater of action plus the ensuing storm of shells and bombs that caused correspondents to refer to the Battle of the Ebro as the Verdun of the Spanish Civil War.

Not waiting for dawn, Captain Lamb's Company 1 of the Lincolns had infiltrated the town during the night. Minor skirmishes drove defending Civil Guard units into the hills beyond. The rest of the battalion awoke to find that Christmas had arrived in July. An *intendencia* (supply depot) had been captured. There was bread, canned squid, sardines, oysters, meat in Italian tomato sauce, and chocolate. There were cookies, too, and every kind of tobacco from *puros*, Spanish and Italian cigars, to excellent cigarettes and sacks of loose tobacco for pouches and pipes. The first hours of morning saw the battalion distributing wheat, flour, sugar, canned goods, and all that the *intendencia* held to the townspeople, warning them to take it and to leave immediately, that the rebel bombers would arrive at any moment.

Wolff states that contact was then made with the Third Division's commander and staff officers. Fatarella, they exclaimed angrily, was to have been their town. The *intendencia* was rightfully theirs. In the midst of a heated argument which can only be explained by the general poverty of all Republican units, information arrived that the Fifty-ninth was heavily engaged. Wolff broke off the debate. The Lincolns were ordered to the aid of the Fifty-ninth.

Within minutes they met their first opposition, enemy troops that had failed to make their escape. Company 1 threw out an immediate skirmish line to outflank and invest the rebel positions. The fighting was brief. The enemy had no heart for it. More than 250 prisoners were taken, along with rifles, machine guns, and other equipment. Alvah Bessie writes:

> They were patently terrified. They kept their hands over their heads even when ordered to lower them. They timidly offered us cigarettes, of which they had a considerable supply. They emptied their pockets of anything that might be called a weapon, even pocket-knives—which were immediately returned to them. They had expected to be shot on sight by the "Reds" and their officers had obviously removed any insignia they might have been wearing. But instead of being shot they had to stand around on the road for about two hours, while their *avión*—observation planes and bombing squadrons—wheeled and inspected the terrain.

Two sections of Company 3, headed by Sergeant Joe Taylor and Corporal Jim Lardner, escorted the prisoners to the river. By midnight, the men were camped on another hill in an olive grove. A fire fight developed then between guards screening the American positions and enemy units attempting to move down the road. These were quickly driven off, with the Lincoln Company 4 commander, Lieutenant Paulo, becoming the battalion's first casualty.

Dawn of the second day had found the Canadians moving into deserted Corbera where they too discovered an *intendencia*. Again, it was Christmas. Shoes for everyone—this time Italian soft leather boots, canned squid, *puros*, marmalade, and anchovies. As at Fatarella, the townspeople and peasants were asked to bring bags, carts, boxes, anything to hold the sugar, wheat, flour, and canned goods to be given away. The

Mac-Paps loaded their cavalry with boxes and cartons. The Fifteenth's headquarters sent trucks to rescue some of the provisions for themselves and for the Thirty-fifth Division. The danger of bombing hung like an omnipresent cloud. Indeed, Fatarella and Corbera, *all* the towns within the arc of the Ebro were shortly to be almost totally destroyed.

Attack orders came through at 0200. The Mac-Paps moved out on a battalion front to the south of the Gandesa-Corbera road. A machine gun section moved behind each company as it advanced steadily toward Gandesa.

It was an impressive sight. The nature of the terrain was such that the entire Canadian Battalion could be seen, as could the British to the south, and other troops to the north— all advancing on a three-battalion front. At two kilometers from the town, the entire enemy line opened up: mortars, machine guns, the works. The battalions then deployed, infil- trating by squads and companies over the fields. Their for- ward movement was beautiful, executed with the strong precision of contained discipline. The time was approx- imately 1630 hours.

Insurgent skirmish lines were quickly driven back on the town. There was simply no halt in the forward movement. The British occupied the foothill zone known as El Puig del Aliga, to the southeast, where they linked with advancing Spaniards of the Fifth Corps. They were confronted with one final hill, however, on their right. Marked "Hill 481" on their maps, it was one of those that would prove disastrous to all their plans.

The Mac-Paps, coming up fast to within 600 meters of the first houses, were also prevented by this hill from any further advance. The battalions of the Thirteenth and Eleventh to the north had now partially encircled Gandesa from that direc- tion. As dusk fell, the sky to the west was ablaze with the oncoming lights of what seemed like hundreds of trucks from the gathering divisions of the Corps of Morocco.

The rapidity of the Republican advance was guaranteed to lead to confusion. Tales are told of the capture of entire com- panies by just handfuls of men. On the morning of the third day, for example, Lieutenant Jack Cooper of Cleveland (a former union leader there) was captured with eight men. Earlier, Major Valledor had assigned the brigade machine gun company to set up a defensive perimeter of guns and to send out patrols in the vicinity of the Crossroads (Venta de los Campesinos). There Cooper and his squad ran into two companies of the enemy. Cooper's story is excerpted from the *Volunteer for Liberty:*

"In a matter of minutes, we were surrounded and taken prisoner." They were relieved of their arms and Cooper was stripped of his possessions, pistol, wallet, etc. They were then threatened with execution, but were finally taken to a hill where the officers of the group were gathered. Lt. Cooper was brought before them for questioning.

"And I gave them information," he says. "All they wanted and more! I told them we had Gandesa and that by tomorrow (the 27th), we would be in Calaceite. When they asked where our forces were, I answered 'way ahead.' How many? they questioned. Without hesitation I answered, 'Five Army Corps.' They were impressed and worried . . . During that afternoon and evening we developed friendly conversations with two of their officers, who had friends in New York and Chicago, so they said, and with some of their *soldados* as we discussed generally the conditions on the Fascist side and on our own . . .

"The following morning they were in a more or less panicky state. Added to their growing strain was the fact that they had been three days without food. Finally, while we waited to see what would happen, their six officers held a conference, at which they decided their game was up. They surrendered themselves to us.

"It was dark most of the time we were with them, and they were pretty-well scattered. It was not until we marched them to Brigade H.Q. that I discovered there were 208 of them. Among whom were the six officers and nineteen sergeants.

"My kids (the Spanish recruits) could have escaped or made their path easier many times, especially when we were being threatened with death. But they didn't, because they figured that would mean my death—that's loyalty!"

By dusk of the second day Lister's Fifth Corps had seized the Sierra de Pandols and Caballs and had advanced to the gates of the villages of Bot and Prat de Compte. The count of prisoners approached the 6,000 mark. The storming of the village of Pinell had brought a magnificent haul. A train, crammed to the wheels with troops and war materiel, had been sent in answer to desperate appeals of the enemy. Once across the bridge outside Pinell, it was surrounded and captured. The entire convoy, officers, munitions, and men, fell into Lister's hands.

On July 27, 1938, Edward Rolfe wrote in his diary:

> Deployed after three kilometers march against positions on hills held by the enemy. Drove them from wooded height, then over another hill where our command post was established. Then our men drove them off another ridge. Lamb, Hoshooley, Tabb, Mendelson wounded.

The most important item in Rolfe's entry was that the enemy had now established a line, for they too had been advancing, and from fortified positions. Companies 1 and 2 of the Lincolns had suffered heavily in the assault of the last hill. At one point Companies 1 and 4 fought it out within forty feet of the enemy on the crest. The Americans persisted; the enemy fled. Their retreat exposed them to a concentrated fire by the Lincoln guns, so that many were cut down as they attempted to cross the valley.

"We fought with grenades at close quarters," says Arthur Munday, wounded in the engagement. "Then when they broke and ran for it, one of our gunners, Red Shenker, a veteran of Aragón, had a field day before he himself was killed." Every man in Munday's section, with the exception of Dick Rusciano and Ben Holtzman, was wounded. Holtzman pulled Munday to safety.

"The Fascists," says Donald Thayer, now commanding Company 4, "were trying for the hill, too. But we took it and they ran. They didn't have the staying power. I recall Luchell McDaniels, amongst others, heaving grenades with both hands." McDaniels was the young Black worker from San

Francisco who went on to win the name of *El Fantástico* among the young Spaniards.

Wolff also describe seeing two enemy cavalry companies dismounting and moving into the lines in the late afternoon. The Republican Third Division had not yet appeared on the Lincoln's right flank, so there was no protection from enfilading fire from the village of Villalba to the north. The third did arrive as dusk fell, and all that night the lights of troop convoys were seen to move up from south and west

Dawn of the twenty-eighth revealed the Lincolns occupying a ridge facing a broad valley. On the near slope was the Villalba de los Arcos-Gandesa Road. There were terraces between their positions and this road. Beyond it were vineyards and wooded slopes leading up to the enemy positions— a distance of about 600 meters. The ridge faced southwest. Northwest, from a valley to the rear of the Lincoln ridge, was the village of Villalba—rumored to be the site of the executions of Robert Merriman and Dave Doran. Its distance was about two kilometers. At the mouth of the valley, receiving fire from three sides, was a small wooded island. On the island were two machine gun crews under the command of section leader George Cady, with gunners Nat Gross, Charlie Bartolotta, and a Greek-American named Scarlettos.

The Lincolns attacked at 6:00 in the morning, again at 10:30, and again in the afternoon. Other than the supporting fire of their maching guns, they had nothing. The enemy, on the other hand, had some artillery and had moved in a great number of maortars. The situation was again predictable. With each attempt, the companies would push down the slopes, cross the road, and infiltrate the trees toward the enemy positions. Artillery ranged the valley. Mortar shells fell in profusion. Once a squadron of Heinkel fighter bombers swept in from the rear, strafing and bombing. In the late afternoon, the rebels counter-attacked. Their dead joined the dozens of American and Spanish bodies now strewn over the terraces and vineyards.

The Lincoln attack was but a small part of the attack by the Army of the Ebro, which still pressed forward everywhere, without artillery, planes, or tanks. Its objective? To *guarantee* that upon Ebro would fall the full weight of the Franco armies. Only in this way could time be bought, Valencia saved, and the immense disparity in arms somewhat negated. Also, there was always the possibility of victory, however small.

To the immediate south, the Fifty-ninth Battalion had been badly mauled. Among its dead was the courageous American machine gun commissar, Arnold Reid, about whom James Lardner had written: "He knows more than anyone I've met here of what it's all about."

On the following day the Lincoln companies were again thrown into the assault, with the same results. The enemy was now too strongly fortified. Shells burst over every inch of the Lincoln lines. Flights of Jus swept the valley in relays before and behind the American positions. Lieutenant Wheeler tells of forty to fifty on the morning of the twenty-ninth alone.

By evening fewer than 400 Lincoln cadres were still in the lines. Fifty were dead, 250 wounded. Rolfe writes of the Lincoln first-aid post:

> Dr. Simon worked calmly and swiftly during the action, soon moving his post to a point directly behind the lines and a few yards in back of Wolff's C.P. The twenty-five-year-old Battalion *médico* was not really a doctor; he had left medical school in Philadelphia almost two years before to go to Spain, and had served in almost all of the battles since Jarama, and had been a front-line doctor with the rank of Captain, for a longer period than any other medical man in Spain. The men respected him for his courage and competence under fire.

Companies 1, 2, and 3 lost their commissars: Murray Goldstein with shrapnel in his arms and legs; Harold Smith with the same; Larry Lustgarten shot through the throat. Tom Paige, a Black sergeant of Company 3, had been hit, as had Sergeant Joe Taylor, also Black, of Company 1. A courageous veteran of every action since Brunete, Taylor had been shot through the shoulder. Among the many dead was Joseph Cuban, one of the seven to volunteer a second time for Spain, and Wilfred Mendelson, leader of the last contingent.

A singular point in respect to casualties: for each of the American dead, there were three Spaniards—because in all International battalions, Spaniards now constituted seventy percent of the personnel.

The world press lauded the resurgence of Republican strength, while soberly detailing the furious response of the Fascist military. A new German tank had made its appearance, as well as a new antitank gun. The all-purpose German 88s, used sparingly at the beginning of the offensive in Aragón, were now present in batteries. In the face of the 88s, the superior Russian tanks were essentially obsolete.

The Canadians at Gandesa were attacked the first night by Moroccans of Barrón's Thirteenth Division. They were driven back with heavy losses. On the following morning, the Mac-Paps moved against Hill 481, reached through a *barranca* on their left flank, and were driven back in turn. The contending units then attacked furiously back and forth so that the *barranca*'s floor was soon carpeted with the dead and dying. It would be known to both sides as the "valley of death."

Lawrence Cane, Mac-Pap machine gun company adjutant, writes:

> We attacked two or three times in the next three days. Could not advance. Failure of the British to take the dominating hill, "the *pimple*," prevented this. We were actually within grenade-tossing distance of the first houses of the town.
>
> The British had terrible losses—no success. Lots of Mac-Paps lost from fire of enemy hill. I was first aware of the 88s on the third day. Mainanen, a Finn from Canada, together with another Finn named Myllikanges, was directing cover fire to allow our pinned down men to retire. An 88 shell drove us to the bottom of the trench. I felt something on the back of my neck, warm and wet. I thought the back of my head was blown off. It was brains. Both of the Finns were dead, blown to pieces.
>
> I remember the first flight of our planes over the front by this time some planes had arrived from the Levante front as well as a few tanks and guns from across the river]. They were driven back, literally, by the 88s. It was a devas-

tating gun. On the same day three tanks attacked in front of our Company 2 positions. If they had any success we were to follow them in. The 88s got every one of them. Two Spanish tankists were the sole survivors.

Heavy enemy shelling and aerial bombardment had begun. Every day and all day. It was a crescendo from morning 'til evening. No infantry attacks now. They had stabilized and were bringing up reserves.

That the "pimple" held was not because the British didn't try. William Rust writes:

> If the Battalion had failed gloriously on Hill 481, it was not for lack of audacity but for lack of artillery. Armed only with M.G.s and mortars, and unable to get tanks and heavy guns across the river, the Republicans had dashed into the very heart of the Fascist fortifications.
>
> Every company commander and commissar of the British Battalion was either killed or wounded in the five day fight for the hill. The cadres were decimated. Lieutenant Lewis Clive, Company 2 commander and a distant relative of the original *Clive* of India, so associated with British imperialism, was killed on the last day, as was David Guest, son of the Labor peer, Lord Haden Guest.

The Mac-Paps tried for the pimple again on August 1. Company 2, under Henry Mack, and Company 4 almost reached the crest. But again they were forced to retreat with heavy losses. Sam Nahman, of Company 4, states:

> We should not have attacked. Company after company went into action there. It was futile. Sol Rose was killed and Ben Barsky, and many others. The top of the pimple was heavily fortified as well as the base. It should have been shelled. One battery and we would have had it.

Karl Cannon, of Toledo, Ohio, a Mac-Pap veteran of the first days (he had been wounded at Fuentes, and again at Teruel), says simply that the enemy positions were so strong and Republican preparations against them so lacking that each attack was but an exercise in futility. "At one point we drove through the fortifications at the base and were actually exchanging grenades with the Fascists at the top. But it was useless." Cannon recalls seeing Milton Cohen from Chicago, another Mac-Pap veteran of every battle, trying, with revolver in hand, to rally the men for one last effort. But that too failed.

On July 31, the Lincoln and Fifty-ninth battalions arrived from Villalba to make their try. Rolfe writes in his diary:

> *August 1, 1938:* Moved across hill at 3:30 A.M.; took up positions under artillery fire on side of hill behind the 59th. Our artillery opened up at 11:00 A.M. After a short barrage the 59th went into an attack. The Lincolns went to their positions over "Valley of Death." Enemy artillery shelled us all day. Our planes came over three times, bombing Gandesa.
>
> Evening, enemy shelled again in "Valley of Death." Place stank with dead Moroccans and Tercios. Enemy shells came over our ridge into valley behind, killing evacuated wounded and men with canteens at the waterhole. Shells screamed directly overhead as we lay against rockwall of a terrace, dropping twenty, thirty, fifty meters away. Hugged wall. As dark came, enemy began to use tracer bullets, the bullets tracing a horseshoe against the sides of the bottle-neck shaped gulley systematically. Bodies stank. Men screaming *"Socorro! Socorro!"* or groaning, *"Madre mía!"* long-drawn out. Kept up all night long, intermittently, with hand-grenades, machine guns, artillery just over the valley. Men dead by the hundreds, mostly the enemy. Millman, commander of the 59th, killed, bullet clean through the head. Frank Stout badly wounded, trench mortar fragments in gut and groin.
>
> Longest day I've ever spent.

On the following night the Lincolns and Fifty-ninth relieved a unit to the north of the road. The four battalions of the Fifteenth were then in line for the first time since the beginning of the campaign. At midnight of August 6, they were relieved in turn by a brigade of the Twenty-seventh Division. Alvah Bessie writes of their march through Corbera:

As we approached the outskirts of the town the stench of the dead nauseated us. There was nothing left of the place. The Fascist aviation had bombed it. There was not a sound as we marched through, except the shuffling of our feet on the broken pavement; the smell of the dead still buried beneath the refuse—women, children, old men— was rotten sweet in the deserted moonlit streets; the shell-like houses cast wide fantastic shadows on the road. No one spoke as we passed through; there were no words to say.

There now began that gigantic battle described by Republican General Rojo as "an unequal and terrible struggle of men against machines, of fortifications against all the elements of destruction, of the media of the air against those of the earth—and of abundance against poverty."

For the first few days, the men simply ate and slept. On the fourth night, they went to the river and swam in its warm waters for hours, not wanting to leave, relaxing in an almost other-worldly atmosphere of night sounds, tepid water, a ghostly moon—and the muted drums of artillery in the distance. Their clothes were cleaned by delousing machines. For a few days, until the lice reasserted their primacy in that domain of war, the men felt quite human.

On August 11, Leonard Lamb came up from Barcelona with Ernst Toller, the famed German poet and reporter, Joseph North of the New York *Daily Worker*, and Daniel Roosevelt, a nephew of the president of the United States, who at that time worked as a correspondent for the *Brooklyn Daily Eagle*. They spent but a short time at brigade headquarters, hiking instead to the Lincoln Battalion Command Post to share a garbanzo stew with the men.

"They spoke for a long time," Rolfe writes,

> the young man [Roosevelt] diffident and casual in his questions, the writer searching, painfully sincere. As they rested, talking with Bessie and the men, as many as twenty-seven bombers flew over the encampment; to be followed by others. Each time the two visitors looked up, calm but apprehensive, past the leaves of the tree into the

*189*

clear sky. . . . The planes returned as the group waited; this time Lamb looked up too, shading his eyes from the sun. Turning quietly to Toller and Roosevelt, he said calmly, "All right, now lay back flat." In a moment there came the horrible, tearing sound and the great rush of air as the bombs fell; then the explosions just beyond the hill to our right. In a few moments they saw the geysers of smoke and dust rise above the crest. "All safe now," Lamb said. "Better get going."

Before Daniel Roosevelt left Spain he would, like Lardner, give all his clothes and personal nonessentials to the Americans in the field and the wounded in the hospitals.

Supplies other than military were generally plentiful now. The Auto Park was doing an effective job despite the rain of bombs. This had not been true in the first days, however. From the third to the eighth day, the brigade had had but six trucks to service all its needs. The lack of transport in this critical period was especially felt by the medical service. William Pike, heading the Fifteenth's medical service, describes the scope of the problems and how they were met:

Late that night July 25, the bridge for heavy transport was finished—munitions and guns first. In the early morning, the Brigade *Sanidad* consisting of two ambulances, a coach, a truck loaded with all the sanitary material and an autobus formed part of that clamoring mass which crowded the road that led in clouds of choking dust to the bridgehead. Hour after anxious hour went by as we cursed the ammo trucks that moved in ahead of us. Then, when the first faint light of day appeared the horrible news filtered back to us—the bridge was broken!

We gave orders for the *sanidad* transport to cross as soon as the bridge was repaired and three of us left to cross over the foot-bridge. Our task seemed hopeless, no possible means of evacuating the wounded, but we had to contact our forces fighting many kilometers ahead.

*Walking,* we reached the "crossroads," where we heard of the advances and the still more relieving news that the troops were resting. We set up a joint ambulance post with the 13th Brigade, sent runners to apprise the battalion doctors of the line of evacuation, and returned to the river. That afternoon the road behind the *Sanidad* post was cut by a battalion of Fascists. Rifle fire cracked all around until they were dispersed or captured.

At the river temporary arrangements were made to ferry the wounded across and additional relays were posted. Still no ambulances! Back to the Brigade!

Our personnel was strung along the road; they were ordered to the established post. Far into the night we trudged along picking up *artolas* [litters to carry the wounded on mules], and mule carts abandoned by the fleeing Fascists. Men were sent to look for mules.

The next afternoon we were able to send our improvised, non-motorized transport into action—*four mules, two carts, three artolas*. Relays of stretcher bearers were sent to places where we had no mules to carry the wounded. All available men were utilized. The Army Corps sent over *one* ambulance. Pitifully inadequate! The wounded kept piling up. All trucks returning from the front were mobilized for the transport of the wounded.

The third day—news that one of our ambulances was being held at the river. No ambulances permitted across the ferry. Loud arguments! Threatened arrest but we got the ambulance across.

The wounded suffered greatly. Hour after hour of riding on heavy trucks which vibrated pain through every fibre of their bodies. Then the terrible waiting at the river in the dusty tunnels, trucks rumbling by raising thick clouds of dust which stifled them, the anxious waiting while the gray Italian and German bombers circled overhead, the constant bombing that tore at their straining nerves. Once the cables of the ferry broke—it was overloaded with wounded—they heard the descending horror of the whistling bombs and they were powerless to move.

These first terrible days were finally over. The line of evacuation was changed, more ambulances arrived, and the wounded could be speedily taken from the front-line medical posts.

On August 7, a small bridgehead across the Ebro in the Mequiñenza-Fayón sector, fell to the enemy. The destruction of this pocket was the first phase of the insurgent counter-offensive; the second phase was then the all-out assault against the Sierra de Pandols. On August 8, two Francoist divisions were hurled against Lister's Fifth Corps. The roar of exploding shells, guns, grenades, machine guns, mortars, and bombs joined in one monstrous cacophony of sound; the resulting carnage, plus the terrible heat of mid-August, obliterated both attacker and attacked. Rebel archives tell of violent assaults and counter-assaults wherein hills of the Pandols changed hands time and again. In the end, no advance could be made without Republican line troops being literally blasted from their positions.

On August 14, with the Fifth Corps decimated and exhausted by the unending inferno (its casualties amounted to between fifty and seventy percent), the Thirty-fifth Division was again ordered into action. The march to the lines, a distance of twelve kilometers, began at early twilight. Bessie describes passing through Pinell:

> then over a steeply uphill path, bounded on one side by a precipitous gorge out of which came the sudden, sickly smell of the dead, and on the other by towering peaks and crags that would have been fantastic even in the daytime. Ahead, muffled by distance, was the sound of artillery in the night.

For the Lincolns there had not been, nor would there ever be, positions quite like those in the Sierra de Pandols. It has been described as a place of precipitous hills—jagged, rocky, bare stone in some places, others covered with scrub oak and pine. But even this simple description belies the truth. Archie Brown, Company 1 commissar, gives his own description:

> We got there at night. There was simply nothing like it. All the terrain was steep and rough. Morning showed a scene of a blackened, war-torn and destroyed land. Dead burros lay everywhere. Bodies were everywhere too. They stank. Everything was burnt to a crisp. All was rock. We couldn't dig in. We piled shale rock for parapets.

And Lawrence Cane of the Mac-Paps writes:

It was one of the most difficult positions we were ever in. First of all, the Goddamn place was almost sheer rock, precipice. We had one mule path as the only point of entrance to the Mac-Pap positions. There was no way of getting vehicles up there at all. They had to stay on the road three or four kilometers to the rear. The mule path came up a deep ravine.

The Pandols had originally been lightly wooded. This cover was now burnt off. When we first arrived, the area was still burning from incendiary bombs. It wasn't possible to dig in. It was solid rock. We couldn't bury the dead. Bodies were everywhere, ours, theirs—all in various stages of decomposition. We stacked them like cordwood. They stank and the smell was hideous.

We wore camphor bags around our necks to counter the smell. We evacuated our own dead. It was impossible to get supplies except at night—water, food, and ammo. We couldn't even evacuate the wounded during the day. Every man had to be hand-carried or taken by mules the three or four kilometers to the ambulances. Men with gut wounds were automatically finished—and this applied to *any* man needing immediate surgery.

The Fifteenth's position was designated Hill 666 on their maps. It was a series of three overlapping hilltops, with the Lincoln Battalion occupying the extreme right, the Canadians the center, and the Fifty-ninth the far left. The British Battalion was in reserve. The Lincoln sector of 666 faced an enemy knoll across a shallow saddle of ground. To the front of the Mac-Paps and the Fifty-ninth, the area of no man's land resembled a great saucer-like valley, sloping upward to the higher, enemy-held ridges.

Lieutenant Donald Thayer's Company 4 was on the Lincoln's right flank. *His* right was simply a precipitous drop of some 200 feet to the Pinell-Gandesa Road. Across the road, reputedly, were units of the Eleventh Thaelmanns.

The first day saw a fruitless attempt to dig in. Sandbags were brought up, but there was nothing to fill them with but rock slivers. The Canadians were heavily bombed in the afternoon. In the midst of the waves of concussion, water and food arrived. The water, laced with iodine and cognac, was warm, and did little to cool the men from the sun's brazen heat or the heat from the bare volcanic rock which burned to the touch.

The Lincolns were slated to attack the knoll at mid-afternoon. At exactly 3:00 P.M., as many as two Republican batteries opened up on the enemy, and five *Chatos* arrived, to strafe for all of ten minutes before retiring. The companies had gathered on the back of the hill to await orders; None came. Instead, the insurgent guns began a sharp reply to the Republican 75s. Their shells first fell on the British in reserve, then crept up the reverse slope of 666 searching for the Lincolns.

Bessie describes the men as simply ignoring this fire:

> We looked around at the hundreds of men, calmly lying there as the explosions moved back up the mountainside toward us; they did not move; they were cleaning their guns or eating or lying on their sides talking, or trying to catch a few winks of sleep.

They attacked that night instead. Companies 1 and 3 spearheaded the movement. Speaking of the plan to attack the knoll, Wolff says that Major Valledor had previously called a meeting of all commanders, during which he proposed that they hold those positions:

> counter-attacking at every opportunity, even if we were cut off. He told us that Brigade was laying in enough food and ammo to stay indefinitely. We simply had to hold. The whole purpose of the Ebro offensive depended on us holding.

The concept of holding can hardly be questioned. The poorly planned organization of the attack, however, is something else. The two companies were simply met with a hosing from many machine guns and were driven in a disorganized rout back to their trenches. The Company 3 commander, García Abad, was killed. Lieutenant Aaron Lopoff of Company 1 was shot through the head, and would die later in hospital at La Sabinosa. Aside from the wounded, many were missing and presumed dead. Bessie writes:

> You couldn't find anyone in the dark. Stretcher bearers had disappeared; the men were all mixed up by squads, sections, and companies; the wrong information, or worse, no information at all, as to the extent of the enemy fortifications.

To compound the original stupidity, the British were brought up and thrown against the knoll just before dawn— with the same results; a hosing of machine guns, the pink explosions of grenades, the weird, ululating chanting of the Moroccans, and the British straggling back in ones and twos, cursing and carrying their wounded. What had begun in the afternoon as a planned attack with some meaningful support—six to eight 75s and a flight of *Chatos*—had degenerated into a foolish and ill-conceived venture.

The men settled in on their rock cliffs. More sandbags were brought up. Barbed wire was strung before all positions. Trenches were literally carved from the stone of the mountain. The four battalions would now await the enemy's move.

The third phase of the counter-offensive began, its front extending from the Pandols to the Heights of Gaeta between Corbera and Villalba de los Arcos. The main drive was directed at these heights. But the right flank of the drive, the Pandols, was also hit hard. More than 600 guns were in line for the Fascist attack, bolstered by complete batteries of 88s. Planes and tanks were thrown in in equal proportion.

The Pandols were hit first, hard! It was a feint, actually, to distract the Government's attention from the chosen area of penetration—Gaeta!

For two days the Fifteenth Lincoln Brigade was subjected to a horrendous bombardment. On the afternoon of the second day the enemy infantry advanced in swarms, and were driven back. The process continued with each attack shattered before the Lincoln parapets. "The attacks against our positions," recalls Cane of the Mac-Paps,

> were constant and general. The pattern would be the following: tremendous artillery—as many guys were killed by shell-blasted rock fragments as by shrapnel—to be followed by infantry. There were two especially heavy attacks in which we slaughtered them. The Brigade did a helluva job in the Pandols. *Lesser troops could never have held.*

Bessie writes:

> They were pounding the shallow lines on the hill crest; with artillery and antitank shells they were hammering away from left to right and back again, and it hurt to watch. They hammered at the lines and the men ran out from behind the parapets, seeking shelter on the bare back of the hill; then they came back to the lines again. They pounded at the same place time and time again, and you would see forms that looked like moving picture dummies rise slowly in the air and fall back again. You knew that they were men.
>
> All day, hour after hour, they kept it up. They covered our parapets and every inch of the backside of the hill. They wanted, by the sheer weight of their steel, to blow us off that hill. Hour in and out they kept it up, and the body was utterly exhausted and indifferent to conscious fear, but straining to the snapping point. There was sweat and there was internal pain; the word "waiting" came to mean something more than it had meant before, for you were definitely waiting for them to find you and to finish you. . . . The boys in the trenches were hammered, their rock parapets smashed down; there were many wounded; many killed; many missing. There was no connection with the Battalion, and you twisted the handle of the field-set just the same, knowing that you would not get an answer.
>
> The pauses were worse than the shelling, before and after, waiting for them to cool their guns. When they are dropping the mind is impersonal even if the body is not, but waiting for them to begin again. . . . A fly is attracted to your bloody hands and you think, "At least you're safe,

you louse," and laugh. Dry lips, rising gorge, sweat, and shaking limbs. You look at your hands, filthy and covered with the blood of two men who have finally been taken— where?

For six hours no word from the Battalion, no connection; and then, coming up through the bursts of fire there are two men, one of them bent with the weight of a spool of wire on his back, reeling it out across the bare *barranca*. Orders. You speak calmly, trying to keep your voice even and level: "What's happening up there?" "They're throwing the shit all around." "Keep a few men in the lines and let the others seek what cover they can find; the Mac-Paps are extending their lines toward your left flank; the British are coming up with reenforcements. In the event of an attack, put all the men back in the line, get up munitions now!" That is Wolff's voice speaking, a young man who is not here.

The attack came in the early twilight. The artillery had lifted. The Lincoln machine guns, what there was left of them, opened up. The men stood up in the shallow trenches and hurled grenades. The attack was beaten off. Bessie writes that the next day,

> it began again about ten in the morning; not quite as intense, but much more accurate. Their batteries pounded our parapets viciously with shell after shell and mortars, smashing them to pieces. The men ran out, sought shelter and returned; the Fascists advanced under cover of the barrage, and received hand grenades for a reception. They withdrew and our morale rose visibly—and audibly. Archie [Brown] had the men singing *The Star Spangled Banner* in the lines—and the barrage began again.

The Abraham Lincoln Batallion's defense of Hill 666, amidst the welter of their dead and their destroyed trenches, is one of only a few examples of such heartfelt courage and patriotism that exist in the annals of American military history.

On August 25, the brigade was relieved by units of the famed Spanish Forty-third Division. The brigade had not given an *inch* to the attackers. Indeed, the trenches were now cut deep into the solid rock and were faced with excellent parapets and lines of barbed wire. It had also left in shallow graves some of its finest veterans, among them the now-legendary Joe Bianca.

Bianca, commanding a section of two heavy Maxims, had been mortally wounded by a direct hit on one of the gun positions. "Bianca asked me," Wolff relates, "if he was going to make it. He was in great pain." Bianca's last moments, his stomach and groin laid open by shrapnel, were similar to those of the famed British Major, George Nathan, at Brunete. Wolff, a friend of Bianca's from the first days, told the men not to move him any further. Then he and the battalion officers, and those of Bianca's comrades who had carried him off the hill, stayed with him until he died.

Britt Webster, writing in the *Voice of the Federation*, organ of the Sailors Union of the Pacific, expressed his feelings about a brother seaman frankly:

> Joe Bianca was a Communist. As a Communist he first fought for union organization where there was none. As a Communist he fought for unions to be controlled by the membership rather than any clique. As a Communist he advocated unity of all workers, regardless of affiliation, and as a Communist he advocated resistance to Fascism and proved his sincerity by giving his life in a real and meaningful defense of democracy.

For those susceptible to the anti-communist syndrome, it should be known that another close friend of Bianca's, a man who helped carry him from the line, was Kenneth Shaker. Shaker, an avowed *anti*-communist, was the elected political commissar of Bianca's platoon.

The Fifteenth International Brigade was cited by both the Thirty-fifth Division and the Fifth Army Corps for its stubborn defense of Hill 666. The Lincoln Battalion was given special recognition for its role in the fighting. The insurgent General Galera of the Eighty-fourth Division writes that Hill 666 was the *key* to the Pandols. The Lincoln Brigade had occupied it for ten of its most brutal and critical days.

The fourth phase of the counter-offensive was directed

against Corbera, to cut off the Fatarella-Camposines Road. It began with the rebel General García Valiño, driving south and east with four divisions and Yagüe north and east, with two. They were confronted only by the Eleventh of Lister, the Thirty-fifth of Tagüena, the Forty-third of Beltrán, and the Twenty-seventh. Each had been in the fight since the beginning, and had as yet received no reinforcements.

Division after fresh rebel division was hurled into the melée. A second attempt against the heights of Gaeta used 600 guns, 150 tanks, and 300 planes in a single assault, which was again thrown back by the Twenty-seventh Division and the Twelfth International (Garibaldi) Brigade.

On that same evening, September 3, correspondents of Western newspapers filed copy in Barcelona to the effect that the opening barrages of this new phase could be heard in Barcelona, at a distance of 150 kilometers! They would file similar reports throughout the defense of the arc of the Ebro.

To describe the ensuing weeks as anything but a monstrous hour-on-hour holocaust of steel and explosives would be to deny reality. It is estimated by *all* sources that the insurgent army expended no less than 1,250,000 shells in the hundred days of the Battle of the Ebro. The historian Hugh Thomas writes that each day also saw the dropping of 10,000 bombs, and all of this within an area of twenty-by-thirty kilometers. The Republican General Vicente Rojo writes:

> There was no "art" to it; what there was was actually the application of the new "science of *aplastamiento*"—the total crushing of an enemy by a weight of steel and explosives—and under conditions wherein he cannot reply.

With the slogan *Resistir es vencer* ("To resist is to win"), the Army of the Ebro dug in rapidly and desperately in a race against time. Lines of trenches were constructed in depth. Lines and lines of barbed wire were strung before these positions. Literally thousands of machine gun nests were created, whether there were guns for them or not. There was to be no breakthrough in the accepted sense. If a line were lost, there would be another 300 meters to the rear—and behind that another and another.

And in the skies, above the cauldron of flame and ear-splitting cadenzas, the Republican air force—it was all Spanish now—would go freely into that most unequal of struggles. The little green *Chatos* and Moscas would dip their stubby wings over the embattled trenches in salute to their comrades below. They would then rise in their coveys of sixes to pit their diminishing strength against the swarms of Fiats, Heinkels, and Messerschmidts. And they would win, with losses of three to one in the Republic's favor. But, like their comrades on the ground, their victories would be hollow, for the Fiats would be replaced on the morrow—and the *Chatos*, never.

Until the final battles of mid-November, the enemy, for all its weight of steel, would advance just two kilometers toward Pinell, eight in the direction of Camposines, and four toward Fatarella.

The fourth phase, however, did expose the political climate of the day. The battle now was openly on two fronts: in the arc of the Ebro and in the chancellories of Europe! Spain's and the world's fate would hang in the balance.

European Fascism, as represented by the Axis powers of Italy and Germany, was agressive, dynamic. It was the means, perhaps the answer, to controlling the peoples of Europe. Or so reasoned important sections of Europe's power elite. It was no accident; therefore, that the rearming of Germany and Italy went unopposed. Indeed, the very process had been underwritten by the banking interests of Europe and the United States! The House of Morgan advanced loans of more than 100 million dollars to Mussolini; Dillon Read and Company and the Chase National Bank of New York did as much for Fritz Thyssen in the financing of Hitler's regime; and the list went on.

The results? Every pact born of the League of Nations, from Versailles to Locarno, was in shreds. The creation of new military blocs was instantly followed by the incorporation of the Saar into the body of Nazi Germany, the invasion and seizure of Ethiopia by Italy, the annexation of Austria, the moves toward Danzig and the Polish Corridor—and the ongoing, open invasion of the Spanish Republic by divisions of the Axis armies.

Indeed, on September 6, 1938, Adolf Hitler demanded the immediate ceding of the Sudeten areas of Czechoslovakia to the Third Reich. *The Czechs, however, had dared to refuse!* Forty Czech divisions, the finest in central Europe, were actually moving to challenge the Nazi armies. At this, Hitler ordered the Wehrmacht to the Czech and French borders, and *France ordered her armies to the Maginot line!*

It was then, at that critical moment in world history and with the fate of humankind itself in the balance, that England's conservative leadership committed the final perfidy. Neville Chamberlain, prime minister, dispatched Lord Runciman to Czechoslovakia with orders to Czech President Benes to withdraw the forty divisions and to negotiate the surrender of the Sudeten lands.

But Benes refused again. Indeed, he threw down the gauntlet of war to Nazi Germany, outlawed the Nazi Party in Czechoslovakia, and declared martial law in all the border provinces. That very night Karl Heinlein, *fuehrer* to the Sudeten Germans, fled the country—and on that very night the prime minister of England, hat in hand, flew obsequiously to Berchtesgaden to meet with Adolf Hitler.

And in the arc of the Ebro, on September 6, the Abraham Lincoln Brigade was again ordered into the maelstrom. Captain Radomir Smerka, Fifteenth Brigade chief of information, a Czech who had been wounded twelve times and who spoke excellent English, recorded the following:

> *Sept. 6th:* We are standing by. A hectic night. The enemy continues his pressure, accompanied by a tremendous concentration of fire. Counted more than a hundred Fascist planes in the air. Front has been boiling since dawn.
>
> Finally our orders. We are to move in immediately to prevent a threatened breach. Within twenty minutes the Brigade is on its way. To get there faster we are using *camiones*—eight trucks going back and forth on the shell-swept highways, picking up the marching men and depositing them closer to the lines.
>
> The enemy pressure increases. Shells are bursting all over and the Fascist planes are continuously overhead and

bombing. There is considerable excitement in the staff. The troops of another unit, unable to hold any longer, gave way, permitting the Fascists to advance. The Lincoln Battalion is rushed into the breach and succeeds in stopping the Fascists. A small advance on a narrow sector—This has been the result so far of the much-heralded "decisive offensive on the Ebro."

A day later, the lines holding, the Lincolns moved to another threatened point at some distance from the road, and into a long and narrow ravine. A command post was established and Companies 1 and 4 spread to the south on low flanking hills. Lieutenant Luke Hinman writes that: "That night the Brigade scouts went out to check the ridge ahead of us and a big black bitch [hill] beyond. Their report was that the hill was not occupied."

Upon which Wolff ordered Wheeler's Company 3, with seventy men remaining, to occupy and hold it. Jerry Cook, a veteran of Brunete, and a platoon commander of Company 3, writes:

> We moved into position at night. Directly in front of us was a hill occupied by the enemy. To our rear-left was a much higher hill.
>
> Shortly after our arrival a night attack was launched against that hill. All night we watched the flashes of grenades and machine guns, measuring the route of the Fascist advance. It was obvious to all of us that if they reached the top we would be outflanked and in the soup. The battle ended before dawn. The enemy was now behind us. Larry Lustgarten was sent to Battalion H.Q. to report, and to get the order for us to get the hell out of there.

Herman (Gabby) Klein continues:

> When the sun arose we could see no one to left or right. Firing was sporadic, some of it coming from behind. We were outflanked. The firing increased in intensity from both front and rear.
>
> I infiltrated across the crest of our hill, yelling to Wheeler: "We're being attacked from the rear!" At this point they were actually coming up the left-rear slope

carrying red and gold flags. They were coming en masse. The occupied hill to our front opened up with heavy fire to pin us down so we couldn't fight off the attack. Some of our guys replied to the guns across the valley, others fired into the oncoming Fascists causing considerable casualties. But they came on and they were yelling: "Surrender! Put up a white flag!" A Spanish sergeant, one of ours, waved a white rag and yelled that he was surrendering, upon which Tom Paige [back with the Battalion with his Villalba wound unhealed] shot him. The Fascists continued to swarm up the hill. One of our guys, Abe Cohen, turned full around from firing toward the front and shot the standard bearer through the head, and a second man who reached for the falling flag.

I was with Wheeler now. We had found a light machine gun but no ammo pan. Larry Lustgarten came along the spine of the hill yelling for everyone to evacuate—"Go! Go! Go!"

The Fascists were now in our trenches. There was hand-to-hand fighting everywhere. An officer grabbed Harry Hurst. Hurst smashed him in the face and made it over the parapets. He was shot five times, but he got away.

In the ensuing free-for-all, few Americans escaped. Klein and Wheeler, carrying Hurst, Jerry Cook, Thomas Paige, Abe Cohen, Norman Berkowitz, and the commissar, Lustgarten, were all who made it to safety. Cook writes:

It was like running a gauntlet. I ran behind Gabby, and to close my mind to the firing coming at us from three sides, I concentrated on the bullets tearing into his old trench-coat which streamed out behind him as he ran.

Wolff was waiting at the top of the ravine. He ordered Dave Smith of Company 4 to advance with a section of men. But Smith was shot down at the rise of the first terrace and Wolff ordered the section to withdraw.

Radomir Smercka's entries in his diary for the next days read as follows:

*Sept. 8:* At 1400 hours, the enemy starts a new attack following an intense artillery preparation. I go to the lines to lead the Mackenzie-Papineau Battalion into position. I hold a meeting with the Battalion officers while John Gates meets with the commissars. We are under fire. A shell lands near Gates, wounding one of the commissars. The meeting continues.

The Mac-Paps go forward in a brilliant attack, reoccupying positions that had been taken by the enemy.

The enemy artillery concentrates on the Mac-Paps but they continue their advance, although the promised flank support fails to materialize. They advance a full kilometer and reoccupy a large commanding hill—one of the most important heights dominating the Gandesa-Corbera road. This Mac-Pap counter-assault [keeps] the entire Fascist front from advancing. The Brigade is doing an excellent job. The Lincolns, the 59th, and the Mac-Paps have all retaken the positions designated in a brilliant manner and are holding fast. The Fascists attack with tanks, but we hold our ground. Four tanks are turned back by rifle fire alone.

*Sept. 9:* A 15.5 shell lands right in front of the Brigade staff. Dunbar is again wounded, fifteen fragments in face, chest and leg. He refuses to be evacuated and puffs calmly on a cigarette while his wounds are dressed. Three deserters from the Fascist lines are brought to me for interrogation and they are rather interesting, different from the usual "we-only-receive-one-can-of-sardines-a-week" type.

Their first answer to the routine question, "How did you get over here?" is very interesting. They came over through the *Cotas de las viudas, huérfanos y novias* is their answer—through the Hills of the Widows, Orphans, and Sweethearts.

This is a new one to us. We have never heard of these hills. They explain. These are the hills where our positions lie. They have lost so many men attacking them that the name [has] become natural.

Lawrence Cane, who at that point had advanced to machine gun company commander of the Canadians, says this of the Caballs:

We came into the Caballs, actually, during an infantry attack. We moved into positions with units of the 13th

Brigade. Together we threw the Fascists back with extremely heavy losses. We had so many machine guns in the line the Fascists didn't know what hit them—dead all over the place. The Fascists retreated with their flags in wild confusion. We remained in the Caballs a week or so. The positions we created were excellent; deep trenches, heavy bunkers, and so on.

The ensuing days witnessed attack after attack beaten off and the enemy frustrated in all its attempts. Nevertheless, like the Lincolns and British, the American veterans of the Canadian Battalion were dying one by one. Dead in the Caballs were the Company 4 commander, George Carbonel, the last of three brothers, the young Company 1 commissar, Wade Ellis, and the much-loved Company 2 commander, James Hill. All had fought through from their first entry into battle with the tank attack at Fuentes del Ebro. Hill was from Oklahoma City. Like Joe Bianca, he had been in so many battles he'd been considered indestructible.

The Caballs held fast, though Corbera itself fell to the Thirteenth Division of Barrón. A single hill, 343, changed hands four times in one afternoon, as the defending Spanish soldiers fought tenaciously against the sheer mass and ferocity of the rebel onslaught.

On September 13, the brigade was again relieved—to be told by the Spanish government that the long-rumored withdrawal of all International volunteers from military service was fast approaching. Also, Spanish newspapers delivered to the battalions at rest—the influential *La Vanguardia* (Republican), *Solidaridad Obrero* (Socialist), and *Frente Rojo* (Communist)—all proclaimed the crisis of the still unresolved Axis gambit in Czechoslovakia.

On September 16, President Benes was simply *ordered* by England and France to surrender unconditionally all of the Sudeten areas with their mountain defenses. Benes was told that he could expect no help from either country if he ignored their demands.

*All of Spain watched with intense emotion!*

The Fifteenth moved nearer the front again. Correspondents Herbert Matthews and Vincent Sheean, together with a number of others from Western newspapers, came up to visit the bivouac area, to share briefly with the men the omnipresent peril of the guns in the near distance and the bombings, and to view the constant dogfights overhead.

The appearance of the volunteers at the end of the second month of the campaign—flesh blackened by the sun, faces ingrained with the earth of trenches and a thousand foxholes, eyes that bespoke the weariness of the combat soldier—gave witness to all that had transpired, the Aragón, Teruel, the retreats, and now the Ebro.

The men were friendly to the correspondents, but, except for Matthews, Hemingway, and Sheean, whom they regarded as their own, they and the reporters were worlds apart.

Phase five of the Francoist counter-offensive, already underway, had been launched against Government forces increasingly incapable of a strong defense. Along the entire length of line, the Republican divisions that were already legend were dying. Attrition, when translated into the simple terms of flesh and blood against so many thousands of tons of bombs and so many salvos of shells, was the grimmest of reapers. That the Army of the Ebro could hold at all in the face of the juggernaut that would soon claim all of Europe seemed a miracle of the Spanish people.

In the early dawn of September 18, as if to implement the Nazi demands upon the Czechs, the full weight of the rebel armies were thrown against the defenses of the Corbera Road on a front of but five kilometers. The objective: to smash through to Venta de los Camposines, and to then drive south and east, outflanking the Pandols and the Caballs. The defending Republican troops in the sector were the Forty-fifth International Division and brigades of the Spanish Twenty-seventh and Forty-third Divisions. Needless to say, in the ensuing tornado of shells and bombs and men, the Republican units, down to one-third of their strength, were stunned and shattered. Those who had held in the Pandols, at Gaeta, and at Girondeses, had already given their life's blood. The decimated Eleventh Thaelmann Brigade was thrown in on the northern flank and came under immediate attack. Battalions of the Thirteenth Dombrowskis, too, were then moved up. And finally, amidst a sea of explosives, the Fifteenth International Abraham Lincoln Brigade was ordered into what would be its final battle.

On the afternoon of September 22, the Lincoln Battalion moved to reserve positions directly behind the front. The British, preceding the Americans, moved into trenches still partly occupied by remnants of a Polish battalion. The Mac-Paps, too, though coming up later than the Lincolns, were positioned to the left of the British. The line-up, then, for the morning of the twenty-third, was the Canadians and the British—with the latter's right flank anchored to the south of the Corbera Road—the Lincolns in reserve, and the Fifty-ninth in active reserve as the left flank of the Forty-fifth Division.

The day of September 22 had borne witness to a number of untoward events. All of Barcelona's newspapers, for example, carried Premier Juan Negrín's announcement, before the League of Nations at Geneva, that every foreign volunteer was to be removed from the front lines without delay and repatriated as soon as a League commission could reach Spain to oversee the job.

The big decision had been made!

Edwin Rolfe left Barcelona with all the papers he could carry, and headed for the Ebro. Crossing the river in the late afternoon, he was told that the men were already in action, even though they knew of the withdrawal orders. "As early as the nineteenth," according to Alvah Bessie, "the battalions were blazing with rumors of our imminent departure." Whatever the circumstances of the decision, and although efforts had been made to conceal it from the men, there wasn't one of them who didn't know of it—and who didn't want to survive that last day.

On September 22, Neville Chamberlain again met with Hitler, this time at Godesberg, where Der Fuehrer demanded additional Czech territory—in effect, partition, demobilization, the destruction of Czechoslovakia and its armies.

Again the Czechs refused. This time they called for general mobilization. Hitler then let it be known that the German army would be fully mobilized by September 28. At this, the Soviet Union informed President Benes that even if Britain and France failed in their declared commitments under mutual treaties, Russia was prepared to come to Czechoslovakia's aid.

On the Ebro the battle raged. In the early twilight an officer of the Thirteenth Dombrowskis appeared at Captain Wolff's command post: "The lines," he said, "are breaking. You must come immediately!"

Wolff hastily assembled the companies and moved quickly to the aid of the Poles. They crossed the Corbera Road to the north, where the day-long battle had been most ferocious, making for a group of low-lying hills across a flat plain. That it was twilight, a condition of poor visibility for enemy artillery observers, greatly aided their movement. The companies had deployed in open, artillery formation, and well they did, since they came under observation and were subjected immediately to a searching fire. Shells fell everywhere. One source describes them as "going through the barrage at a dead run."

The hill they had occupied was 281 on the map. The Lincolns left flank was anchored on the road, across which was the British Battalion. Their right flank sloped down to a section of plain to the north. The men dug in, strengthening the shell-shattered emplacements.

Harold Smith, having gone to the rear to organize food and munitions details, found James Lardner there with Sam Nahman and a half-dozen others who had just returned from the hospital. Nahman went off to the Mac-Paps, Lardner and the others to the Lincolns. There began the series of events leading to Lardner's death.

On Smith's return, he was ordered by Wolff to check out Company 4, which was thought to be temporarily lost somewhere on the right flank. Smith went off in that direction. He didn't find Company 4, but he did find the remnants of a Polish company in a blasted trench section. Unaware of the Lincolns' presence, and thinking themselves cut off, they had vowed not to surrender. They were prepared to die there; they expected no help. They were mostly Polish and Palestinian Jews, a part of the Botwin company attached to the crack

Polish Palafox battalion. The knowledge that they had been relieved, says Smith, was like a reprieve from death.

Smith then ran into James Lardner, who had been sent out by Lieutenant Dick Rusciano to contact Spanish troops—also thought to be on the right flank. Smith and Lardner, noticing a hill to the north and west, continued toward it. Approaching quietly, they heard voices and the sounds of entrenching tools. Smith assumed that the hill was enemy occupied, since entrenching tools for the Lincolns had as yet not come up. They returned to the battalion.

In the meantime, Company 4 had been found echeloned somewhat to the rear and, as assumed, on the right flank. Lardner, heading up a three-man patrol, then went back to the hill in question, to check it further. Jerry Cook writes:

> After an interval we heard machine gun and rifle fire and saw bursting grenades in the vicinity of the hill. Nowakowsky [the second member of the patrol; the third was Spanish], returned in a couple of hours alone. He reported that proceeding in the darkness they had heard voices. Lardner instructed the others to remain while he checked them out. A few minutes later firing broke out, and grenades. The young Spaniard was instantly killed. After waiting a considerable time for Lardner's return, Nowakowski made it back to our positions. We do not know whether Lardner was killed outright, or captured and then executed. The next morning, the twenty-third, we paid dearly for that open gap to our right.

In his article "Somebody Had to Do Something," Ring Lardner, Jr. writes of his brother's death:

> Weeks later Ernest Hemingway, seeking definite confirmation of Jim's death, learned through a correspondent with the Fascists that a corpse had been found on that battlefield with press credentials. We never received any more definite confirmation than that. He was among the last losses, perhaps the very last of the American forces in Spain.

After that, according to Sidney Levine,

DEATH IN THE OLIVE GROVES

there was a meeting of all company commanders: Pappas, Thayer, Rusciano, Lancer and myself. Wolff informed us that, "I just got a call from Gates. We've got to hold for just one more day. You get it?—*One more day!*" By morning everyone knew what was going to happen. That last day was one son-of-a-bitch!

Lawrence Cane, also commenting on the general awareness of the Negrín decision, says, "The men knew of the withdrawal order. The last day was psychologically very bad. Everyone wanted to live."

The morning of September 23 began with a large flight of Republican planes, as many as eighteen, the most the brigaders had seen for some time. They swept back and forth over the brigade front, pinwheeling and strafing the rebel trenches. Simultaneously, shells from a nearby Republican battery began a sporadic but accurate fire. The rebel artillery unlimbered and began to reply, their salvos mounting in number as new batteries opened up. Their guns soon switched to the Fifteenth's trenches, and high explosives lashed back and forth along the lines of the four battalions. It was soon obvious from the intensity of the shelling that an attack of some strength was coming. Rolfe writes:

> The insurgents did not begin their heavy work until a few minutes before ten o'clock. But when they started, they unloosed hell over the entire sector. Their planes came over in waves all day long, some bombing, others strafing the lines. Once, in an excess of zeal and a slight miscalculation, they dropped an entire load on their own positions. Their rapid-fire batteries never ceased for long, transforming the hills and valleys into a landscape of flying metal and huge, low-hanging clouds of smoke and dust."

The barrage is estimated to have come from as many as a hundred guns. The ensuing events are best seen through the eyes of the participants. Arthur Munday, adjutant to Donald Thayer of Company 4 (Munday would be wounded for the *fifth* time in this last engagement), says that to the right flank the barrage was tremendous and shattering. In the middle of it, a Polish lieutenant came running along the crest of Company 4's hill:

> He pointed a hundred yards to our rear to another small hill, and told me he was going to set up his guns there. He had some Spaniards with him and twelve Poles. Some of our Spaniards joined him—all was confusion. Captain Lamb was hit again, shrapnel in the neck. Lots of shrapnel casualties among our Spaniards.

Thayer, on the other hand, states that other than the barrage, his company was not under frontal attack; that as the fighting progressed, he was ordered to fall back by Jack Egan of the battalion staff. This was accomplished in good order, with a tight control of the company.

Nevertheless, all data points to the right flank of the Lincolns as the breakthrough area of the oncoming waves of insurgent infantry. Jerry Cook describes the battle thusly:

> All morning their guns were trained right into our trenches. By noon, or later, there were only a handful of men left in Rusciano's company on the extreme right, which was the prime target of the attack. Most of these had only side-arms left, the rifles and M.G.'s having been smashed by shell-fire. When the Fascists and some Moroccans appeared advancing from the right and *rear*, the line crumbled. Those on the far right retreated directly to a hill to their rear. The rest of the Battalion, pushed out of their positions in a running battle, with the enemy swarming down the trench line, fell back across the Corbera road and into a long ravine paralleling the road.

Lieutenant Sidney Levine recalls:

> The shelling really started then, with heavy bombing too. Jerry Cook peered into our dugout from time to time; then suddenly we heard Jack Hoshooley and Cook yelling that they were coming [the Fascists]. I ran to my mortar crews yelling, *"Tirar! Tirar!"* ["Fire! Fire!"]. One Spaniard

wrapped his legs around his mortar and was firing as fast
as he could—straight at the oncoming enemy. Still, many
men were falling back. Jerry Cook had a man wounded in
both legs and was carrying him. Suddenly there was no
one around but myself and the mortar crew. After a year
and a half of carrying a pistol, I was using it for the first
time—firing point-blank at Moors who had broken into
our trench section. I yelled again to the mortar crew to
leave, and Jack Hoshooley came up and I yelled "Jack! Get
out of here!" We made it back through bursts of fire to new
positions where Hoshooley and I took over a Tuckeroff
from a young Spanish crew and turned it on our erstwhile
trenches.

Jerry Cook continues:

The position we now occupied was a poor one, and it
was clear that when the enemy finished knocking out the
British and turned back to us, we wouldn't have much of a
chance. Sitting in our hastily prepared lines we watched
the attack proceed across the road, heartsick at what
we saw.

To Milton Wolff, the limited retreat was simply, "The most
painful part of my whole period in Spain."

The British were indeed in serious trouble; so were the
Canadians. Rebel war journals of the Thirteenth Rebel Divi-
sion list those attacking the Fifteenth Brigade at that precise
moment as the Fifth and Sixth Tabors of Mellila, the Third
(Vitoria) Battalion, and the Fourth and Sixth Banderas of the
Foreign Legion.

Tanks now moved through the abandoned Lincoln positions
to attack the British. Two were knocked out on the road.
Another three succeeded in penetrating to the rear of the British and Mac-Paps. Artillery in profusion lashed the lines again,
obliterating in many places the defending trenches. The
majority of the British guns were quickly knocked out. Lieutenant Cane of the Mac-Pap machine gun company ordered a
heavy Maxim crew led by Butch Goldstein, a veteran of the
first days, to the aid of the British. Butch's crew wasthe only
one that spoke English; the others were either Finns or Span-

iards. He and his crew arrived just in time for the second attack. Cane describes the Mac-Paps' effort to hold:

> Battalion was in position. Harry Schoenberg, Matti Matison [Brigade staff officer], a Spanish *carabinero* captain being groomed for battalion commander. Tremendous artillery barrage began at nine or ten in the morning. Stayed in position until two or three in the afternoon. Fascist tanks broke through then—three in the Mac-Pap area. These got between the Mac-Paps and the British and got to our rear.

Maury Colow, a New Yorker and a Mac-Pap platoon leader of Company 2, remembers:

> Artillery, mortars, machine guns; all hell broke loose. Guys everywhere bleeding from nose and mouth; concussion awful—chewed on twigs [to lessen the force of it]. Lieutenant Henry Mack, Company 2, was ordered to leave the hill by Battalion. Fascist tanks coming through on both flanks, right and left. British were under heavy assault on the right—grenades going off. Most of our guns were knocked out by artillery. The Fascists were swarming into the trenches. Hand-to-hand fighting. A lot of Canadians killed—and a lot of Fascists. Three of the company staff killed there too. I fell back with Henry Mack, Lieutenant Jiménez, and the company commissar, who had been shot through the knee. Others were trying to fall back too and we were running a gauntlet of tank and machine gun fire. We reached a second line where a number of guys were setting up guns. We were instantly and heavily bombed but we managed to hold.

Lawrence Cane continues:

> Battalion H.Q. retreated. Our orders were to hold at all costs—but—the Thirteenth had been driven back, then the Lincolns, then the British. The British had lost their hill, a low-lying one about two hundred meters to our right front. We had sent Butch there and had seen his position overun.

Tanks were attacking again from the rear. We hit them with two heavy M.G.s. Drove them toward the road. Two of them made it. We disabled the third. The two tanks moved back through the British positions. Only the Mac-Paps were holding! We—Harry Schoenberg, Matti Matison, the Spanish captain and myself—decided to continue wearing our insignia. We never expected to survive, but we would stand and go out like men.

On the third attack-wave the Fascist infantry broke through and into our remaining positions. They were just twenty-five yards away and we were firing with light machine guns and pistols—succeeded in driving some of them back. But Canadians were dropping all around and we were now too few. We had no choice but to make a break for it.

Cane survived, as did many of the staff. The four battalions—the Fifty-ninth had been mainly in reserve—had retreated at best but 500 yards.

In the hours before dawn, September 24, 1938, men of the famed Forty-sixth Division arrived to relieve the Fifteenth International Brigade. The skeleton Lincoln companies then moved silently onto the road for the last march to the bridges of the Ebro. El Campesino's men, knowing that these *foreigners* had fought their last battle on Spanish soil, offered *abrazos* and handclasps and softly spoken words of thanks and friendship. They asked the Lincoln men—the Americans, Canadians, British, and Latin-Americans—to return again, when Spain was free and at peace. And the volunteers said they would and gave away their cigarettes and other things they would no longer need.

"Waiting at the Brigade Command Post," writes Alvah Bessie, "we heard the marching feet, the shuffling feet, dragging on the road, moving toward the river. It was a slow shuffle; there were no voices; there was no singing."

The war, for the Americans and other Internationals, was over. The roar of artillery, the flights of bombers overhead, would no longer concern them in exactly the same way. By a decree of the Spanish government, reflecting a humanism that refused to allow the remnants of those who had given so generously of their blood and lives to be led to the final slaughter, they were soldiers of the Republic no longer. They would be repatriated by the League of Nations. *They were going home!*

To be immersed in war at its lowest, most murderous, and brutal level, and to then be suddenly free of it is in itself a trauma. That which the volunteers had come to do had yet to be concluded; still, after almost two years of war they were going home! There was hardly a man who did not want this, and understandably so. But many, like Milton Wolff, confess to a certain sadness. "I never felt right about leaving," he says. "I had signed up for the end, and I wasn't prepared, psychologically, to leave."

The Lincolns moved to a nameless valley, the other battalions, likewise. For the Mac-Paps, the third night brought an additional measure of cheer. As they ate a dinner of garbanzos and mule-meat in the gathering dusk, their valley rang with a long, drawn-out shout: "*Comidaaas! Comidaaas! Comidaaas!*" (Food! Food! Food!). The shouter was Butch Goldstein, whom everyone thought had been killed in the last bloody minutes of action on the British hill.

Others would not return. The dead of the campaign were ever present in the minds of the survivors: men who had fought at Jarama, such as Paul Wendorf, who had lived through so much only to die in the last days in an aerial bombing; Jack Freeman and William Sachs of New York, veterans of Brunete, both killed in the Caballs; Herbert Schlessinger and Felix Salter; Thomas O'Flaherty and Eugene Collins; Archie Kessner, who had been with the Mac-Paps since its first days, and who, in almost the last hour of action, was struck down by the Fascist steel. "I was beginning to think they would never get me," he said, and died moments later.

As on most of the major battlefields of the Spanish war, there are small markers in the Pandols and Caballs denoting the graves of the many American dead, among them Joe Bianca, Jim Hill, and John Cookson. Cookson, a mathematics instructor at the University of Wisconsin before coming to Spain, commanded the Lincoln Transmissions; he too was killed in the last days. Years later, Abraham Copeland, visiting Catalonia, found Cookson's headstone "erected at an uncultivatable spot near the country road leading to our billet near Marsa." The inscription on the stone read: "John Cookson, Sgt. Transmissions, 15th Brigade, August, 1938." Copeland reports that the stone, "had a few patches of moss on it. The ground had been weeded. Flowers had been deposited there from time to time. It was a treasured possession in the village."

While awaiting the arrival of a League commission to oversee evacuation, officers made preparations to move the men closer to the French border. Archie Brown and Howard Goddard went ahead to arrange billets with the officials of the town of Ripoll. Some men were already there, since Americans from hospitals and other units in the process of disbandment were being sent directly home rather than to Marsa or Falset. Rolfe writes:

> Then one day the final official episode in the history of the Americans in the Battalions took place. While twenty-five government planes were locked in combat with fifty-five enemy chasers, some directly overhead and others over a wide sky area to the west, the four companies of the Lincolns lined up in the football field at Marsa . . .
> The orders were simple: all Internationals were to fall out of the ranks and re-form in one group in a far corner of the field. As the order was given, the Americans stepped out. Wolff and Commissar Watt turned over their posts to their successors, two young Spanish officers who had been trained by the Americans. The Lincoln Battalion, for the first time in its history, was now completely Spanish.
> I counted the Americans as they lined up to be photographed against a terrace wall at one corner of the field. Officers and men, *there were sixty-one in all.*

Similar "last parades" took place in the other three battalions, and in each the number of British, Canadian, and Latin- and Spanish-Americans slated to go home hardly equaled the thinned ranks of the Lincolns.

*  *  *

Alarmed at the Czechoslovakians' will to fight, and their preparations to do exactly that, Prime Minister Chamberlain, together with Mussolini, arranged one last meeting with Hitler at Munich, on September 29, 1938. Within an embarrassing few hours, Chamberlain, Daladier, Hitler, and Mussolini had agreed to a pact depriving the Czechs of twenty-nine percent of their territory, thirty-four percent of their population, and their forty splendid divisions.

Benes was forced to acquiesce. But Jan Masaryk, Czech foreign minister, when given the ultimatum by Chamberlain and Lord Halifax, said quietly: "If you have sacrificed my nation to preserve the peace of the world, I will be the first to applaud you. . . . But if not, gentlemen, then God help your souls."

The Spanish war, which had endured for over two years of blood and horror, would continue for another six months. Its final tally would be one million dead. No one recalling the infamy at Munich can fail to remember Spain and the saga of a people who stood alone on the field of battle, in absolute confrontation with European fascism, while Austria was surrendered, while Czechoslovakia was given away, and while the first of the Italian *Bersaglieri* were landing on the coast of Albania.

Far from removing the danger of world conflagration, the signers of the Munich Pact had in fact made it inevitable. The bombs that fell on Madrid would now fall on Paris and London. Czechoslovakia would be invaded, partitioned, and utterly destroyed even before the Spanish Republic fell, right in the face of the cringing Chamberlain. Within weeks, the shouts for Memel, for Danzig, for Tunisia, for Corsica, and even for sections of the French Riviera would ring above the cadence of marching feet and the roar of tanks.

The high point before the Americans' final departure from Spain was the Republic's farewell to the International Brigades in Barcelona. The date was October 29, 1938; the time, 4:30 P.M. The line of march was down the length of the wide *Diagonal* to the reviewing stand on which stood Premier Negrín and his War Cabinet. Planes flew overhead to guard against attack. Hundreds of thousands of people jammed the curbs and sidelines. According to reliable sources, there never was, nor has there been since, a parade in Barcelona to match the cheers, the warmth, the plaudits, and the *tears* of that one.

There were perhaps 2,000 Internationals marching, all who were capable of doing so, gathered from the hospitals and dissolved units. There were as many as 200 to 300 Americans, led by Wolff, Gates, Thayer, Lamb, Watt, and Goddard. "We cleaned up like we never had before," Lieutenant Will Carroll writes, "And we never marched better in our lives."

Wolff says, "We were never what you call very good at parade marching, and when we got on those streets with flowers up to our ankles, I guess we did a kind of shag. It was a pretty good show."

Edwin Rolfe writes that none of the marchers drew as much applause as the Americans.

> It was the most thrilling sight, we agreed, that we had ever seen. The planes flew overhead, dipping recklessly above the heads of the hundreds of thousands of men, women, and children who lined the streets, perched on benches, hanging from balconies and from palm trees that lined the avenue. As the Internationals went by, hundreds of girls in native costumes rushed forward, kissing them, pressing huge bouquets of flowers into their arms.

The entire foreign press was there, as well as photographers and newsreel cameramen from some of the world's most important news agencies. Vincent Sheean reports:

> I saw a lot of photographs of it afterwards: Capa, Buckley, Matthews, and others had kept their cameras busy. You never saw so many weeping people all at once as there were in those photographs. André Malraux told me about it a day or so later. "*C'était toute la Révolution qui s'en allait*" ["That's the entire revolution that's going away"], he said. Perhaps that was why the people wept. These boys, all these *Lardners*, their average age about twenty-three, had come to Spain to help save the Republic. The impulse which had sent all these Lardners to Spain had been a reflex of the conscience of the world.

On the morning of December 2, 1938, the first contingent of Americans entrained for France. Within a week, the second and last major grouping would also leave. The first train arrived at the Spanish border town of Puigcerdá two hours early. The mayor and other officials were there to greet the men and to bid them *salud!* The men crossed into France on the first stage of the journey to the channel port of Le Havre—and passage home.

At precisely noon, the original time for the Lincoln's scheduled arrival in Puigcerdá, two squadrons of Fascist bombers appeared and heavily bombed the town's now-deserted station. That this was done even though the Americans were now noncombatants bespoke a sickness of fear and irrational hatred in no way confined to Spain's Fascist military. The forces unleashed at Munich were soon to be loosed upon the world.

On December 23, 1938, 350,000 Fascist troops were hurled against the Republican provinces of Catalonia. They were spearheaded by the Italian army of General Gambara, consisting of six full divisions and the equivalent of a seventh. Two Republican armies with a total strength of 100,000 men defended Catalonia.

Within two weeks, the defenses of the Ebro and the Segre were destroyed. What few weapons there had been were lost, so that the Catalan army falling back upon Barcelona possessed but 37,000 rifles—and nothing else.

Still on French soil were 500 pieces of artillery, 10,000 machine guns, over 400 aircraft, and an equal number of tanks and shells. This equipment, according to Spain's last foreign minister, Alvárez del Vayo, had been purchased from the Soviet Union by the legal government of the Spanish Republic, and had then been denied to the Republic's armies by the governments of England and France. This act was nothing short of criminal, and made a mockery of every aspect of international law.

One of the tragedies and scandals of the modern history of France concerns this thwarted massive supply of modern armaments. Few historians are aware of it or have chosen to mention it.

After the catastrophes in Aragón and Teruel, where most of the Republic's heavy armament was used up or lost, Republican Prime Minister Negrín dispatched General Cisneros, the commander of the Republican air force, on an urgent and secret mission to Moscow. Upon arrival, Cisneros met in the Kremlin with Stalin, Voroshilov, and Molotov. He informed the Russians of the desperate shortage of all weaponry in the Republic's arsenals. He then presented a list, drawn up by the Republic's general staff, of the minimum requirements to reestablish the front. Stalin studied it, paused for a few moments, and then said, "Do you Spaniards wish to leave us disarmed?" He then told the General to return the next morning. At the next meeting, Stalin informed the General that, by agreement with the French government, the requested arms—all of them—would go by ship convoy from Murmansk to Bordeaux.

The convoy arrived without incident at the French port. The arms were then shipped to Toulouse for transshipment to Catalonia. However, a shift to the right in the French Cabinet at the beginning of the crisis in Czechoslovakia halted the resupply of the Spanish Republic's battered divisions. The armaments would still be in warehouses near Toulouse when the German army occupied southern France in 1942!

So Catalonia fell. The world witnessed the tragic exodus of 300,000 refugees: women, children, old men, and the wounded and sick from the hospitals. All braved the bitter heights and raging snows of the Pyrénées, seeking the now-questionable freedom of a reluctant France.

The appearance of this huge, defenseless caravan of misery on the snowy roads of Catalonia evoked a strange response from the remnants of the International Brigades. In the many hospitals and convalescent centers of Catalonia were all those who had not been able to depart with the thousands who had marched proudly through Barcelona a few months before. When these men—mostly Poles, Czechs, Hungarians, and Bulgarians—whose homelands were in Fascist hands learned of the plight of the refugees, learned of the collapse of the Catalan regiments, they demanded back their rifles and machine guns. Five thousand strong, a miniature International Division, many still bandaged, many supported by canes, they constituted the rear guard that held at bay the surging Fascist army, and shepherded the exile columns to the putative shelter of the Pyrénées. It remains only to add that once in France, the Spaniards and International Brigadeers were thrown into concentration camps by the French authorities. One year later, the victorious German Wehrmacht marched unopposed into Paris.

All central Spain succumbed a few months later, not to the Moroccan levies of Franco, nor to the armor of Italy and Germany, but to the treason of the infamous junta of Madrid's Colonel López Casado. Capitulators and cowards had prevailed where two-and-one-half years of bloody war had not. The Spanish Republic was given to her executioners.

On the eve of the death of the Spanish Republic, a morose American president stated bluntly to Claude G. Bowers, U.S. Ambassador to Spain, "We have made a grave mistake; you have been right all along."

Had Franklin Roosevelt taken Bowers's advice, to send arms to Spain, the Spanish tragedy might have ended differently. Indeed, all of subsequent history might have been different. Unfortunately men such as Henry L. Stimson, Sumner Welles, Senators Nye and Pittman, and so many others, spoke up too late against "that frightful error in American foreign policy."

Within four days of Roosevelt's remarks, Italian and Moroccan divisions drove through Madrid's Toledo Gate. And five short months later, World War II, the catastrophe that the Lincoln volunteers had fought and died to prevent, was unleashed upon the world.

The volunteers had come home. For a short time, they became again what they had been, students, teachers, sailors, writers, workers, and organizers of the American labor movement. For those in need of extended medical care, funds were raised and care was given. For the others, the new veterans organization could do little. There were still some 16 million unemployed in the land. For Lincoln veterans, "severance pay" consisted of a ticket home, an *abrazo* or a handshake from Steve Nelson, Leonard Lamb, and Milt Wolff, who boarded each outbound Greyhound bus to bid them goodbye, and a cash advance of perhaps twenty or thirty dollars from the local Veterans of the Abraham Lincoln Brigade—and that was that.

But not quite. With the rain of bombs upon Pearl Harbor and the immediate American declaration of war on the Axis powers, both East and West, Lincoln veterans were among the first to volunteer. More than 600 of the approximately 1800 who had returned were enrolled in the American army, navy, marines, and air force. Of the remainder, a majority of whom had been rejected from service because of war wounds and the like, over 400 then served in the merchant marine. Their dedication and courage have rarely been matched. It is no accident that a joint Yale University/Ford Foundation survey on "The Nature of Fear and Courage in Modern Warfare" compiled on the eve of World War II, numbered among its subjects over 300 veterans of the Abraham Lincoln Brigade.

These men were among the first to fight again: at Guadalcanal, Leyte, Anzio, Omaha Beach, the Ardennes, and in Germany itself. Their casualty rate was high: over 400 of them were killed or wounded in action. Some sixty to seventy former volunteers became commissioned officers. And they were highly-decorated: Captain Herman Bottcher, better known as the "one-man" army of Buna and Leyte, received a field commission and a Distinguished Service Cross with oak-leaf clusters; so too did Robert Thompson, former commander to the Mac-Paps. Lawrence Cane and Harry Schoenburg became captains; Captain Kenneth Shaker, a machine gun section leader in Spain, commanded a company of the famed 509th Parachute Battalion of the Eighty-second Division at Anzio, in southern France, and at the Battle of the Bulge.

Lincoln Brigaders formed a central part of the original core of the Office of Strategic Services (OSS), under General "Wild Bill" Donavan, serving with valor behind enemy lines in North Africa, Italy, Yugoslavia, and France. Captain Irving Goff was one of these. In Spain, he and Captain William Alto, also with the OSS, had helped lead a guerrilla detachment to free 300 prisoners behind Franco's lines. Captains Vincent

Lossowski and Mike Jiménez, winners of the Legion of Merit, along with Lieutenant "Toots" Fajans, were also with the OSS, as was Milton Wolff, who as a major had commanded the Lincoln Battalion in some of its toughest campaigns.

The list seems unending; riflemen, corporals, and sergeants, bedecked with combat ribbons, Bronze Stars, and other decorations, in totals out of all proportion to their numbers. A final summation of the achievements of the men of the Abraham Lincoln Brigade both in Spain and in World War II would suggest that in battles fought, in men lost, and in honors received, they might easily surpass any other group of fighting men in the military history of the United States.

# Epilogue

FOUR DECADES HAVE PASSED since that final hour of betrayal and bitter defeat when, in Spain, the defenders of the Republic went to the seacoast for the ships that weren't there; to the mountains for whatever short lease on life their protection would afford; to their homes and villages—to await the arrival of Franco's executioners.

The "long night" has now finally come to an end. Fascism is irrevocably *dead*.

The return to constitutional government has elicited a new and quite lively interest among Americans in the affairs of that country, including its civil war. Immediately obvious to any serious student of Spanish affairs is that today's democratic freedoms and pluralistic political system were created by precisely that same coalition of Republicans, Socialists, Communists, and liberals who in that far time of 1936 to 1939, were the heart and soul of Spain's resistance to Fascism and Nazism.

In Spain today the deeds and valor of *La Brigada Lincoln* are well-known. Returning Lincoln veterans, gray-haired but with a certain sparkle in their eyes and a spring in their steps, need but mention who they are to attract an admiring crowd in any village, bar, or plaza. The Spanish media, in all its forms, has told their story many times.

The question persists: Whence came the men of the Abraham Lincoln Brigade? The answer is simple: From that vast majority of the American people who, across the years and without exception, have been basically liberal, progressive, and humanist. From 1936 to 1939, this anti-Fascist segment was the majority of the American people—polls at the

225

time put this figure at seventy-six percent—and this majority solidly supported the Spanish Republic.

The key word here is "anti-Fascist." It refers to Fascism in *all* its forms, and wherever it may be found, whether in various rightist dictatorships in both hemispheres, or, more subtly perhaps, but just as dangerously, in the parliaments and congresses of the Western world.

Lincoln Brigaders thought "anti-Fascist" was a key word, too. Indeed, despite differences in their political viewpoints, it was this term which they invariably used to describe themselves, this term on which they could always agree. To see this, one need only see the way the men described themselves in their International Brigade service books: Phil Dentro, anti-Fascist, Joseph Gordon, anti-Fascist, and on. The term was the catalyst, the thing that more than any other brought the men together, that allowed Roosevelt Democrats, members of the I.W.W., Socialists, Communists, and ordinary students and workers to find a common ground, a unity of action without which they could have had no success in what they had set out to do.

A prime manifestation of Fascism is the denial of human rights and basic freedoms; in this sense, the American Constitution, the Bill of Rights, and the Declaration of Independence are *anti-Fascist documents by their very nature.* By assisting the Spanish people in their fight for freedom, the Lincoln Brigaders were simply carrying out the spirit of these documents, giving them a proper, real-life definition.

So much then for the "Stalinist dupes," "premature anti-Fascists," and all the other bugaboos promulgated by the American right about the Lincoln Brigaders.

Above all else, it must be remembered that the men of the Lincoln Brigade were *never* the product of any one single tendency or belief. Instead, it can be honestly argued that they were but the continuation of the American Revolution, the fight against slavery and oppression, the fight for workers' rights, and the fight against discrimination—in short, they were attempting to expand America's progress, its *promise,* to the people of war-torn Spain.

226

In the end, we must remember that the men of the Lincoln Brigade were the few of their time to face up to this responsibility, to face the most profound social crisis of their time. Their heroism in this will be remembered for all time.

# Afterword

SCATTERED THROUGH the pages of this book are references to the careers of some of the participants in the long sequel to the Spanish conflict—particularly their participation in World War II. Landis mentions, for example, that the liberation of Paris—the great insurrection of the French people—was commanded by French veterans of the International Brigades. One should also add that the armored columns under the Free French General Leclerc, were spearheaded by tanks bearing on their sides placards with the inscriptions MADRID, EBRO, TERUEL. The crews were Spaniards. Fifty thousand Spanish Republicans fought with the French *Maquisards* and were instrumental in liberating vast areas of southwest and southeast France. Long before this, Spaniards took part in the ill-fated Allied expedition to Norway (1940), and it was they who covered the retreat of the Allied troops to the evacuation ships. It was Spaniards who played a major role in the terrible struggles on the perimeter of the beaches at Dunkirk. Many of them, lacking papers, were refused permission to board the ships! Thousands of them were left to the tender mercies of the Germans and perished in Nazi slave-labor camps. It was not only in France that veterans of the International Brigades carried on the struggle against Fascism. In Yugoslavia, where a People's Army of 300,000 was organized by Marshal Tito, a one-time recruiter and organizer for the International Brigades, eleven of his thirteen generals were veterans of the Spanish conflict. Spain-tested combatants were also instrumental in organizing the partisan armies in Greece and Albania. The Italian partisans, who eventually numbered in the hundreds of thousands, drew many of their leadership cadres from the veterans of the Garibaldi Battalion of the Twelfth International Brigade. It was a patrol of the Garibaldi who captured and executed Benito Mussolini in the closing days of the Italian campaign.

Even in the far-off Soviet Union, Spaniards who had found refuge there in 1939 played important roles in the massive partisan armies on the eastern front. Symbolically, the son of Dolores Ibarurri (La Pasionaria) died defending the ruins of Stalingrad, as a lieutenant in the Soviet army.

As for the Soviet officers who came to help the Republic, at least 200 were killed in the field. Many remained in Spain long after the International Brigades were withdrawn (in November 1938) and had to be literally plucked out of a small airfield near Alicante as the surging rebels closed in on the last enclave in the Republic.

Of those who returned home, many rose to the highest rank, as marshals in what the Germans called *Operation Barbarossa* and the Soviets called The Great Patriotic War. Batov held the last road to Moscow; Meretskov held Leningrad and later commanded the armies that destroyed the Kwantung army in Manchuria; Eremenko, Chuikov, and Rodimstev between them commanded the troops that made the battle of Stalingrad the turning point in World War II. Vatutin liberated Kiev. Krylov led the defenders of Odessa and Sevastopol. Smuskevich commanded the fliers who covered the retreat of the Chinese armies to the interior of that country. Voronov, who commanded the few batteries that defended Madrid in November 1936, became marshal of all the artillery forces of the Soviet army. When his 10,000 batteries ringed Berlin in May 1945, his order was: "Open fire on the fascist capital. The first salvo is in honor of Madrid!" Malinovski, who advised the Spanish Republican forces that defeated Mussolini's expeditionary divisions at Guadalajara, commanded armies from Budapest and Vienna to Mukden.

Special mention should be made of two Polish volunteers. One, who used the *nom de guerre* General Walter, commanded first a brigade, then a division on the Spanish front. Later he commanded the Polish field army that fought with the Red Army from the Vistula to Berlin. Another Pole, who used the *nom de guerre* Alexander Schmidt, returned to his native Warsaw in 1940 and later went over the wall of the infamous ghetto in order to organize the epic uprising.

On the Axis side, it should be noted that the professional officers of the Wehrmacht and Luftwaffe who made up the Condor Legion that guaranteed Franco's victory received invaluable postgraduate training in Spain. It is not surprising, therefore, that from their ranks came General Heinz Guderian, supreme organizer and commander of Hitler's dreaded Panzer Divisionen. Field Marshal Rommel's Afrika Korps had as chief of staff Von Thoma. Hitler's fliers, who devastated half of Europe, drew many of their top commanders from the ranks of the pilots who had bombed Barcelona and tested pattern bombing on the defenseless Basque city of Guernica. Nor in this epilogue should one forget that General Francisco Franco, before he moved from benevolent neutrality favoring the Axis to neutrality, sent the 50,000-man Blue Division to fight on the eastern front. His agents in the Caribbean, acting as spies for Hitler's wolf-pack submarines, helped turn that American lake into a graveyard of ships.

In the strange moral bookkeeping of Churchill and Truman, Franco was rewarded with thirty more years of undiminished power and undiminished support.

The foreigners who have been mentioned in the above paragraphs received gratitude and high honors from their liberated countrymen. The experience of the American volunteers was somewhat different. After Pearl Harbor, many were barred from participation in the armed forces because a suspicious if not hostile government branded them with the ambiguous denotation of "premature anti-Fascists." Yet through perseverance approximately 800, or half of the survivors from Spain, found service in the varied armed forces and the merchant marine. Approximately half of those who enlisted died, a frightful percentage compared to other groups of the same size. They landed with the first waves on the beaches of Normandy, Leyte Gulf, Anzio. They fought with Stilwell in Burma and served as Donovan's shock troops in Italy. They died in the Solomons and with General Carlson's Raiders in the central Pacific. Yet years after the end of World War II, their families have had to go to court to gain the right to have them buried in Arlington National Cemetery.

Despite a spate of books appearing in this fiftieth anniversary year, one can say that the record of the American volunteers in Spain is still a page torn from the history of our country. To justify this, it is often alleged that upward of fifty percent of the Lincolns were members of the Communist Party or the Young Communist League. One is reminded here of the response of the exiled Norwegian King Hakkon when told by his advisers that Communists in occupied Norway were organizing armed resistance groups. Said Hakkon, "I am also king of the Norwegian Communists!"

Is it too much to hope that, eventually, this broad and beauteous land that calls itself the home of the free will one day be as generous to some of its forgotten sons?

ROBERT G. COLODNY

# Suggestions for
# Further Reading

IN ORDER not to burden the text with innumerable citations, we have not provided footnotes. All of the quotations from the participants are taken from taped interviews or private correspondence. Much of this material is now available to historians in the Spanish Civil War collection of Brandeis University in Waltham, Massachusetts.

This bibliography is not intended to be exhaustive. Its modest purpose is to serve as a guide to the vast literature that was mentioned in the Foreword. The attentive reader will have noted that the men whose life and death in Spain has been chronicled by Arthur H. Landis were profoundly aware of the international context of their struggle. For this reason, a large number of the books listed below are selected so that this global landscape can be at least partially illuminated. The titles are divided into eleven categories. When a book deals with several categories, it has multiple listings. This is for the convenience of students approaching the subject for the first time.

There are many elements of this history that are still in violent dispute among professional historians. We cannot here hope to resolve these scholarly arguments, nor have we tried to indicate the particular bias of any of the authors. Some historians have attempted, in our judgment, with only partial success, to compile such an analytic account of this corpus of books. Such discussions are found in the books of Payne, Southworth, Eby, and Bolloten. Many of the books listed in this bibliography are analyzed "in terms of their content" in Colodny, *Spain, the Glory and the Tragedy*. It is obvious that the volunteers who wrote about their experience made no specious claims about objectivity. Perhaps their "biases" are the heart of the matter. As the fiftieth anniversary of the Spanish conflict passes into history, only ten percent remain to celebrate. It seems most probable to this writer that they would prefer to be remembered not as mythic folk heroes but merely as examples of how uncommon the common man can be.

## 1. Spanish socio-political background

Alvárez del Vayo, Julio, *Freedom's Battle*, London, 1940.

Amat-Piniella, J., *K. L. Reich, Miles de españoles en los campos de Hitler*, Barcelona, 1963.
(This title also appears under category 11.)

Ansaldo, Juan Antonio, *¿Para que . . .¡ (de Alfonso XIII a Juan III)*, Buenos Aires, 1951.

Aznar, Manuel, *Historia militar de la guerra de España*, 3rd ed., 3 vols., Madrid, 1963.
(This title also appears under category 3.)

Barea, Arturo, *The Forging of a Rebel*, New York, 1946.

Beltrán, Güell Filipe, *Preparación y desarrollo del alzamiento nacional*, Vallodolid, 1939.

Bolloten, Burnett, *The Spanish Revolution: The Left and the Struggle for Power during the Civil War*, Chapel Hill, 1979.
(This title also appears under category 7.)

Brenan, Gerald, *The Spanish Labyrinth: An Account of the Social and Political Background of the Civil War*, 2nd ed., Cambridge, England, 1950.

Brouè, Pierre and Tèmime, *La revolution et la guerre d'Espagne*, Paris, 1961.

Carr, Raymond, ed., *The Republic and the Civil War in Spain*, London, 1971.
(This title also appears under category 7.)

Chase, Allen, *Falange: The Axis Secret Army in the Americas*, New York, 1953.
(This title also appears under category 2 and category 11.)

Díaz-Plaja, Fernando, ed., *La historia de España en sus documentos: el siglo XX; la guerra (1936–39)*, Madrid, 1963.
(This title also appears under category 10.)

Foltz, Charles, Jr., *The Masquerade in Spain*, Boston, 1948.
(This title also appears under category 4.)

Fraser, Ronald, *Blood of Spain: An Oral History of the Spanish Civil War*, New York, 1979.
(This title also appears under category 7.)

Great Britain, *Parliamentary Debates: House of Commons Official Report*, 5th Series, London, 1937.
(This title also appears under category 10.)

Ibarruri, Dolores, *El único camino*, 3rd. ed., Mexico, D.F., 1963.

Jackson, Gabriel, *Historian's Quest: A Twenty-Year Journey into the Spanish Mind*, New York, 1969.
(This title also appears under category 7 and category 11.)

Koestler, Arthur, *Scum of the Earth*, New York, 1941.
(This title also appears under category 6 and category 11.)

Largo Cabellero, Francisco, *Mis recuerdos: Cartas a un amigo*, Mexico, D.F., 1954.

Maíz, B. Felix, *Alzamiento en España: De un diario de la conspiración*, Pamplona, 1952.

Martín, Blásquez José, *I Helped to Build an Army: Civil War Memoirs of a Spanish Staff Officer*, London, 1939.
(This title also appears under category 5 and category 7.)

Matthews, Herbert L., *The Yoke and the Arrows: A Report on Spain*, New York, 1961.
(This title also appears under category 7.)

Merin, Peter, *Spain between Death and Birth*, New York, 1938.

Miller, John, ed., *Voices Against Tyranny: Writing of the Spanish Civil War*, New York, 1986.
(This title also appears under category 8.)

Olivera, A. Ramos, *Politics, Economics and Men of Modern Spain 1808–1946*, London, 1946.

Payne, Stanley G., *Falange: A History of Spanish Fascism*, Stanford, 1961.

Payne, Stanley G., *Politics and the Military in Modern Spain*, Stanford 1967.

Regler, Gustav, *The Owl of Minerva: The Autobiography of Gustav Regler*, New York, 1960.
(This title also appears under category 6 and category 11.)

Robinson, Richard, *The Origins of Franco's Spain, the Right, the Republic and the Revolution, 1931–1936*, Pittsburgh, 1970.

Sencourt, Robert, *Spain's Ordeal: A Documented History of the Civil War*, London, 1940.

Sender, Ramón J., *Counter-Attack in Spain*, Boston, 1937.
(This title also appears under category 7.)

Southworth, Herbert Rutledge, *El Mito de la Cruzada de Franco*, Paris, 1963.

Stein, Louis, *Beyond Death and Exile: The Spanish Republicans in France, 1939–1955*, Cambridge, Mass., 1979.
(This title also appears under category 6 and category 11.)

Whelan, Richard, *Robert Capa, A Biography*, New York, 1985.
(This title also appears under category 6.)

## 2. International diplomacy and the global context

Correspondence between Franklin D. Roosevelt and William C. Bullitt, *International Press Correspondence*, Special Spain Issue, London, 1938.

Barros, James, *Betrayal from Within: Joseph Avenol and the League of Nations, 1933–1940*, New Haven, 1969.

Bell, J. Bowyer, "The Non-Intervention Committee and the Spanish Civil War, 1936–1939." Unpublished doctoral dissertation, Duke University, 1958. (Available in bound manuscript copy, University of Michigan, Ann Arbor.)

Bowers, Claude G., *My Mission to Spain: Watching the Rehearsal for World War II*, New York, 1954.

Chase, Allen, *Falange: The Axis Secret Army in the Americas*, New York, 1953.
(This title also appears under category 1 and category 11.)

Churchill, Winston, *Step by Step, 1936–1939*, London, 1942.

Ciano, Galeazzo, *Ciano's Diplomatic Papers*, London, 1948.

Cockburn, Claude, *The Devil's Decade, The Thirties*, London, 1973.

Cot, Pierre, *The Triumph of Treason*, Chicago, 1944.

Dalton, Hugh, *The Fateful Years: Memoirs 1931–1945*, London, 1957.

Degras, Jane, ed., *The Communist International, Documents, Vol. III, 1929–1943*, New York, 1965.

Dimitroff, Georgi, *The United Front*, New York, 1938.
(This title also appears under category 5.)

Dzelepy, E. N., *The Spanish Plot*, London, 1937.

Farago, Ladislas, ed., *The Axis Grand Strategy: Blueprints for the Total War*, New York, 1942.

Fischer, Louis, *Men and Politics: Europe Between the Two World Wars*, 3rd ed., New York, 1966.

Furnia, Arthur H., *The Diplomacy of Appeasement: Anglo-French Relations and the Prelude to World War II, 1931–1938*, Washington, D.C., 1960.

George, Margaret, *The Warped Vision: British Foreign Policy, 1933–1939*, Pittsburgh, 1965.

Jerrold, Douglas, *Georgian Adventure*, New York, 1938.

Little, James Douglas, *Malevolent Neutrality; The United States, Great Britain and the Revolution in Spain, 1931–1936*, Ithaca, 1985.

Padelford, Norman J., *International Law and Diplomacy in the Spanish Civil Strife*, New York, 1939.

Puzzo, Dante A., *Spain and the Great Powers, 1936–1941*, New York, 1962.

Schuman, Frederick L., *Europe on the Eve: The Crisis of Diplomacy, 1933–1939*, New York, 1939.

Sheean, Vincent, *Not Peace but a Sword*, New York, 1937.
(This title also appears under category 6.)

Southworth, Herbert R., *Guernica! Guernica! A Study of Journalism, Diplomacy, Propaganda, and History*, Berkeley, 1977.
(This title also appears under category 4 and category 7.)

Traina, Richard P., *American Diplomacy and the Spanish Civil War*, Bloomington, Indiana, 1968.

Watkins, K. W., *Britain Divided: The Effect of the Spanish Civil War on British Political Opinion*, London, 1963.

Windell, George G., "Leon Blum and the Crisis Over Spain," *The Historian*, XXIV, 1962.

## 3. General military history: campaigns and battles

Aznar, Manuel, *Historia militar de la guerra de España*, 3rd ed., 3 vols., Madrid, 1963.
(This title also appears under category 1.)

de Lojendio, Luis María, *Operaciones militares de la guerra de España*, Barcelona, 1940.

## 4. Axis intervention: Germany, Italy, and Portugal

Abshagen, Karl Heinz, *Canaris*, London, 1956.

Belforte, General Francesco, *La guerra civile in Spagna*, 4 vols., Milan, 1939.

Beumelberg, Werner, *Kampf um Spanien: Die Geschichte der Legion Condor*, Berlin, 1939.

Busch, Fritz Otto (Lieutenant Commander, German navy), *Kampf vor Spaniens Küsten: Deutsche Marine in spanischen Bürgerkriege*, Berlin and Leipzig, 1939.

Cantalupo, Roberto, *Fu la Spagna: Ambasciata presso Franco, Febbraio–Aprile 1937*, Verona, 1948.

Coverdale, John F., *Italian Intervention in the Spanish Civil War*, Princeton, 1975.

Department of State, *Documents on German Foreign Policy, 1918–1945*, Series D, Vol. III; *Germany and the Spanish Civil War, 1930–1939*, Washington, D.C., 1950.
(This title also appears under category 10.)

*Deutsche kampfen in Spanien: Herausgegeben von der Legion Condor*, Berlin, 1939.

di Giamberardino, Oscar (Admiral, Italian navy), *La politica bellica nella tragedia nazionale, 1922–1945*, Rome, 1945.

Einhorn, Marion, *Die okonomischen Hintergrunde der faschistischen deutschen Intervention in Spanien, 1936–1939*, Berlin, D.D.R., 1962.

SUGGESTIONS FOR FURTHER READING

Feis, Herbert, *The Spanish Story: Franco and the Nations at War*, New York, 1948.

Foltz, Charles, Jr., *The Masquerade in Spain*, Boston, 1948.
(This title also appears under category 1.)

Guariglia, Raffaele, *Ricordi, 1922–1946*, Naples, 1950.

"Hispanicus," ed., *Foreign Intervention in Spain: Documents*, London, n.d.

Korth, Eugene H., "Economic Aspects of German Intervention in the Spanish Civil War, 1936–1939," *Mid-America: An Historical Review* XLII, 1960.

Kuznetsov, N. G., "Before the War," *International Affairs*, Moscow, Serialized 1966, May, No. 5 through 19.

Mattioli, Guido, *L'Aviazone legionaria in Spagna*, Rome, 1940.

Merkes, Manfred, *Die deutsche Politik gegenüber dem spanischen Bürgerkrieg, 1936–1939*, Bonn, 1961.

Raeder, Erich (Grand Admiral, German navy), *My Life*, Annapolis, 1960.

Roatta, Mario, *Il processo Roatta*, 2nd ed., Rome, 1945.

Southworth, Herbert R., *Guernica! Guernica! A Study of Journalism, Diplomacy, Propaganda, and History*, Berkeley, 1977.
(This title also appears under category 2 and category 7.)

Spielhagen, Franz, *The Nazi Conspiracy in Spain*, London, 1937.

von Stackelberg, Karl Georg, *Legion Condor: Deutsche Freiwillige im Spanien*, Berlin, 1939.


## 5. Soviet role, military and political

Cattell, David T., *Soviet Diplomacy and the Spanish Civil War*, Berkeley, 1957.

Degras, Jane, ed., *Soviet Documents on Foreign Policy, Vol. III: 1933–1941*, London, 1953.

Dimitroff, Georgi, *The United Front*, New York, 1938.
(This title also appears under category 2.)

Ehrenburg, Ilya, *Memoirs: 1921–1941*, Cleveland, 1964.

Koltsov, Mikhail, *Diario de la guerra de España*, Paris, 1963.
(This title also appears under category 6.)

Maisky, Ivan, *Spanish Notebooks*, London, 1966.

Malinovsky, R. et al., *Bajo la Bandera de la España Republicana; Recuerdan los voluntarios soviéticos participantes en la guerra nacional en España*, Moscow, n.d.

Martín, Blásquez, José, *I Helped to Build an Army: Civil War Memoirs of a Spanish Staff Officer*, London, 1939.
(This title also appears under category 1 and category 7.)

Potemkine, V., ed., *Histoire de la diplomatie, Vol. III: 1919–1939*, Paris, 1947.

Vaoupchassov, S., *Quarante Ans dans les Services Secrets Sovietiques*, Moscow, 1978.

## 6. *International Brigades*

Acier, Marcel, ed., *From Spanish Trenches: Recent Letters from Spain*, New York, 1937.
(This title also appears under category 9.)

Alexander, Bill, *British Volunteers for Liberty, Spain 1936–39*, London, 1982.

Baumann, Gerold Gino, *Extranjeros en la Guerra Civil Española: Los Peruanos*, Lima, 1979.

Brome, Vincent, *The International Brigades, Spain 1936–1939*, New York, 1966.

de Bayac, Jacques Delperrie, *Les Brigades Internationales*, Paris, 1968.

Francis, Hywel, *Miners Against Fascism: Wales and the Spanish Civil War*, London, 1984.

Geiser, Carl, *Prisoners of the Good Fight*, Westport, Connecticut, 1986.
(This title also appears under category 9.)

Györkei, Jenö, *Magyar Önkéntések a Spanyol Polgárháborúban*, Budapest, 1977.

Hoar, Victor, *The Mackenzie-Papineau Battalion*, Toronto, 1969.
(This title also appears under category 9.)

Johnston, Verle B., *Legions of Babel: The International Brigades in the Spanish Civil War*, University Park, Texas, 1967.

Kantorowicz, Alfred, *Spanisches Tagebuch*, Berlin, 1949.

Kantorowicz, Alfred, *Tschapaiew: Das Bataillon der 21 Nationen*, Rudolstadt, n.d.

Koestler, Arthur, *Scum of the Earth*, New York, 1941.
(This title also appears under category 1 and category 11.)

Koltsov, Mikhail, *Diario de la guerra de España*, Paris, 1963.
(This title also appears under category 5.)

Longo, Luigi, *Las Brigadas Internacionales en España*, Paris, 1966.

Regler, Gustav, *The Owl of Minerva: The Autobiography of Gustav Regler*, New York, 1960.
(This title also appears under category 1 and category 11.)

Renn, Ludwig, *Der Spanische Krieg*, Berlin, 1955.
(This title also appears under category 7.)

Romilly, Esmond, *Boadilla*, London, 1937.

Rust, William, *Britons in Spain: The History of the British Battalion of the XVth International Brigade*, New York, 1939.

Sheean, Vincent, *Not Peace but a Sword*, New York, 1937.
(This title also appears under category 2.)

Sommerfield, John, *Volunteer in Spain*, New York, 1937.

Stansky, Peter and Abrahams, William, *Journey to the Frontier. Julian Bell and John Cornford: Their lives and the 1930s*, London, 1966.

SUGGESTIONS FOR FURTHER READING

Stein, Louis, *Beyond Death and Exile: The Spanish Republicans in France, 1939–1955*, Cambridge, Mass., 1979.
(This title also appears under category 1 and category 11.)

Weinert, Erich, *Camaradas: Ein Spanienbuch*, Berlin, 1951.
(This title also appears under category 8.)

Whelan, Richard, *Robert Capa, a Biography*, New York, 1985.
(This title also appears under category 1.)


## 7. General military-political operations

(This was a highly political conflict in which politics and military operations mutually interacted.)

Bolloten, Burnett, *The Spanish Revolution: The Left and the Struggle for Power during the Civil War*, Chapel Hill, North Carolina, 1979.
(This title also appears under category 1.)

Carr, Raymond, ed., *The Republic and the Civil War in Spain*, London, 1971.
(This title also appears under category 1.)

Colodny, Robert G., *Spain: The Glory and the Tragedy*, New York, 1970.

Colodny, Robert G., *The Struggle for Madrid: The Central Epic of the Spanish Conflict (1936–1937)*, New York, 1958.

de Cisneros, Ignacio Hidalgo, *Memorias*, 2 vols., Paris, 1964.

Fraser, Ronald, *Blood of Spain: An Oral History of the Spanish Civil War*, New York, 1979.
(This title also appears under category 1.)

Jackson, Gabriel, *Historian's Quest: A Twenty-Year Journey into the Spanish Mind*, New York, 1969.
(This title also appears under category 1 and category 11.)

Jackson, Gabriel, *The Spanish Republic and the Civil War, 1931–1939*, Princeton, 1965.

Jellinek, Frank, *The Civil War in Spain*, London, 1938.

Lister, Enrique, *Nuestra Guerra: Aportaciones para una Historia de la Guerra, Nacional Revolucionaria del Pueblo Español 1936–1939*, Paris, 1966.

Martín, Blásquez, José, *I Helped to Build an Army: Civil War Memoirs of a Spanish Staff Officer*, London, 1939.
(This title also appears under category 1 and category 5.)

Matthews, Herbert, *Half of Spain Died, A Reappraisal of the Spanish Civil War*, New York, 1973.

Matthews, Herbert L., *The Yoke and the Arrows: A Report on Spain*, New York, 1961.
(This title also appears under category 1.)

Nenni, Peitro, *La guerre d'Espagne*, Paris, 1959.

Renn, Ludwig, *Der Spanische Krieg*, Berlin, 1955.
(This title also appears under category 6.)

Rojo, General Vicente, *España Heroica*, Buenos Aires, 1942.

Sender, Ramón J., *Counter-Attack in Spain*, Boston, 1937.
(This title also appears under category 1.)

Southworth, Herbert R., *Guernica! Guernica! A Study of Journalism, Diplomacy, Propaganda, and History*, Berkeley, 1977.
(This title also appears under category 2 and category 4.)

Thomas, Hugh, *The Spanish Civil War*, rev. ed., New York, 1965.


## 8. Fiction

Hemingway, Ernest, *For Whom the Bell Tolls*, New York, 1943.

Malraux, André, *Man's Hope*, New York, 1938.

Miller, John, ed., *Voices Against Tyranny: Writing of the Spanish Civil War*, New York, 1986.
(This title also appears under category 1.)

Regler, Gustav, *The Great Crusade*, New York, 1940.

Uhse, Bodo, *Lieutenant Bertram*, New York, 1944.

Weinert, Erich, *Camaradas: Ein Spanienbuch*, Berlin, 1951.
(This title also appears under category 6.)


## 9. American battalions

Acier, Marcel, ed., *From Spanish Trenches: Recent Letters from Spain*, New York, 1937.
(This title also appears under category 6.)

Bessie, Alvah, *Men in Battle: A Story of Americans in Spain*, New York, 1939, 1954.

Bessie, Alvah and Albert Prago, eds., *Fighting the Good Fight: An Anthology of the Veterans of the Abraham Lincoln Brigade*, New York, 1987.

Eby, Cecil, *Between the Bullet and the Lie: American Volunteers in the Spanish Civil War*, New York, 1969.

Geiser, Carl, *Prisoners of the Good Fight*, Westport, Connecticut, 1986.
(This title also appears under category 6.)

Gerassi, John, *The Premature Anti-Fascists*, New York, 1986.

Guttman, Allen, *The Wound in the Heart: America and the Spanish Civil War*, New York, 1962.

Hoar, Victor, *The Mackenzie-Papineau Battalion*, Toronto, 1969.
(This title also appears under category 6.)

Landis, Arthur H., *The Abraham Lincoln Brigade*, New York, 1966.

Merriman, Marion and Lerude, Warren, *American Commander in Spain, Robert Hale Merriman and the Abraham Lincoln Brigade*, Reno, 1986.

Nelson, Steve, Barrett, James A., and Ruck, Robert, *Steve Nelson, American Radical*, Pittsburgh, 1981.

Rolfe, Edwin, *The Lincoln Battalion*, New York, 1939.

Rosenstone, Robert A., *Crusade of the Left: The Lincoln Battalion in the Spanish Civil War*, New York, 1969.

Tisa, John, *Recalling the Good Fight: An Autobiography of the Spanish Civil War*, South Hadley, Massachusetts, 1985.


## 10. Official documents

Department of State, *Documents on German Foreign Policy, 1918–1945*, Series D, Vol. III, *Germany and the Spanish Civil War, 1930–1939*, Washington, D.C., 1950.
(This title also appears under category 4.)

Díaz-Plaja, Fernando, ed., *La historia de España en sus documentos: el siglo XX; la guerra, 1936–39*, Madrid, 1963.
(This title also appears under category 1.)

Great Britain, *Parliamentary Debates: House of Commons Official Report*, 5th Series, London, 1937.
(This title also appears under category 1.)


## 11. 1939–1945, History of Spaniards and International Brigades, World War II and later

Amat-Piniella, J., K. L. Reich, *Miles de españoles en los campos de Hitler*, Barcelona, 1963.
(This title also appears under category 1.)

Chase, Allen, *Falange: The Axis Secret Army in the Americas*, New York, 1953.
(This title also appears under category 1 and category 2.)

Jackson, Gabriel, *Historian's Quest: A Twenty-Year Journey into the Spanish Mind*, New York, 1969.
(This title also appears under category 1 and category 7.)

Koestler, Arthur, *Scum of the Earth*, New York, 1941.
(This title also appears under category 1 and category 6.)

Regler, Gustav, *The Owl of Minerva: The Autobiography of Gustav Regler*, New York, 1960.
(This title also appears under category 1 and category 6.)

Stein, Louis, *Beyond Death and Exile: The Spanish Republicans in France, 1939–1955*, Cambridge, Massachusetts, 1979.
(This title also appears under category 1 and category 6.)

Vidali, Vittorio, *Diary of the Twentieth Congress of the Communist Party of the Soviet Union*. Newport, Connecticut and London, 1974.

# Index

Abad, Garciá, killed at Ebro, 194
Abraham Lincoln Battalion (ALB), *xxv,*
  8, 11, 18, 49; at Belchite, 77–85; at
  Belchite II, 123–132; in Brunete
  Offensive, 39–57; at Caspe, 136;
  encircled at Gandesa, 144; at Hijar,
  132; loss of officers at Pingarròn, 23;
  members in WWII, 222–223; morale
  of, 32; at Pedigrosso, 118–119; at
  Purburell hill, 74; line at Fuentes,
  90; new officers of, 66; at Quinto,
  70–92; recognition of, 198; re-estab-
  lishment of (ALB "new"), 164; songs
  of, 33; and Teruel campaign, 94–98,
  100–114
Abraham Lincoln Battalion "new"
  (ALB "new"), 164; attack at Ebron,
  184–185
*Abraham Lincoln Brigade* (Landis),
  *xviii*
Adams, Franklin P., 35
Addes, Bernard, at Brunete, 51
AFL, 35
Aiken, George, 97
Aitken, Commissar, 23
Albacete, 5
Abirti, Rafael, 157
Alcalá de Henares, 12
Aldo, Commissar, at Belchite, 78
Alexander, William, 114
Alfambra, 105
Alfonso XIII, King (Spain), *xxii*
*All Right,* 177
All Union National Conference, 97
Allison, James, 14, 63
Almería, shelled, 65
Alto, Capt. William, with OSS, 222
American casualties, 95
American Communist party, and
  recruitment of volunteers, 3–4
American flyers, 62–64
American hospitals, in Spain, 13, 65,
  86–87

American Medical Bureau, 13, 25
American mobile hospital unit, 98–99,
  100, 104
American Socialist Party, 3
American Student Union, 81
American Trade Union Committee for
  Relief to Spain, 35
American volunteers: first, 4–5;
  and commissar system, 10; de-
  scribed by Matthews, 7; training of,
  11. *See also* Abraham Lincoln Bat-
  talion
Ames, Bernard, 36
Amlie, Lt. (later Capt.) Hans, 36; at
  Belchite, 78–79; casualty at Brunete,
  47; in command of ALB, 66; repatri-
  ated, 81
Amlie, Rep. Thomas, 36
*Among Friends,* 97
Anarchists: in Aragón area, 67; nega-
  tive role of, 68
Anderson, Ivor, 37; at Ebro, 38
Anderson, Melvin, at Quinto, 72
André Malraux International Squad-
  ron, 61
Anglo-American Company, 38
Aragón front, 67–120
Aranda, Gen., 103, 108
Arganda, 12
Arion, Ernie, at Brunete, 47
Armas, Rudolfo de, 19
Armitage, Joseph, at Brunete, 42
Army of Africa, *xvii, xx–xxi*
Arraras, *xx*
Arrow divisions (Italian), 27
Ascencio, Col., 17
Ashley, Charles, at Teruel, 113
Associated Press, 105–106
Astor, Mary, 36
Atkinson, Brooks, 35
Austria, annexation of, 200; occupied
  by Germany, *xvi*
Autonomous Council of Aragón, 68

*Index*

Pindoque Bridge, 14–15; massacre at, 55

Pingarrón battle, 19–29, 25

Pittman, Sen., 221

Plymouth, Lord, *xxii*

Poland, threatened by Axis, 159

Ponte, Gen. Mugnel, 82

Popular Front Government, election of, *xvi*; membership of, 68

Portuguese Army, *xx–xxi*

Pozas, Gen., 17

Prago, Al, at Belchite II, 127

Probaska, Commander (Dimitrov Bn.), later mayor of Prague, 86

Protectorate of Morocco, *xix*

Purburell hill, 170; British at, 74, 75

Quinto del Ebro: battle of, 69–75; church at, 73; enemy losses at, 77; volunteer peasants from, 94

Rackley, Mildred, at Mataró, 167

Ramírez, Nicolas, on Fuentes tank charge, 90

Rappaport, Milton, killed, 24

Rasantes (Soviet bombers), 62, 89

Raven, Robert, at Pingarrón, 26

*Regulares of Tetuán*, 18

Rehill, Joseph, 167

Reid, Arnold, at Ebro, 185

Reiss, David: at Belchite II, 123–124, 127; at Pedigrosso, 118

Republic: and aid from USSR, 27; in last year of war, 159; victories of, at Teruel, 101

Republican Eighteenth brigade, 12

Reuters Agency, 105

Riffin troops, *xvii*

Rintz, Dr. Norman, at Alcorisa, 100

Río Valdemembro, 11

Roach, Douglas, 19

Robbins, Dr., 53–54

Robeson, Paul, 96

Robinson, Commissar John Quigley (Robbie), 66; at Belchite, 78–79

Rodimstev (Russian), 230

Rogers, Frank, at Belchite II, 127

Rojo, Gen. Enrique, 134

Rojo, Gen. Vicente, *xv*, 41, 199; on Ebro offensive, 172; on Valencia campaign, 170

Rolfe, Edwin, 207; on Ebro, 210; on Teruel, 103; on American volunteers, 87; on Barcelona parade, 218; on breakup of ALB, 148–149; on capture of convoy, 183; on Caspe,

135; on final "parade" of Americans, 216; on first-aid post, 185; on Franco artillery, 64–65; on Gandesa retreat, 146–147, 154–155; on Hemingway, 31–32; joins ALB "new," 165; on Lamb/correspondents meeting, 189–190; on Lardner, 169; on Fuentes, 92; on war, 121

Roosevelt, Daniel, at Ebro, 189

Roosevelt, Pres. Franklin D.: on embargo, 161–162; and non-intervention, *xxi*; and policy toward Spain, 221; warns of Nazism and Fascism, 93

Rose, Sol: at Gandesa retreat, 154; at "pimple," 187

Rose (with Mac-Paps), at Belchite II, 131

Rosenblatt, Sid, at Belchite II, 128

Rosner, Hy, 30

Runciman, Lord, 201

Rusciano, Dick, at Ebro, 183

Rust, William, 22; on Brunete, 41–42; on Gandesa, 140, 155; on "pimple," 187; on Teruel, 111–112

Ryan, Frank, at Gandesa, 140

Saar, annexation of, 200

Sachs, William, in Caballs, 215

Saklatvela Battalion, *xxv*

Salter, Felix, at Ebro, 215

*San Diego Sun*, 49

*San Francisco Chronicle*, 49

Santillán, Diego Abad de, 68

Sastre, Commissar José María, 164

Scarlettos, (Greek) with ALB "new," 184

Schlesinger, Herbert, at Ebro, 215

Schmidt, Alexander (*nom de guerre*), 230

Schoenburg, Harry: at Ebro, 213, 214; in WW II, 222

Schrenzel, Isidore, at Fuentes, 91

Scott, John, 11, 14, 19; aka Inver Marlow, 11

Seacord, Douglas, 11, 19; as commander of machine gun company, 11; as field commander, 23

Second Esquadron (First Regimento de Tren), 66; losses of, 166

Secundy, Lt. Louis: in command of Auto Park, 66; joins ALB "new," 166; at Teruel, 101

Seldes, George, 30–31, 34

Selles, Chang, at Brunete, 62

Sennett, Commissar William, 66

*Index*